R

NUNNELLY
MYSTERIOUS
KENTUCKY

It takes the unique individual, in the midst of a strange state like Kentucky, to serve up the kind of great stories and sightings that hold the readers' interest. Bart Nunnelly is our guide here, and we should be happy he is, for the book he's given us is a treat to behold. You won't be disappointed. Join him on your journey into Mysterious Kentucky.

Loren Coleman, cryptozoologist and author, Mysterious America and others

Bart Nunnelly has compiled a most impressive compendium of weird events that have occurred throughout the Bluegrass State for over 200 years. It represents a groundbreaking effort and is an eye-popping collection of accounts of the creepy, bizarre, and the unexplained. Bart Nunnelly s Mysterious Kentucky is truly the way of the future for cryptid, paranormal, and bigfoot research. This book is a must for students of the mysterious and the unexplained."

Thom Powell, author of The Locals: A Contemporary investigation of the Bigfoot/Sasquatch Phenomena

For anyone and everyone interested in the mysteries of this world and beyond, Bart Nunnelly's book is one that you cannot afford to miss. Packed to bursting point with eerie tales from Kentucky's strange skies to its murky waters, and from its shadowy woods to its haunted cemeteries, Mysterious Kentucky is one of those books that is best read by candlelight on a dark and stormy night. You thought those old horror movies you watched as kids were mere fiction? You are wrong, my friends. Dead wrong. As Bart demonstrates time and again, dark and diabolical entities lurk in deepest Kentucky, including werewolves, Bigfoot, phantoms, and...well, I will leave you to learn the macabre delights for yourself. Read and enjoy - and keep a careful watch over your shoulder too...A great read - really excellent!'

Nick Redfern, author of Three Men Seeking Monsters and Memoirs of a Monster Hunter.

The state of Kentucky grows things far stranger than blue grass, and plays host to creatures furrier, bigger, and much, much meaner than its famed thoroughbred horses. Bart Nunnelly's Mysterious Kentucky , a full-throttle safari through weird places not found in official Kentucky tour guides, details them all. Nunnelly has not only compiled a veritable Smoky Mountain of unexplained phenomena; he has documented his own treks into Kentucky's most isolated swamps, forests and caves. And as an accomplished artist, he provides first class forensic illustrations of the cryptids he has been lucky enough to spot. Nunnelly also delves into the state's crazy UFO incidents -- replete with little green men -- as well as ancient Native American puzzles. This book is for anyone willing to open his or her cranium to the mind-bending realization that humanity does not yet know it all. Barton Nunnelly doesn't claim to know everything either, but his book is one heck of a documentation of the strangeness that is Kentucky."

Linda S. Godfrey, author The Beast of Bray Road: Tailing Wisconsin's Werewolf; Hunting the American Werewolf; Weird Michigan; Strange Wisconsin and co-author Weird Wisconsin.

Mysterious Places from Whitechapel Press

MYSTERIOUS KENTUCKY
The History, Mystery & Unexplained of the Bluegrass State
BY B.M. NUNNELLY

- A Whitechapel Press Book from Dark Haven Entertainment -

Original Cover Artwork Designed by
© Copyright 2007 by Michael Schwab & Troy Taylor
Visit M & S Graphics at http://www.manyhorses.com

Original Photographs and Illustrations by B.M. Nunnelly
Additional Photograph Credits Noted in the Text

Editing and Proofreading Services: Jill Hand

This Book is Published By:
Whitechapel Press
A Division of Dark Haven Entertainment, Inc.
15 Forest Knolls Estates - Decatur, Illinois - 62521
(217) 422-1002 / 1-888-GHOSTLY
Visit us on the internet at http://www.prairieghosts.com

First Edition -- August 2007
ISBN: 1-892523-53-1

Printed in the United States of America

MYSTERIOUS KENTUCKY
TABLE OF CONTENTS

FOREWORD

Just like my father before me, I've always loved a good story. My dad, Sidney T. Nunnelly, was a master storyteller. The entire family spent many an evening in my childhood just sitting and listening to the yarns he'd spin. We didn't even need a television or a radio. And all his stories were true. That was the part which enraptured us, his audience, and kept us riveted to every well-crafted word. When he passed on in 1994, the region lost one of the great unknown orators of his time.

My father was one more member of a swiftly vanishing generation of Kentucky storytellers who were taken too early, their stories unrecorded, lost forever to us all. In this day and age, amid the death spasms of oral tradition, family stories have been replaced with videos and personal computers. People are too busy. They hardly speak to each other anymore, it seems, and the loss is a great one to society as a whole. Paradoxically, the love of the story remains unchanged. Nearly everyone feels the yearning to be swept away to mysterious places, to see fantastic sights and experience unexplainable enigmas through the power of the written or spoken word.

True stories are especially intriguing. Even more so if they are of a controversial, fantastic, bizarre, anomalous or mysterious nature such as the ones this book attempts to chronicle, many for the very first time. Included as well, are my own personal experiences with the unknown, which force me to view every strange tale that I have collected herein with an open mind. Skeptics will contend, I'm sure, that my view of these mysteries is, perhaps, too liberal, but incredible things really do happen to ordinary people, and I present these accounts as they either happened or were given to me.

I have always deemed it absolutely necessary to refuse to let my own views, opinions and/or beliefs influence the data that witnesses present, or the manner in which it is collected. I am capable of either accepting or dismissing each account on its own content and merits according to my own paradigms. It is certainly not my place, however, to do this for everyone, although many researchers have no problem doing so. They choose to accept only the anomalous data regarding a given topic which supports their own preconceived notions as to the topic's nature or origins, to the exclusion of any and all evidence to the contrary. Not only is this tendency wholly unscientific, but it shows a curious lack of foresight regarding mysteries about which almost nothing is known for certain.

I consider these researchers akin to a detective investigating a murder with a preconceived notion about the identity of the culprit. He comes across two pieces of evidence, one of which incriminates his suspect. This detective would accept only the evidence which supports his view, entirely ignoring the other. Another analogy would be like taking a large puzzle, sorting through the pieces to remove the ones that don't contain one's favorite color, then trying to complete the puzzle without them.

I prefer to record the data as presented, and rely on everyone else to make up their own minds just as I have done.

Many people are to be thanked for their generous help and inspiration in completing such a Fortean work as this. I humbly thank them all for their outpouring of support. Loren Coleman, Linda Godfrey, Nick Redfern, Mary Green, Chad Arment, Bill Hancock, Stephen Wagner, Ella Howard, Charlie Raymond, Terry Wilson, Joshua Sparks, Angela Barth, Connie Gwinnup, Chris Thompson, Kent Ballard, Ray Crowe, Jan Thompson, Kent Ballard, Doug Tarrant, Pearl Prihoda, Mark Machek, Bill Green, Russell Bedwell, Chris Kavanagh, Troy Taylor and my wife, Audra and son, Jerrod.

INTRODUCTION

If someone were to ask you how well you know your own hometown chances are you could answer "Pretty well." But, unless you're a local historian, if that same person were to ask you if you remember what happened there in 1950, most would find themselves answering, "No. What?" Those born well after the time period in question would have practically no chance of knowing about events "way back then." It's not surprising that, given the passage of nearly six decades, even those living in that era would likely have forgotten all but the most memorable events of their day.

Kentucky, the Bluegrass State, world-renowned home of horseraces and fine bourbons, is also a place filled with intriguing mysteries that have defied explanation since the first settlers stepped onto its fertile soil and began exploring its beautifully forested mountains and valleys. For over 200 years these enigmas have remained. There have been reports of encounters with unknown creatures and frightening apparitions and terrifying, even deadly, experiences with extraterrestrial phenomena and alien entities.

All manner of odd things abound in Kentucky's borders, from discoveries of gigantic human skeletal remains belonging to lost, forgotten or completely unknown races of beings, to sightings of diminutive humanoids who wear bright clothing and pointed hats. In fact, some of the world's most famous and baffling accounts of Fortean phenomena have taken place here. Some of the reports are extremely bizarre and unsettling, as you will see. Since Kentuckians are well known for their staunch resilience and naturally tight-lipped dispositions it can be safely assumed that hundreds, if not thousands, more of these atypical experiences have gone unreported for fear of public ridicule and personal repercussions and remain unavailable to public scrutiny.

This book attempts to bring to light a few of Kentucky's oddities, many for the first time in print, as well as to review some of the more well-known accounts which have been a matter of record for many years. Some researchers of Fortean events tend to dismiss out of hand the more bizarre reports, simply labeling them as hallucinations, misidentifications, misperceptions or outright fabrications. This book will not. All testimony is faithfully recorded in its entirety for the reader to draw his own conclusions regarding the validity of such claims. This book should NOT be considered folklore, containing mere superstitious myth, not to be taken seriously. After all, how does "folklore" leave giant footprints in one's field, turn a doorknob, kill livestock and people, or steal meat from freezers?

Many outsiders view Kentuckians through stereotypical eyes, as backwards hillbillies who lack basic skills, intelligence and technology. This is a highly false impression, as many of the world's most talented athletes, performers and thinkers have hailed from this state.

However, Kentucky is almost completely overlooked when it comes to any type of serious scientific attempts to gather reputable data concerning unexplained phenomena, even though, as we shall see, the state is overflowing with such accounts. This type of cultural data is especially vulnerable to being relegated to the dusty bins of the forgotten. For example, how many people living in Wolf County still remember, or have ever even heard of, the huge fish-shaped airship cruising around in the sky seen by many witnesses back in 1927? Not many, you can be sure. How many citizens of Russellville are aware that a gigantic phantom tiger was seen and even shot at there in 1823? How many people now living in Hopkinsville realize that Edgar Cayce, the man known as the Sleeping Prophet, was born, grew up and received his amazing powers there?

Incidents such as these, which no doubt caused quite the stir back in their own times, are now mostly forgotten to all but the few Fortean researchers who doggedly plow through book after book, article after article, specifically looking for accounts of the unexplained.

Many of the enigmas included herein can still be experienced to this day in Kentucky. Others are now long gone and unheard of for decades. A good portion of this book contains events and experiences of a personal nature, which I can attest to without hesitation. They are gathered from a lifetime of walking along the dark hills and wandering the thick forests and lonely river bottoms of this mysterious state. Many stem from the years I've spent searching for the secrets that lie hidden beneath the hills or unseen at the bottoms of deep, still pools.

In Kentucky, I've lived in stately old houses haunted by malevolent specters, shades of the unseen spirit world. In Kentucky, I've seen creatures which defy belief which haunt the seldom-visited bottomlands even now, creatures which could not (and officially do not) exist in reality, and yet there they were. In Kentucky I've discovered hidden caves and subterranean passages into which men far braver than myself dared not go. Staring into the stygian darkness of places such as these one feels a distinctive chill as some primordial memory stirs within, demanding only that you flee at once and not look back. In Kentucky, I've walked the stony streams and found traces of an unknown and unnamed race that trod there before me, centuries ago. I've seen things that fly through the air, things that swim through the water and things that walk on dry land, upright, like men, but are not. I've seen all these things right here in the Bluegrass State and, I assure you, I'm not the only one. I've listened to and recorded the stories of others like me. Stories told to me first-hand, not as rumor or folklore, but as true instances of remarkable things happening to honest, ordinary people with nothing to be gained from the disclosure. I've seen it all and heard about the rest right here in my home state. And I've written it down, lest we forget that we are not omniscient by any means. We do not know all there is to know about the mysteries of nature.

Hopefully, this book may even inspire some to begin a search of their own for answers to these mysteries, as I did many years ago, inspired by my own experiences and the works of other intrepid researchers such as Loren Coleman, John Keel, Bernard Huevelmans, Jerome Clark, Ivan T. Sanderson and Brad Steiger. Should this be the case, be forewarned. There are precious few answers to be found. Only ever-deepening mysteries which will expand and broaden the way one perceives this wonderfully mysterious planet on which we live.

Enigmas exist to grant us a sense of wonder. They are still there awaiting anyone with enough will and fortitude to undertake the endlessly exciting journey to the borderlands of the unknown.

B.M. Nunnelly
Summer 2007

1. KENTUCKY'S MYSTERIOUS PAST

Archeological Anomalies
Unusual Skeletal Remains
Mysterious Structures
Kentucky: Birthplace of Paleontology

Interest in the collection, categorization and preservation of fossils in North America began right here in Kentucky in 1739 with the discovery of mastodon and giant sloth remains in Boone County. A Frenchman by the name of Charles L. DeLongueil, while on a return trip to Quebec, found huge bones, teeth and tusks in a bog at a location aptly known as Big Bone Lick. DeLongueil immediately changed his plans and set sail for France where he presented his relics of American antiquity to King Louis XIII. They were placed in the king's own cabinet for exhibition, where they aroused so much interest, not only in France but throughout Europe, that another expedition was sent to Boone County in 1766 to acquire a second collection. The very first important paper on the subject of vertebrate paleontology of Kentucky and North America was presented a year later to the Royal Society of London. After examination by one of its members, erudite naturalist Peter Collison, many others soon followed. In London, the Kentucky fossils were examined by one Benjamin Franklin, who wrote down his opinions concerning them on Aug. 5, 1767. In 1801, newly elected president Thomas Jefferson penned his own descriptions of the extinct creatures found as fossils at Big Bone Lick. They were published in book format under the title "Big Bones of Kentucky."

In more recent times, the Bluegrass State has continued to be fertile ground for discoveries of the fossilized remains of extinct Ice Age mammals, with dozens of counties reporting scores of finds. A great portion of Ice Age fauna are well represented in the fossil record of the state, but what of the ancient peoples who once inhabited Kentucky? Who were they and what were they like?

THE MYSTERIOUS KENTUCKY MOUND BUILDERS

Throughout the state can be found thousands of artificial hills of dirt. These mounds are believed to be creations of the Native Americans and long held to have been constructed exclusively for the purpose of burying the dead, though recent discoveries have shown this to be an erroneous assumption. The earthworks have been attributed to a mysterious culture known as the "Adenas", or Mound Builders. They were an unusually tall people with large, rounded heads who tamed the wilderness of Kentucky and wandered here for nearly a thousand years. The Adena culture introduced farming and the creation of beautifully crafted vessels of pottery and clay. They are also presumed to be largely responsible for the creation of many of the mounds of immense size and enigmatic shapes that can be found within the commonwealth. However, consensus holds that only about half of the mounds the Adenas left behind have anything to do with the actual burials of Adena dead. What the other half were used for and why they were built still remains a matter of conjecture.

The Adena folk were unusually tall and powerfully built; women over six feet tall and men approaching heights of seven feet have been discovered. It would seem that a band of strikingly different people of great presence and majesty had forced their way into the Ohio Valley from somewhere about 1000 B.C.,' wrote Robert Silverberg in *Mound Builders of Ancient America.*

While the largest examples of both burial and effigy mounds are located in other states, Kentucky can lay claim to more than its share of these enigmatic earth works. Unfortunately, as no artifacts of everyday life have been found in association with supposed Adena sites, almost nothing is known about the people themselves. Who they were, where they came from, what they called themselves. All unknown. It is commonly believed that this race was 'absorbed' into the advancing Hopewell cultures over a period of time. However others feel that the Adena people, for unknown reasons, seem to have disappeared as suddenly as they appeared. Where they went and what became of them remains an archeological mystery.

In 1989, a Union County farm owned by a family named Slack was pillaged by artifact hunters. A once well-preserved site was left a vast stretch of gaping holes and ravished graves. This incident led to strict laws being passed making any attempt to expose the contents of ancient burial sites a felony punishable with a lengthy prison term

But legislation came too late for thousands of mounds which have fallen prey to looters of every type for generations, people from all walks of life eager to take advantage of the lucrative black market artifact trade or, perversely, those who dug into mounds out of admiration for the craftsmanship of the objects contained within. However, long before the artifacts themselves were considered to be monetarily valuable, the principal interest lay in the occupants of the mounds. In the past, numerous attempts to solve the riddle of who was actually responsible for the creation of the mounds resulted in many of the earthworks being opened and the contents exhumed by both the trained and untrained, professional and amateur archeologists alike. Some of what was found to be interred in these hills of earth proved to be intriguing to say the least. Perhaps even sensational.

ANOMALOUS ARTIFACTS

In the late 1800s some 10 mounds in Henderson County, located just across the Ohio River from Diamond Island, attracted some attention. A professional excavating firm was called in from out of state and they immediately busied themselves with the task of digging up only two of the 10. To everyone's surprise it was announced that the mounds held the remains of a "pre-Indian" culture. Many artifacts of decidedly "un-Indian" appearance were brought forth, most of them made of glass. A. J. Anderson, the owner of the property, was also involved in the dig. Anderson claimed that the trinkets of glass were handsomely carved and, no doubt, belonged to a culture which existed long before the arrival of the Native Americans to whom mounds of this nature were invariably attributed.

Colonel A. H. Majors also found mounds on his own Henderson County property and dug into them. He, too, claimed to have discovered evidence linking the mounds to a pre-Indian race though I can find no record or descriptions of any artifacts that he may have unearthed. It is interesting to note that in both these early accounts there is a curious absence of the discovery of any human skeletal remains inside the mounds. I visited this area on several occasions and was able to walk some of the many ridges and cultivated fields there. The 10 mounds have long since disappeared beneath the farmer's plow and the devastating effects of soil erosion. I was able to find two good examples of worked glass on my first trip. They appeared to be examples of hand-held scrapers or "skinners" as they are called. Though they were not "handsomely carved" they did appear to be genuine artifacts and, although it is known that glass was unavailable to early cultures and so not worked into tools by them, these did appear to be of American Indian construction.

The Mound Builders, it would seem, most likely consisted of not one but several very different and unrelated peoples, but they were by no means the only mysterious culture to have lived in the Bluegrass State in the distant past. Other enigmatic groups, about which nearly nothing at all is known, evidently made their home here as well. Few have ever even heard of the" Kentucky Stone Graves" people. This is due mainly to the fact that nearly everything about this race lies shrouded in mystery. They were a people unto themselves and did not follow or share the customs of their prehistoric counterparts. They did not burn their dead or bury them in mounds but in shallow graves marked by massive head and heel-stones - two large stones that are placed upright, or standing, with the cadaver interred between them. They did not inscribe the stones with markings of any kind and, unlike similar burial sites found in neighboring states, no artifact of any sort, not so much as a thread of clothing, has ever been found in association with these Kentucky burials. Also, the Stone Graves skeletal remains were found to be of smaller stature than contemporary Indians and, whereas the Mound Builders' earthworks proliferate over an extremely large area, by contrast, fewer than 10 Stone Grave burials have been found. All of them in northern Kentucky.

This archeological riddle still waits to be solved but, when and if it ever is, there are still others of some merit waiting to take its place. In spite of all evidence and testimony to the contrary, mainstream archeology still does not officially recognize one single example of a "pre-Indian" culture as existing in North America. It has, for generations, been a commonly held scientific "fact" that neither humans nor their progenitors lived on this continent at all before the last great ice-age, when much of the earth's ocean water dramatically froze, becoming glaciers and causing tremendous drops in sea levels around the globe, thus creating a natural land-bridge of ice between Asia and the Americas. Many different species of prehistoric animals, including mammoths, then wandered across this bridge, soon followed by nomadic stone age hunters - the ancestors of today's Native Americans. No one knows why these intrepid adventurers decided to journey thousands of miles across a sea of fatally cold ice or what they even expected to find on the other side but, in theory, that is exactly what they did. Gradually, as the earth's climate warmed back up and the glacial ice-caps began to melt, the waters rose once again to flood back over the land bridge and effectively strand forever anything and anyone that had previously crossed over. This bridge was located in the Bering Straits and it has been taught that all of this supposedly happened a mere 12,000 to 20,000 years ago. Knowing all this it would seem safe enough to assume that the words "mysterious" and "pre-Indian" are synonymous since, geologically speaking, no human presence was to be found in the Americas before the arrival of the Indians' ancestors. Therefore any artifact or evidence pointing to a pre-Indian race could not exist.

But recent archeological evidence found in North America has shaken this long held notion and forced academia to reconsider, revise or erase completely much of what has been written and taught about the first peoples of this continent for generations. It is only now being grudgingly conceded that man has lived here for tens of thousands of years longer than all previous guesses-no matter how learned they may have been. Recent archeological discoveries in states like California, for example, have pushed the envelope of human occupancy as far back as 70,000 years! But, incredibly, even the people who walked the earth during that distant era were mere geological infants compared to those who apparently once roamed the dark hills of Kentucky.

Evidence of human presence has been reported from sites in the Bluegrass State which goes far back into the dimness of mankind's past, and far beyond, to a time when no man of any type was supposed to be walking around on two feet, much less leaving behind him evidences of structured societies.

We know from scores of fossil recoveries from across the state that many species of Pleistocene vertebrates, or ice-age mammals, thrived within Kentucky's boundaries, with the mastodon (*mammut americanum*) being the most plentiful, having adapted extremely well to the area's climate and ecology. Since it is officially believed that these huge, elephantine colossuses became extinct long before early man developed any type of recognizable civilization, no evidence of civilized man, geologically speaking, should be discovered anywhere but above strata containing fossilized remains of mastodons. Certainly no artifact of man could possibly exist in the earth far below the remains of mammoths. Right?

A prehistoric site found in Blue Lick, Nicholas County, cries out in contradiction. Excited workers excavating there at a depth of 12 feet discovered the bones of a mastodon. They dug even deeper in the hopes that more big bones might be found and then, three feet below the mastodon remains, they made a remarkable discovery. A set stone wall of "perfect design and craftsmanship." So obvious was it to all who beheld it that no act of nature could have formed and executed such a structure, that each witness was entirely convinced of its origins by the hands of some form of early man. The wall seemed to continue into the hill in both directions and, even now, has never been entirely excavated or adequately explained. Simple logic, however, cries out that man, of some intelligent, wall-building sort, was in this location long before the arrival of the mastodons. And this is by no means the only example. If it were it might be easy to dismiss the structure as some type of accident or freak of nature.

In 1886, workmen quarrying rock on the Frankfort Pike, one mile from Frankfort, were astonished to find another such man-made wall of stone, this one encased in Limestone 30 feet below the ground's surface. The massive structure, completely mortared and with well-dressed joints and seams, was described as being constructed with such skill that it would be greatly envied by the best stone masons of the day. Since the formation of limestone takes millions of years to complete it would seem that this profession is a far older one than any historian has ever dreamed! If the data that has been recorded in Kentucky is accurate, the implications are staggering.

Another find, this one in Jackson County in the previous year, 1885, had already caused quite an uproar in the scientific community. There, in the Cumberland Mountains at a place then known simply as Big Hill, a well-used wagon trail had eventually worn down the earth far enough to uncover a layer of sandstone upon which were found 300 million-year-old tracks of several prehistoric creatures including bears and horses. Although it is believed that horses were not native to North America, only being introduced here at a much later date, the sensational aspect of this find was the fact that, alongside the animal prints were the clear impressions of two footprints of a human being. Following a thorough examination of the tracks, Prof. J. F. Brown, of Berea College announced his opinion that the prints were of human origin and that they "...were of good size (or larger than normal for a man), with toes well spread and distinctly marked."

Decades later, in 1938, Dr. Wilbur S. Burroughs, head of geology at Berea, announced his discovery of no less than 10 fossilized human footprints on a farm owned by one Mr. O. Finnell. The tracks measured nine and a half inches long by six inches wide across the toes with a stride of 18 inches. Photographs taken through a microscope and infrared photography revealed no signs of carving, or pecking such as the Native Americans were known to employ in the creation of petroglyphs. Also, a sand grain count revealed that the prints had been formed by the impact pressure which came directly from the feet that made them, actually rolling up sand particles around the outer edges of the tracks. This effect was, to any Indian rock artist, completely impossible to duplicate. The rock formation upon which the tracks were impressed was reportedly 250 to 300 million years old. No further investigation was possible due to the prints' subsequent destruction by vandals attempting to chip them free of the surrounding rock.

Other examples of curious artifacts found in Indian mounds exist as well, such as the iron fork found in a prehistoric mound near Eddyville in the summer of 1959. The announcement was made by Dr. Douglas Schwartz, director of the Museum of Anthropology at the University of Kentucky. Schwartz and his group had unearthed the object, described as having two well-rusted tines and a bone handle, while excavating a prehistoric site in Lyon County. Also found, within a few feet of the fork and in the same strata, were a number of Indian skeletal remains, flint knives, projectile points and pottery vessels. By virtue of these artifacts the site was dated to around 1200 B.C. Schwartz, realizing that early Native Americans possessed no utensils of worked iron and forks were certainly unknown to them, offered his academic peers the only explanation he could think of as to the presence of the anomalous artifact. It was weak, he freely admitted, but his theory was that perhaps a wayward traveler might have dropped the fork into an ash-pit at a much later date.

This fanciful solution obviously created more questions than it was meant to answer. Questions which went unasked. Incredibly, this explanation seemed to satisfy everyone involved and the incident faded quickly from public attention. Simply put, the fork could not have been "dropped" down to the level at which it was found if dropped from the surface at a much later date. It is much more feasible that the Indians obtained the object from members of a contemporaneous culture which had some knowledge of metallurgy and the ability to mine and work iron.

Other anomalous artifacts found in Kentucky include coins such as the ancient Hebrew coin found in 1952 by Robert Fox from Park City. The coin was positively identified by Dr. Ralph Marcus of the University of Chicago, a leading scholar of Hellenistic culture, as well as three other independent professional analysts, and dated at the year A.D. 133. Other Hebrew coins of the same era were found in Pleasure Ridge Park in 1940 and in Hopkinsville in 1950. A coin found by Mr. L. B. Redding while tending his garden in Lexington in 1928, turned out to be a 15th century Italian medallion dated A. D. 1446.

STORIES IN STONE

Kentucky's Mysterious Rock Carvers
Curious Kentucky Petroglyphs and Pictographs

It might be considered only logical to ask, if creatures such as the "Spottsville Monster" and the "Beast of LBL" have been running around Kentucky for so long, wouldn't the Indians have known about it? The answer is yes. Nearly all Native American tribes have their own oral histories regarding these dangerous, hairy "man-beasts." Unfortunately, they did not possess a written language. Instead they conveyed ideas using both petroglyphs (rock carvings) and pictographs (rock paintings.)

In Edmonson County, there is a placed called the Asphalt Rock Site, where a series of three ancient rock shelters lie beneath the shadow of a line of cliffs overlooking the Green River. In the middle of this trio, painted in dull red on the upper portion of the rear wall in what is one of only two documented pictographic sites in the entire state, is a bizarre humanoid figure which stands as one of the best examples of ancient "Beast Man" images I have seen. The figure is depicted standing up like a man with its arms above its head, its clawed fingers spread menacingly. It has a cat-like, muzzled face, hairy body and either horns or pointed ears. The lower portion of the image is heavily weathered, a testimony to its great antiquity and authenticity as an actual Native American pictograph.

It is believed that for more than 12,000 years all parts of Kentucky were inhabited, or at least well traversed, by many tribes of early Native Americans. Much is known of the history and culture of many of these tribes but the meaning of the strange symbols and images which they are given credit for carving, or pecking, into the rocks of Kentucky in ancient times remains largely enigmatic to this day. Therefore, this chapter on Kentucky's mysterious past should not conclude without some mention of this interesting topic.

Twenty-seven counties in the Bluegrass State have been officially recorded as possessing examples of ancient petroglyphic or pictographic art forms. In these counties, 71 sites of this nature have been documented. It can be safely assumed that, just like the curious mound platforms that proliferate here, many more examples remain undiscovered by modern man, having been swallowed up over the centuries by dense growths of trees and thickets. And no one can say how many darkened caves exist with strange images decorating their walls which have never been, or may never be, gazed upon by the eyes of the white man. No one knows of a certainty who was responsible for many of these images or what they might mean. So let us examine just a few of them. Though all are extremely interesting from an historical standpoint, some are particularly so, for they depict images of an anomalous nature or atypical to what might be expected to spring from the hands of early Amerindian artists.

In Carter County, at a place known as Carter Caves, can be found one of only two known pictographic sites in the entire state. There, at the base of a limestone cliff, can be found the painted image of a cross within a circle and, beside it, the representation of a gigantic human foot measuring 24 inches long from toe to heel. It remains the only limestone pictograph as yet discovered in Kentucky. The circled cross conjures images of European origin and much resembles the insignia used by the Knights Templar though, in the end, this is merely speculation. Who can guess as to the meaning of the gigantic footprint? Perhaps the images were meant to convey to future generations that giant Europeans once lived or passed through the area. But, then again, this might be accrediting this early culture with a simplicity to match even our own. Examples of petroglyphic sites which contain similar images of giant, seemingly human footprints abound within the state, but seem at odds regarding the number of toe-digits that these images display. Four, five and even six digits are all represented in the carven images.

A particularly interesting example of giant, four- toed footprints can be seen in Powell County, at the Ledford Hollow petroglyphic site. The two huge footprints, carved side-by-side, are portrayed with well-defined arches, which suggests to many the usage of some type of shoes.

The only other known pictographic site in the Bluegrass State can be found in Edmonson County. The images depicted here are even more mysterious. They are located on a sandstone rock shelter, the middle of three, at the base of a line of cliffs which overlook the lush and mysterious Green River Valley. Generations of zealous artifact hunters have extensively dug into the floor of this shelter but, amazingly, not a single one of them has ever defaced the paintings which overlook the site from the upper portion of the back wall. There, painted in red and somewhat faded by the passage of ages, is the image of a strange type of creature. Human-like, though not quite human, it sports two short pointed ears or horns on the top of its head and stands on two legs with its sharp talons raised on human-like arms above its head. It seems to be covered with hair or fur and has a most unusual, almost catlike, face with no visible mouth. Unrecognizable symbols are painted there as well alongside smaller, fainter, representations of a raptorial bird with another puzzling image below the horned creature. This one seems to show an animal of some type rearing up on the back pair of four short, thick legs. It has a long, slim tail and an even longer, slimmer neck topped by a small, round head. It resembles, for all the world, nothing so much as a certain type of dinosaur with which most of us are familiar.

In Butler County, southeast of Reedyville, also within the shadow of the Green River, can be seen more bizarre images. The petroglyphs here lie along a small creek bank on an outcropping of sandstone known as the Caseyville Formation and seem remarkably un-Indian. Some might say even alien. Again the symbol of a cross within a circle is present, this time encased within a larger half circle positioned next to strange markings which resemble ancient runes or unknown letters. But the most interesting part of the Reedyville petroglyphs is the enigmatic human figure standing with outstretched arms upon a bisected circle surrounded by other circles. The figure appears to be helmeted and standing over a particular planet in deep space.

At a petroglyphic site in Estill County we find even more otherworldly carvings. These seem to show, from antiquity, depictions of what modern day Forteans would call the 'classic' grey aliens allegedly from outer space. Here, alongside other boulders which contain human stick figures and fertility symbols, rests a large boulder bearing the petroglyphs of three large humanoid heads. They are bulbous and round, completely without hair or noses and are depicted with large, round eyes. One head is completely circular with rays of lines radiating from it like shafts of light. Yet another Kentucky site inscribed with human-like figures with big, round heads with no hair can be found in Livingston County.

Who were these ancient artists and what were they trying to depict? The list goes on. In Madison County there appear carvings of human, or human-like, stick figures with small heads and big, round feet which sport only three toes. Also depicted, rather boldly, is a raptorial bird. A thunderbird perhaps? With a short tail and four toes.

But those crazy early artisans in Lee County may have gone too far. There can be found the carven image of an animal with a long neck, upright pointed ears or horns, six legs and what appears to be a pair of feathered wings sprouting from its back!

So just how accurate were all those tedious history lessons in high school? Ultimately, history is only as good as those who record it. In Wolf County was found a boulder inscribed with the date 1717 upon its face amid many other Amerindian markings known as "bird tracks." The date inscribed seems much older and more weathered than the markings attributed to the Indians and yet, the first documented visit to Kentucky by outsiders was in the year 1750. It is interesting to note that, of all the rock carvings known to exist in this state, these bird tracks are far and away the most common and widespread. When carved upright they are best described as looking like a simplified three-pronged trident. If these are indeed symbols then some meaning must have been ascribed to them by these ancient stone carvers. These simple tridents have been found at prehistoric sites all over the world. Sometimes even in the most unexpected locations such as the ocean floor and, once in 1958, 7,000 feet below the Arctic ice. Unfortunately for us, the meaning of these strange marks remains just as mysterious as the people who carved them. Curiously, the trident has long been considered the symbol which represents the legendary lost continent of Atlantis which, according to most accounts, sank beneath the waves of the Atlantic Ocean over 10,000 years ago. Very strange.

CURIOUS SKELETAL REMAINS

According to Lewis and Richard Collins' "History of Kentucky," 19th century spelunkers, while exploring a cave in Muhlenberg County, discovered the remains of four mummified people dressed as Romans. Bizarrely, also found in the burial chamber was the corpse of a monkey. All the remains, including the monkey's, were petrified. No Romans in Kentucky, you say? What about Vikings? In 1932, near Louisville, a mound was reportedly found to contain the remains of several Indians and a blonde-haired, bearded Viking warrior, complete with metal shield, spear, sword, knife and helmet. Later, after examining the contents of the Indian medicine man's pouch and finding it filled with Indian Head pennies, one of the men who made the discovery reportedly committed suicide. When authorities were brought to the scene the burial cavern was empty save for the shield, an unusual silver peace-pipe and the pouch of old pennies. All the bodies had disappeared. The site was roped off and then ordered bulldozed by local authorities. The shield was identified as Viking in origin by a large university and given to a museum in Washington, D.C. No explanation as to the origin of the pipe or the disappearance of the bodies was forthcoming. Then, eight years later, in 1940, a man named Elias Calloway was squirrel hunting directly above the former burial site when he found three large stones decorated with strange looking symbols and curious markings, obviously writing of some sort. Since he found himself unable to decipher the meanings of the marks he contacted a prominent museum and two archaeologists were soon dispatched to the Calloway home. They were amazed to find the stones were actually Viking rune stones telling how a contingent of warriors became ship-wrecked on the Virginia coast and made their way westward, dying one by one from sickness and hostile Indian attacks, until they came to the Ohio River. The last remainder of this group had apparently befriended the local Indians and was buried in the mound, which was thought to have been at least 200 years old. Native American Indian legends claiming knowledge of the presence of blonde, or red haired, 'Nordic' types which pre-date the arrival of Europeans have circulated for at least two centuries.

Digging even deeper into the past, let us now focus on some even more bizarre skeletal anomalies.

GIANTS IN KENTUCKY

Bracken County
Augusta, Ky., 1792.
According to author Lewis Collins, an early settler, General John Payne, made a startling discovery while building his house along the Ohio River.

'The bottom on which Augusta is situated is a large burying ground of the ancients...They have been found in great numbers, and of all sizes, everywhere between the mouths of Bracken and Locust creeks, a distance of about a mile and a half. From the cellar under my (Payne's) dwelling, 60 by 70 feet, over a hundred and ten skeletons were taken. I measured them by skulls, and there might have been more, whose skulls had crumbled into dust...The skeletons were of all sizes, from seven feet to infant. David Kilgour (who was a tall and very large man) passed our village at the time I was excavating my cellar, and we took him down and applied a thigh bone to his. The man, if well-proportioned, must have been 10 to 12 inches taller than Kilgour, and the lower jaw bone would slip on over his, skin and all. Who were they? How came their bones here?'

Adair County
From the *Louisville Courier-Journal,* Jan. 30, 1876
Columbia, Ky. 'Two young men named White, while idly wandering in a large tract of wild, dense forest, in the south-eastern part of our county, discovered what they supposed to be a sink-hole or fox-den, and with that idea proceeded to explore it. After a little trouble in making their way through the entrance, the cave (for such it proved to be) became large enough to admit of their walking upright. They had proceeded thus in this passage probably 150 yards, when they emerged into a large and picturesque gallery, the beauty and grandeur of which will rival that of the old Mammoth (Cave) itself. The room, according to their calculations, is about 150 by 100 feet, and abounds in all the varieties of the stalactite and stalagmite

But it is not the things we naturally expect to find in caves that we wish to mention particularly, but the curious remains that we discovered therein. In the northeast corner of the first gallery, (which there are five that we will speak of) about five feet from the ground, they noticed some strange characters, or hieroglyphics, neatly carved in the wall which, upon close examination, proved to be the head-rock of a vault. A few minutes prying served to loosen this and disclose to view the interior of an enclosure in the solid rock of about five by ten feet, which contained the remains of three skeletons which measure eight feet seven and a half inches, eight feet five inches and eight feet four and three quarter inches in length respectively. The heads were lying toward the east, each body parallel to the other. Beside them lay three huge (what looked to be) swords, but they were so decayed that, upon being touched, they crumbled to dust.

After examining the remains closely, but finding nothing that would serve to throw any light on the question as to who and from whence they are, they closed the vault, but in doing so, knocked their torch out, which they had contrived before entering, leaving them in anything but a pleasant predicament. After searching some time for their lost treasure, they concluded to try to escape by feeling their way out, but in this they made the matter worse. They stated that after leaving the first large room they struck a good sized branch, and continued following it until forced to turn into another passage, the stream disappearing suddenly in a huge perpendicular gulch which led them into another spacious hall, the size of which they believe to be quite as large as the first.? Out of this second opening, and through what they conceived to be three others similar at least in size, their way seemed to gradually ascend, until their hearts were made glad by the discovery of light ahead, and finally emerged from their ugly confinement through a hole about midway up the cliff of Russell's Creek, having been confined in their subterranean discovery over thirty eight hours. The whole country thereabouts is rife with speculations concerning the interesting discovery, and numbers of citizens will visit it as soon as the Messrs. White finish their work of rendering the entrance less difficult to pass.? The above is a correct account and may be replied on, as the young men are of unimpeachable veracity. With a party from town, your correspondent will start in the morning to further explore and should new curiosities present themselves, will give you the account of an eyewitness.'

According to the *Adair County News*, On Jan. 5, 1858, an Indian mound located on the farm of one Harrison Robinson was excavated and yielded giant human skeletal remains as well.

The late Michael Paul Henson, well-known Kentucky writer and folklorist, wrote in "Tragedy at Devil's Hollow and other Kentucky Ghost Stories," (Cockrel Corp. Publishers, 1985) of another bizarre skeleton found at Holley Creek, Breathit County, in 1965, which he was personally able to examine. A man named Kenneth White, while constructing cattle stalls under a large, overhanging rock ledge near his home, came upon the perfectly preserved skeletal remains of what he, at first, took to be an Indian, as it was buried facing east, a well known Native American custom. Noticing some atypical aspects of the burial, White asked Henson to help further examine the strange bones, which were covered with a peculiar white powdery substance that disappeared when touched. Upon reassembling the bones the two were amazed to find that the unusual fellow, in life, had stood at least 8 feet, 9 inches tall. Moreover, the arms were abnormally long with large hands while the feet of the being seemed small by comparison. The skull measured an astounding 30 inches in circumference, just six inches shy of a full yard! But the most unusual aspect of the skeleton was the facial structure, the likes of which neither had ever before seen or even heard of.

'The eye and nose sockets were slits rather than cavities, and the area where the jaw bone hinges to the skull was solid bone,' Henson reported. Seemingly, this creature had never been able to open its mouth to eat or speak. No weapons, tools or clothing were found in association with the bones which, according to Henson's account, occupied a position five feet below ground, indicating that they had been placed there at least 300 years prior to their discovery. Strangely, Henson related that the burial site looked only a few days old with no sign of dark colored soil usually associated with the decaying of human tissue. The two assumed the remains were those of an extraordinarily large, deformed Indian. In the same area some 20 years prior a 60-pound, double-edged stone axe and a 20-inch flint blade were plowed up by a local farmer.

White later re-buried the peculiar bones and no official examination of them was ever conducted.

Henson died in March, 1995 without ever disclosing the exact location of the burial site.

A JOURNEY INTO SOUTH-CENTRAL KENTUCKY

On a sunny morning in May of 1997 my brother Dean and I set out to explore, for the first time, a few of the mysterious locations which were situated deep within the rugged forests of south central Kentucky. Our base of operations was his home in Summershade, Metcalf County, where he and his family had moved only a short time before. After spending the previous night there and going over our plans, we arose the next morning, armed ourselves with handguns and Bowie knives - two wilderness exploration essentials - and drove to nearby Cumberland County. Our plan was to drive as far as possible along a dirt access road and proceed on foot to a certain "interesting" area my brother had discovered a few weeks previously but had not been able to properly explore at the time. Of particular note was a cave he'd found, filled with old bones and flint shards. He and I had shared a mutual fascination with all places and things associated with Native American Indians since we were small children walking between the rows of corn which grew on the ridges in the bottomlands of Henderson County. That, and the promise of adventure had always proved irresistible to both of us.

Turning off the main road e ascended windingly up the side of an impressive hill and down into the wide, shallow streamed below. The sunshine glimmered on the clear running water as we drove through and up onto a narrow road to begin another ascent. After repeating the process several more times the hills became thickly forested, boulder-strewn mountains that soared upwards to our left. We had driven a couple miles further when I told him to stop the car. I had spotted what looked like the perfect spot for a possible cave in the mountainside about 75 feet above us. We pulled over as best we could in the limited space and set about finding an easy way up. This was soon afforded us in the form of a small stream that meandered down the mountainside. We climbed the streamed until we were level with the large boulders I had seen from below, then set off in their direction.

In the shadow of the rock shelters we found two caves, both with the openings inexplicably blocked by well placed stones of from 20 to 50 pounds each. We knew that it would take several hours to displace the stones and reveal the entrances and we had other sites to explore, so we decided to save this formidable task for another day and continued on our way to the site my brother wished to show me.

This turned out to be a dynamic limestone site. The entrance to the cave was nearly filled in with mud and flint rock so it was necessary to crawl on our bellies for about five yards over the jagged edges of these stones. Many of them were worked, I noticed, into crude blades and the edges were still fairly sharp. The crawlspace opened up into a good-sized chamber large enough to stand up in and move around. Old bones littered the rocky floor. Above our heads we saw a circular tunnel of solid stone about 15 feet in diameter, covered with stalagmites and a few bats, that reached upwards into the darkness for at least 25 feet.

I threw a stone up and over the ledge and judged by the sound of the echoes that another chamber was directly above us. Curiously, along the back of the cave wall were two branching

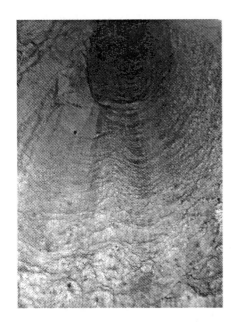

(Left) Vertical Cave Shaft discovered by the author
in south-central Kentucky

(Above) Cave site Entrance

tunnels which had been blocked, just as in the first location, with large, heavy stones that had obviously been brought in from outside the cave. On subsequent visits to the two sites, the stones were removed and tunnel entrances revealed, although they turned out to be uncomfortably cramped and so remain largely unexplored by anyone to my knowledge. The overhead tunnel proved inaccessible and still retains all of its initial mystery. A couple of projectile points from the archaic period were found in these locations which seemed otherwise unremarkable, at least the parts we could see. We carefully inspected the sites for signs of any modern human activity and could find none. No discarded soda cans, cigarette butts or candy wrappers. No discarded or spent shell casings. Not even a hastily scrawled set of initials on any of the cave walls.

My last venture into the wilds of south central Kentucky was in 2001. I had been largely unsuccessful in my attempts at gathering further information regarding the "Littlefoot" creatures and so decided to spend my remaining time in the area exploring the many creeks and mountainsides. We drove to a location that was several miles from the cave sites, took up our walking sticks, knives and handguns, and set off down a rocky creek bed in the middle of nowhere - miles from any apparent signs of civilization. We decided we'd like to know what was on the other side of one particular mountain we were passing so we began our ascent. Soon we came upon what looked like cairns, six or eight good-sized rocks stacked together one atop the other, spaced very 20 yards or so and standing about two feet high. We had no idea who made them, nor what they signified, so we continued on to the summit, breaking out of the woodline onto a series of peaceful looking meadows. These were also constructed one atop the other diminishing in size as they rose. The whole thing strongly resembled the many step pyramids of South America and other places we'd seen pictures of in books.

We stood there, my brother and I, and took it all in before descending once again to the creek and continuing onward. We were about three miles into the trek, walking along down

One example of thousands of curious stones found by the author in a south-central Kentucky stream

the middle of a stream taking care not to step on a water moccasin or timber rattler, when we began finding the curious stones. They lay in and along the creek bed by the thousands, meticulously crafted by unknown hands for unknown purposes into a variety of geometric shapes, the most common being the "wedge" shape, and the "wedge within a wedge" variation. In size, they ranged from just a few ounces to upwards of 20 pounds or so, and came in every color, utilizing in their construction every available local material. We examined many of the strange rocks and could only conclude that they were fashioned in such a manner which allowed them to be placed together piece by piece, like an ancient stony puzzle, to form walls or, at very least, one long wall of rock.

This was exciting stuff! We had both read about the Native American legends of the "Allegewi," fierce 10-foot-tall giants who supposedly inhabited all the lands east of the Mississippi River thousands of years ago. It was claimed that this race was white skinned, had 12 fingers and 12 toes each, a double row of teeth and were completely evil, existing only to kill. Also mentioned was the idea that these white devils constructed houses and walls of stone. After a lengthy and very bloody war, the Native Americans finally succeeded in killing or driving away the Allegewi, and toppling all of their houses and walls until there was not a stone left standing.

Were we standing in just such a location, a location which had remained virtually unchanged for thousands of years? The evidence of such a staggering number of worked stones certainly appeared to support the notion that these rocks had once comprised walls or structures of some sort. No Native American tribe that frequented the area in the distant past, to my knowledge, was known to build and inhabit stone dwellings. It was an intriguing concept to be sure, but one that we couldn't confirm. We found no writings or markings of any type on any of the stones we examined, nor on any of the nearby limestone cliffs. No projectile points or other artifacts could be discovered to possibly shed some light on the mystery. There was nothing to implicate any culture in known American history to this particular mystery site. We searched the immediate area but came up empty handed. I would've given a pretty penny at that moment, to have been able to view an undamaged and intact example of this architecture. A couple of hours later on the return trip back down the creek, I got my chance.

It was completely by accident, of course. We had stopped for a brief rest and, as I sat among the ferns on the creek bank, I heard the sound of faintly running water behind me. I turned to look but saw nothing so I got up to investigate. A couple of seconds later I was staring down at an enclosure which had been built around a natural spring of cold, fresh water which bubbled gently up from the ground. It was rectangular, built entirely with square cut stones and measured some seven feet long by four feet wide by three feet deep. Sank just in

(Above) The mysterious ancient well structure that was built over a fresh water spring. Discovered by the author in south-central Kentucky.

(Left) A close-up of the ancient well

front of the spring was a large, flat, smooth black stone. What I called a "footstone." Two feet above this and slightly behind it a long, square beam about a foot wide and six or seven inches thick was set into the walls. I called this a "seat stone" as it looked to be positioned to serve as a crude chair, perhaps to rest the ancient traveler while he drank his fill. The bottom of the structure was open-ended, allowing for the trickle of spring water to flow out of the enclosure, and capped with a "lintel stone," which was only slightly smaller than the seat stone and of similar appearance. All the rocks used in its construction appeared to be of similar size - about 14 inches long, four inches wide and four or five inches thick. They were well placed, mortarless, and covered with the moss of countless ages.

Who had constructed this mysterious well? Could this be convincing evidence of the truthfulness of the Allegewi legends, after whom the Allegheny mountains were supposedly named? Who can say? I sat down in the structure, bent, and drank from the ice cold, crystal

A closer view of the construction that went into the ancient well.

clear mountain spring just as members of the mysterious, possibly pre-Indian, culture had done many ages ago. I took film footage of the entire area for later reference. The time had come to leave south central Kentucky and make the return trip to my home in the western portion of the state.

As I endured the three-hour drive, I had not only the Littlefoot mystery to contemplate, but also another one concerning the commonwealth's truly mysterious peoples of the ancient past.

11. KENTUCKY'S MYSTERIOUS WATERS

AQUATIC ANOMALIES

One weekend in 1983, two of my brothers and I and an assortment of family friends were fishing on the banks of the Ohio River near downtown Henderson. It was a typical summer afternoon, sunny and hot and the water was calm, broken only by an occasional river barge or speedboat. The catfish were biting and we were all enjoying ourselves when a large object came floating downstream about ten yards out from the river bank on which we all sat. It was round and appeared to have a heavy coat of green moss about three inches thick covering most of its surface. There were bare patches as well, however, and within these I noticed patterns which appeared to resemble such as is found on turtle shells. The surface beneath the moss was smooth and a light tan color.

We were all debating what it could be when I announced that it was a giant turtle. Everyone laughed, of course, at the suggestion. This thing had to be close to the size of a Volkswagen. There were no turtles that big in the Ohio River. Especially not in Henderson. Everyone knew that. They stopped laughing, however, when the big turtle poked its head out from beneath the shell and looked around for a few seconds. Then the head slowly withdrew again and it floated languidly down the muddy river until it was out of sight. Swimming never was the same after that.

Reports of oversized specimens of aquatic "somethings," while more rare than ones concerning land-based cryptids, are not altogether uncommon. People have been seeing unusual things in Kentucky's many rivers and lakes for as long as memory serves. Sightings of not only relatively normal species such as giant turtles and catfish, but also of aquatic, or semi-aquatic, creatures of a more mysterious nature have been reported.

Water has always played an integral part in not only man's bid for survival, but also his ability to entertain himself. Hundreds of thousands of people make use of Kentucky's waterways each year for recreational purposes such as swimming, boating and waterskiing. Anglers of every type roam the rivers, lakes and streams year-round looking for that trophy catch or simply a good meal. Deep, clear water allures and invites, but what might be lying beneath the surface has always been a source of mystery and profound conjecture. When enjoying the proliferation of Bluegrass waterways few expect to see anything more alarming than a snake or two, and none ever expect to encounter anything more mysterious than a mild case of sunburn. Nevertheless, Kentucky's waters, especially its rivers, have proven more than a little capable of holding some surprises for anglers, boaters and swimmers down through the years. In a muddy river, for instance, a swimmer or boater cannot see what might be below him unless or until it gets very, very close. Consequently, when strange aquatic anomalies are encountered and reported, eyewitness descriptions tend to be either extremely vague or precisely detailed and frightening.

An acquaintance once told me that, back in the 1980s, he and some friends were fishing on the Ohio one evening in a twelve- foot John boat when up alongside it swam an alligator gar of tremendous size. Its head was near the bow of the boat, he claimed, while its tail was a couple of feet behind the stern. Also known as "freshwater barracudas," the alligator gar is a long, slender fish with an elongated snout, much like an alligator's, brimming with razor sharp, needle-like teeth. They can be aggressive under the right conditions, much like piranhas, and a 14-foot specimen could pretty much eat anything it wanted. These menacing-looking fish have been known to grow quite big, but they are most commonly seen in the three- to four-foot size range and it is possible that, under low lighting conditions, several of them swimming together might be mistaken for a single fish. On the other hand, that the genetic malady known as gigantism may sometimes occur in species of every genus is simply a matter of record, and it is also possible that the witness saw exactly what he claimed to.

Aside from possible examples of gigantism in known, otherwise normal, species of fish or amphibians, we have other accounts to consider.

GENNY
The Geneva Water Monster

On a sunny morning in the late 1980s, two teenage boys approached the muddy backwaters of the swollen Ohio River in Henderson County. As they walked down Klondike Road, they loaded the small .22 caliber pistol they had brought along with the intentions of getting in a little target practice by shooting turtles off logs. They reached the point where the mighty Ohio flowed over the road and stopped near the edge of the water, searching anxiously for possible targets, which were plentiful. Andy A. went first. His friend, Mike B. had persuaded his father to drive them to this isolated spot in the Geneva River bottoms but had chosen to remain behind in the car to read the daily newspaper. He wasn't far away and could hear the shots ring out clearly as the two boys took their turns.

After shooting for a few minutes, the boys had paused when Andy reportedly saw something bob up from the water just a few yards from where the two stood. It was a green colored, semi-circular "hump." like an auto tire, covered in moss with dark green circles about the size of baseballs spaced evenly about a foot apart along the outsides. He called his friend's attention to it and they both were amazed when another hump surfaced close to the first one. Then another, and another. All they could figure was that someone must've tied a string of tires together which had now come loose in the flood. All together five "humps" surfaced and the boys were starting to get the feeling that something wasn't quite right about the thing. All the humps were segmented and looked a great deal like the skin of a lizard. Then, at the front of the humps, a head arose from the water and the youths froze in their tracks, mouths agape in wonder and shock. They could clearly see the elongated snout and dark black eyes of the thing. The head slowly swung in their direction and, upon seeing them, almost as if surprised by their presence, the creature surged forward and sank very quickly, disappearing beneath

"Genny", the Geneva Water Monster. This illustration was created by the author based on directions and descriptions given to him by a witness

the swift muddy water.

I interviewed one of the witnesses, Andy A., in 1999 and found his story to be credible. He claimed that the creature was over 30 feet long, as big around as a tire, with no scales. He also described a darker line which ran lengthwise down the middle of its side, resembling the coloration which can be found on game fish such as bluegill and bass. When it fled, he claimed, it did not dive head first into the water, but "sank down" extremely fast. It was gone in a couple of seconds and swam by undulating its body from side to side like a huge snake, leaving a large wake that had washed up onto the road after the thing had passed. The entire episode lasted only 10 to15 seconds.

I was able to produce a sketch, under his directions, of this curious Kentucky cryptid. Andy told me that he would not have stuck one toe in the water that day. Not even for a thousand dollars. When asked why they didn't fire on it he said that they had both been so utterly shocked at what they were witnessing that the thought never even crossed their minds. He related that the most frightening aspect of the encounter was the thing's sheer size. He felt sure it was more than large enough to have swallowed either of them whole. In addition, the uncanny speed at which it was able to move, he said, had left them both shaken.

During a follow-up interview in 2005, Andy gave me the exact same details as he did in 1999. He was neither able to add anything to the account nor take anything away from it, which speaks much about the validity of his claims. The other witness, Mike B., just as he has done from the beginning, still refused to talk about the event.

Later, I learned that, at a July 4th camp-out in 2001, a man named James Kennedy reportedly saw a smaller version of a similar creature as it swam close to shore for nearly two hours. It was also described as being snake-like, with a beak which resembled a duck's. It was only about three feet long, about the size of the average water moccasin, but it swam with its head raised up out of the water. He was sure that it was no snake, or anything else he had ever seen before, having been able to watch it for a couple of hours as it swam in the shallows only three or four feet from the banks. He felt that he could've captured it easily, if only he hadn't failed to bring along a dip-net.

This took place within two miles of the Geneva encounter. The location of the these sightings is part of the Sloughs Wildlife Management Area, a ten thousand acre strip of wetlands, forests and well-cultivated fields bordered on the north by the Ohio River. All along the Kentucky side of the river the landscape remains unchanged for hundreds of square miles. The area is very sparsely populated, with long, lonely stretches of bottomland between one dwelling and the next. As a consequence, the odds of seeing the emergence of any aquatic animals other than turtles and the occasional fish are very remote. Nevertheless, sightings of these aquatic anomalies continue to happen again and again.

Personally, I am not unfamiliar with such creatures, having seen on a couple of occasions, and in the company of other witnesses, a similar creature in the Ohio River some twenty miles away in Stanley, Daviess County. Although viewed from a greater distance, the animal was similar to the Geneva cryptid in that it appeared serpentine except for its duck-like bill, or beak. Distance of sighting was roughly 50 yards and its appearance was that of a younger and smaller animal, perhaps a juvenile though not so young as the one Kennedy claimed to witness. The exposed portions were in size comparable to a grown man's forearm jutting from the water's surface. Many factors can sometimes combine to complicate sightings of this nature, most common being distance multiplied by the uneven quality of the river's surface. Some would suggest that it was merely a large duck, but my wife and I watched this creature for almost thirty minutes and it did not behave in an explainable manner. It would surface, then look around several times and sink, not dive, back beneath the waves only to come up again twenty yards away. It repeated this routine until it finally failed to resurface completely. At no time was a body visible above the water; only the neck and head.

On another occasion, I was driving home one afternoon heading south across the Evansville Bridge when I observed what appeared to be a long serpentine neck jutting at least five feet from the river just below me, ending in what looked like a small head. I took it to be a large piece of drift at first but, as I drew parallel to it and then past it, I wasn't so sure. The weather was mild and sunny and the water was, at that moment, calm and relatively clear. From my lofty viewpoint I could see at least three more feet of neck disappearing straight down beneath the water. In all my life along the rivers of western Kentucky, I have never seen or known driftwood to act in this manner, or float perpendicularly with so much extending from the river's surface. It remained perfectly still as the many cars, mine among them, traveled over the bridge. It was a light, sandy brown color and looked for all the world like a certain very famous water cryptid from a certain famous Scottish loch. This happened in the mid-1990s.

Also, from this general area, I was aware of another sighting of a monstrous aquatic unknown, as well as another, even older, account which almost ended tragically. One of the events happened in the late 1970s, also beneath the twin bridges which span the Ohio and connect Henderson, Kentucky to Evansville, Indiana. Back then, there was a floating gas station anchored in the area which provided fuel for the numerous boats and barges which plied the river both for business and pleasure. Randy O., an attendant, was working one night when a huge, terrifying creature rose up from the river just a few yards away. It scared him so badly that, once back ashore, he immediately quit his job and never returned. He is now a Baptist minister and is unwilling to give further details about the physical description of the creature. According to his brother who heard the story first-hand, he would only say that it had been "really, really big," and, evidently, quite terrifying.

Every year, Kentucky's swift-moving rivers claim the lives of many unfortunate people. The bodies of the victims are usually recovered, sooner or later. Some are intact. Others not so. Some are found missing limbs. The very unfortunate ones are never found at all. Boat propellers, turtles and hungry fish like the sharp-toothed gar are commonly at fault concerning drowning mutilations but, if testimony is to be believed, there may also be other more mysterious species of meat-eating creatures lurking beneath the surface. Some of them may even be of a predatory nature, viewing man, alive or dead, as merely another natural food source.

Preposterous, you say? Ask Mrs. Darwin Johnson, the unfortunate victim in this next account which took place only a short distance from the Evansville twin bridges.

On Aug. 21, 1955, Johnson, of Evansville, was swimming in the river with some friends at a place called Dog Town, just across the Ohio River from Henderson, Kentucky, when one of these unseen aquatic mysteries reached up from the depths and grabbed her firmly by the leg, then proceeded to drag her down beneath the murky waves. It was only by kicking her legs and beating her arms frantically beneath the waves that she was able to break free and reach the surface for air - only to be grabbed again and pulled back under once more! Again she managed to kick free and make it to the surface, frantically swimming for a nearby inner tube and screaming to her friends. Again she was grabbed by the leg and pulled under. Miraculously, she escaped the clutches of her would-be killer for the third and final time and, with help from her friends, somehow managed to make it, sobbing and in shock, to the shore and safety. Upon examination it was discovered her attacker had left "green palm stains," as well as various abrasions and bruises where it had repeatedly grabbed her by the knee.

No one has since been able to offer a satisfactory explanation or possible identification of the animal involved in this terrifying encounter with one of nature's unknowns. Fifty-two years later, the case still remains as baffling and unsolved as it did back then.

Interestingly, only a few miles from where most of these water cryptid sightings took place, the Green River empties into the Ohio and could be the source from which many of these unknown aquatic animals originate. The Green River is one of the deepest rivers in the world, second only to the South America's Amazon. Long stretches of this waterway are considered bottomless and it is the only north-flowing river in the entire United States. Many strange things have been seen in and along this waterway. One morning in 1998, I was traveling to work in Owensboro. As I was traveling east over the Spottsville Bridge, which spans the Green River at Beals, Ky., I happened to notice a disturbance in the water below. It was just before dawn and the light was not conducive in revealing much detail, but I could see two slender objects, each about 15 to 20 feet. long, apparently engaged in the act of fighting each other. They were creating large waves as they splashed about and I merely assumed them to be giant catfish which are well known locally to exist there. It has since occurred to me that a twenty-foot-long example of such a specimen most probably would not be so slender in appearance, and the identity of the animals involved have remained a mystery to me.

However, a cryptid sighting did occur in this same area in the early '80s and involved a fisherman who was standing just above the lochs when a creature emerged from the deep channel just offshore. It was described as being long and slender, of immense proportions and had two eye-stalks growing from the top of its head much like a snail's. The fisherman fled, with all due haste, as the thing began to slowly approach.

The actual identity of these aquatic anomalies may never be discovered, but one thing is sure - of the nearly 200 varieties of fish which are known to inhabit Kentucky's rivers and streams, these creatures are not among them, but something else entirely. Much like the creature in a well-known case which reportedly took place in Covington on Jan. 30, 1959.

This peculiar monstrosity was seen by startled witnesses to surface from the depths of the Licking River and clamber up onto the river bank. It was subsequently described as a gray colored, octopus-like creature with ugly tentacles and a bald head surrounded by loose rolls of fat. They also claimed that it appeared, to them, to have a "lopsided" chest. No possible identity for this bizarre-sounding creature, to my knowledge, has ever even been attempted as octopuses are strictly saltwater creatures.

As to the possible identity of the other mysterious aquatic cryptids mentioned in this chapter, one guess is as good as the next. No known examples of fish and/or amphibians held extant in this area seem to fit the bill. In the Johnson encounter, though the species in question was never seen and, therefore, can only be guessed at, no known aquatic freshwater animal's feeding habits can claim even a passing resemblance to the ones demonstrated by her attacker. The fact that she was able to escape its clutches at all, in addition to the stains on her leg, seems to suggest that it had been a hand of some type with an opposable thumb that was used. If it had been a mouth lined with sharp teeth or the crushing beak of an oversized turtle she would at least have lost a leg, and most probably her life, on that day back in 1955. She may even have been added to the ever-growing list of Missing: Presumed Drowned. Fortunately, that didn't happen and Johnson was left with only a scar or two and the memory of something horrible and green which tried to kill her. Others have, perhaps, not been so lucky and their stories will never be told.

On a personal note, though I've swam in both the Ohio and the Green rivers many times in my youth without incident, I count myself fortunate. I took no chances when it came to my own children however, and forbade them from swimming there.

III. KENTUCKY'S UNFRIENDLY SKIES

AERIAL ANOMALIES

Pause for a moment, if you will, to ponder a question: How much time do you spend, during the course of an average day, looking up at the sky?

For most of us the time could be measured in mere seconds. We hurry down our roads to and from our jobs, facing the problems and joys of our intricate lives dead ahead, seldom glancing upward to that which does not directly concern us. Some residents however, when they do bother to look, have been amazed at what they see taking place in Kentucky's unfriendly skies.

Glowing lights, flying men, phantom airships and giant birds or bird-like creatures. Rains of blood and flesh, frogs and fish. All these enigmas have been witnessed and attested to in this region.

My own experiences with aerial anomalies began in 1975 when I was nine years old. Even now, 31 years later, the very first anomaly that I was exposed to at that young age remains, hands down, the most amazing thing that I have ever witnessed.

Several members of my family and I were returning home to Spottsville in Henderson County, from a trip to town for groceries and such. I was sitting in the back seat by the passenger side window. My older brother, Dean, 10, was sitting next to me. We were both clutching as many of that month's issues of important comic books as we could afford and eagerly waiting to make it home to start reading and discussing them.

We had been on the long gravel road, Mound Ridge Road, only a minute or two when I happened to glance up and over the trees to my right. I will never forget what I saw at that moment. A large cloud-bank hung in the distant sky and, as I watched, the middle portion of this began to roll swiftly outward until it had formed a roughly circular hole in the middle of which, I was shocked to see, sat a small castle made of brownish-gray stone. I could see it so clearly that, had I wanted, I could've counted each stone. Two lofty towers rose from the main body of the turreted structure, the one on the left being slightly shorter in height than the one on the right. Each tapered at the top, forming points and, from the spires, a long, thin, bright red banner billowed in the easterly wind. The colors were very vivid, especially the redness of the banners which seemed more brilliant than ordinary. At the front and in the middle of this amazing structure was positioned a broad wooden door, rounded at the top and gilded in what looked like new iron. In fact, the whole thing seemed to be at once incredibly ancient and newly constructed. Stunned, I grabbed my brother's arm, pointed out the window and managed to say, "Look...look..." His mouth dropped open and his eyes lit up, much as my own.

"I see it, Bart," he whispered. "I see it."

As we rounded the last turn in the road some taller trees obscured the sight and, much to our disappointment, when the way was clear again we saw that the hole in the cloud had closed up and the castle was gone forever.

No similar Kentucky account exists, to my knowledge, but it is interesting to note that, when we told our mother what had happened she believed us without question. I thought this strange until she proceeded to recount an episode from her own childhood. Her and her sister, Pauline, now deceased, were out in one of their favorite wooded areas where they used to go to be alone and talk when, upon looking up at the sky, they were astounded to see a little log cabin among the clouds. It was so clear, she told me, that they could count every log. This happened in Smith Mills, Ky., in the 1950s on Klondike Road, then little more than a gravel path.

I remain convinced that the vision my brother and I witnessed was not some waking dream or shared hallucination. This first experience with aerial enigmas so many years ago instilled in me the tendency to look often to the sky and take note of what may be going on above our heads.

I still do.

UFOS OVER KENTUCKY

As a matter of fact and public record, the Bluegrass State claims no less than three of the nation's most highly publicized and thoroughly investigated cases of alleged extraterrestrial attacks, one of which ended with the death of a highly decorated and well-respected citizen of the commonwealth. While the UFO phenomenon is by no means the only air-born mystery to be experienced here, three-quarters of the unexplained aerial activity reported in Kentucky can be attributed to this single phenomenon. And it's a mystery that doesn't seem to want to go away any time soon.

Most people living in today's modern society are free to admit, without much worry, that they have seen something in the sky which they cannot explain. According to a Fox News broadcast on Feb. 3, 2007, 40 million Americans claim to have seen UFOs. It has become the "in" thing in many social circles. But it was not always so. As recently as 30 years ago, those who came forward and admitted UFO experiences were ridiculed, ostracized by their communities and labeled mentally unstable. They often lost their jobs, families, property and all public respect because of what they claimed to have seen or experienced. This is largely in direct contrast with today's public views. Some polls have suggested that as many as two-thirds
of Americans now believe in at least the possibility of life on other planets.

This does not mean, however, that all UFOs are extraterrestrial vehicles originating from outer space.

Many explanations can be, and have been, used in attempts to rationally explain the UFO mystery. Lenticular clouds, ball lightning, weather balloons, unrecognized terrestrial crafts, the planet Venus. One, or all, of these subjects could conceivably, under the right conditions, be mistaken for something of a more unusual nature. However, the first thing to become strikingly apparent to any would-be UFO researcher is the overwhelming amount of data and evidence accumulated in support of the reality of flying saucers. Literally tens of thousands of reports of sightings and/or encounters with aliens of some type are available for consideration. Thousands of allegedly authentic pictures and videos of unidentified aerial objects are viewed or studied each year. Hundreds of thousands of books, articles, websites and films are dedicated to the wide dissemination of the alien life-form hypothesis.

This worldwide enigma is so prevalent in nearly every culture that it simply cannot be comfortably suggested that all the witnesses are either lying or mistaken in their conclusions. If even one of these witness' testimony is correct and accurate, then it would be wise of people around the world to give some serious consideration of the possibilities this notion suggests. If even one person is telling the truth, then we are being visited by frighteningly powerful entities from "somewhere else." Somewhere far beyond our perceptions and powers of scrutiny. And, contrary to popular opinion, they may not have our well-being in mind as they go about their highly mysterious business.

Late one winter night in 1971, in Reed, Henderson County, Mrs. R.N. closed the Christmas catalogue she had been looking through with her oldest daughter, Diona, and rose to exit the room. As she switched off the light she noticed a strange red glow coming through the window from somewhere outside. She walked over and looked out. What she saw frightened her enough to awaken her husband and five sleeping children and flee the location in terror, never to return. According to her, what she saw was a glowing red disc-shaped object as it slowly descended from the night sky and landed behind an old, overgrown barn. An overwhelming feeling of fright came over her as she watched. The family dogs, which usually barked at any visitors to the property, were strangely silent.

The incident took place on Collins Road at an isolated farmhouse which sat near the banks of the Green River and I can personally attest to the fact that the event actually took place as stated. Mrs. R. N. is my mother, and I was among the six children who were forced to beat a hasty retreat that cold night nearly 36 years ago. I was five years old.

Over the course of the ensuing years, I have personally witnessed phenomena of this nature on numerous occasions and remain convinced that misidentification of natural phenomena or conventional aircraft cannot adequately account for all reports of this type.

One night in 1985, two brothers, Charles and David Gee, and myself, all members of a popular local band, pulled into the driveway of 10820 Carlinsburg Rd., also in Reed, to set up for our first practice session at that address. When we pulled to a stop in front of the garage and killed the engine and the stereo, we heard a very loud noise coming from outside. We got out of the car and the sound, which resembled the roar of jet engines, became so deafening that we had to cover our ears with our hands. In the night sky above the house we saw three good-sized points of light flying slowly in a triangle formation.

As it neared the house, the formation stopped for a split second, then each light shot away in different directions and was gone in the blink of an eye, one to the north, one to the south and one shot straight up. The night was clear with very little cloud cover and visibility was exceptional. I was somewhat taken aback by the experience but the Gee brothers just shrugged. They has seen the same thing, they soon informed me, only a couple of months earlier as it flew over their house on Third Street. On that occasion, however, it had flown silently.

In the mid 1990s, another group of friends in Henderson County watched in amazement as several bright, round lights cavorted in the sky above their home on Posey Road. The strange spheres repeatedly darted in and out of a large cloud bank as if they were playing a friendly game of cat and mouse. They were so concerned that they called the regional airport a few miles away in Geneva to ask what in the world was going on. The controllers didn't know, they said, as they could see nothing on the radar. The witness, John Webb, kindly suggested that it might well be time to buy new radar equipment, before terminating the conversation.

Again, the validity and accuracy of this report is beyond question as both myself and my wife were among the group who witnessed the aerial display.

In western Kentucky, the UFO phenomenon has become almost a commonplace occurrence. So much so that it is seldom officially reported. Due to the sheer magnitude of this recurring enigma it can be safely assumed that, for each sighting that is reported, hundreds, if not thousands, more never appear on any report or in any local newspaper. The National UFO Reporting Center, or NUFORC, lists some 428 known sightings from the state of Kentucky. I am aware of no "official" investigations which have taken place in regard to any of these incidents.

My last personal sighting of a UFO, as of this writing, took place on Christmas Eve, 2005 when I and two friends, neither of whom had any interest, nor even believed in the subject at hand, observed a large, red light as it hung stationary in the sky for around 10 minutes. As we talked among ourselves it simply vanished into thin air and was gone. No one in the group was able to explain exactly what it was that we saw but we were all convinced that it was something out of the ordinary.

In any event, these unidentified flying objects have been seen time and again by witnesses of all walks of life in every part of the Bluegrass State.

In 1869 three scientists from Shelbyville in Shelby County, made an amazing announcement. Prof. Winlock, Alvan Clark, Jr. and George W. Dean all insisted that they had observed, and quite independently, small, brilliant lights traveling in straight, parallel lines across the surface of the moon during a lunar eclipse. The only human flights of that time were, of course, of the fanciful variety and no explanation could be given concerning the mysterious lights' origin. One must reckon, however, that the odds of three separate scholars all hallucinating the same thing at the exact same moment must be astronomical indeed.

In the summer of 1927, in Wolf County, a mysterious airship was seen which reportedly resembled a replica of a huge, flying fish complete with tail and perfectly shaped fins extending out near the front and small, short ones near the rear of the craft. Though dirigibles were well in existence at the time, no flights were known to be taking place in the area on that day and, as yet, no one has stepped forward to claim responsibility.

Sept. 7, 1959
A mail carrier in Wallingford, Fleming County, reportedly observed a bluish, disc-shaped object at ground level. While the witness looked on it suddenly flew away on a horizontal trajectory leaving behind a stained ring on the ground. No plausible explanations were forthcoming.

April 23, 1997
Multiple witnesses observed a shiny, triangular-shaped craft with a light at each point and a larger light emanating from a hole in the bottom as it hovered above them in Williamstown, Grant County. It was perfectly noiseless, they claimed, and it shot red beams of light straight up into the sky before it sped off at great speed.

A bit of high strangeness that was subsequently investigated by the late UFO researcher

Kenny Young took place in Morehead, Rowan County, on Nov. 21, 2003. The episode started with a frantic call to 911. A resident of Skaggs Road told the dispatcher that he had heard what sounded like a woman desperately screaming for help from a field located behind his house near Adams Lane. He felt sure that some type of dire struggle had taken place as the woman had yelled, "Help me! Oh God, somebody help me!" for nearly two minutes, followed by a long, terrified, shriek.

Strangely, a UFO was apparently witnessed by as many as five other people descending into this same field moments before the screams were heard. This was immediately followed by the strange craft's departure in a westerly direction after it rose from the field and hovered in the air for nearly a minute.

One witness, Dr. Virgil Davis, a University of Kentucky psychologist, informed investigators that others had heard the screams as well, including his two sons who said it sounded like the woman was being torn apart. Davis later informed members of the Morehead Police Department that he and his sons had observed a strange ball of light which he could not explain for at least 15 minutes just prior to hearing the screams. Within minutes, the scene was crawling with local police and rescue workers who found nothing to indicate that a life and death struggle had taken place in the area. A thermal imaging device was utilized in the search, which lasted for nearly an hour and a half before being called off. The woman was never found.

The area has a history of UFO activity. Morehead is an estimated 45 miles south of Flemingsburg, where a crop formation appeared in a rye field in the spring of 2003.

UFO DOGFIGHT

Just as in a court of law, it is unanimously accepted that the best possible witnesses to any event, Fortean or otherwise, are members of local law enforcement. These brave professionals are reliable, highly trained and skilled observers who often lay down their lives for the citizens whose safety they are sworn to protect. The obvious integrity of their positions ensures that, when officers of the law become UFO witnesses, their reports are taken very seriously. In 1993 not one, but two Jefferson County police officers found themselves in just that position.

Patrol Officer Kenny Downs of the Jefferson County Police Department in Louisville, had been asked to sit in as observer for Officer Ken Graham, an experienced, well-respected helicopter pilot. Graham's partner had recently fallen ill and he needed someone to fill in for him. Downs knew the observer's, or spotter's, job was to watch the ground carefully while the pilot flies the chopper, identifying landmarks and possible obstacles, judging distances and tracking fleeing suspects. He agreed to help out, thinking it would be an interesting switch to fly over the streets instead of being on them, as was his usual routine. Little did he know how right he was.

Downs reported for temporary assignment on Jan. 28, and at 11 p.m. the two men took to the sky. Downs was thrilled to view the ground, which was blanketed with two feet of freshly fallen snow, from so far aloft. It was a crisp night and the skies were clear. What happened next is presented as chronicled in subsequent local newspapers:

Late edition of the *Louisville Courier-Journal*
Thursday, March 4, 1993,

"UFO puts on show - Jefferson police officers describe close encounter" by Gardiner Harris - Staff Writer

Two Jefferson County air unit police officers - described by their lieutenant as "solid guys" - swear they had a two-minute dogfight with a UFO during a routine helicopter patrol Friday night. Two officers on the ground said they, too, spotted the object. The UFO - a glowing pear-shaped object about the size of a basketball - literally flew circles around the helicopter, even though the fliers say they were moving at speeds approaching 100 mph. In one blinding moment when both craft were hurtling toward each other, the UFO shot three baseball-size fireballs out of its middle, all three officers said. The fireballs fizzled into nothing. Officers Kenny Graham and Kenny Downs haven't talked much about their Friday night flight over General Electric Appliance Park because they fear few will believe them. But they are convinced they weren't hallucinating.

"We both go to church every week," Downs said as a way of explaining how normal the two normally are. "In fact, I might start going to church twice a week."

Officer Mike Smith, in his squad car below, said he saw the object for only about a minute. But he confirmed the UFO shot three fireballs into the air and then disappeared.

Officer Joe Smolenski said he tried for more than a minute to catch up to the object in his squad car. "I've been looking for 'em for 14 years, and I guess this is the closest I've come to something I couldn't explain."

Lt. David Pope, who was roused out of bed at 12:30 Saturday morning by a call from the startled officers, attested to their sanity and sincerity. "These guys are totally solid guys," Pope said. "There's no doubt in my mind there was something out there."

The night started out like every other night. Graham and Downs got to work around 6 p.m. and were soon in the air flying a routine patrol. Graham, 39, and an 11-year veteran, was the pilot. Downs, 39, and a five-year veteran, was the spotter. While in the air, they received a call about a possible break-in near Sanford Avenue and Buechel Bank Road. They flew off and quickly reached the area, which is near the northeast corner of Appliance Park, around 11:50 p.m. As they circled, Graham saw something that looked like a small fire off to his left. Dozens of bonfires had been lit around the county that night by revelers delighting in the new snowfall. But Graham soon decided it wasn't a fire. Downs shined his 1.5-million candlepower spotlight on the object, which began to drift back and forth like a balloon as the light washed over it. Then it gradually floated up to the helicopter's elevation about 500 feet above the ground, where it hovered for a few seconds.

"Then it took off at a speed I've never seen before," said Graham, an experienced pilot. The object made two huge counter-clockwise loops and finally approached the helicopter's rear. Graham, afraid the object would ram his tail rotor, pushed his speed above 100 mph. The UFO shot past them and instantly climbed hundreds of feet in the air. It descended again and flew close to the helicopter. Graham tried to close the gap with the object, and it again flew away. As the UFO approached on a parallel course, three fireballs burst out of its core. Scared, Graham banked away from the object.

"When we came back around, it was gone," Graham said.

When the two returned to their base, Graham called the control tower at Standiford Field to ask if their radar had spotted anything unusual. It had not. Downs called the county's radio dispatchers to ask if anyone else had reported sightings. No one had. But the two did get confirmation from two officers on the ground, one of whom was Smith.

"I have no idea what it was," Smith said, but his confirmation cheered the two fliers. "It makes me feel better," Downs said, "that there are grown men out there who are sworn to protect this community and who saw the same thing."

Late edition of the *Louisville, Ky., Courier-Journal*
Friday, March 5, 1993
"The only thing clear is what UFO wasn't"
by Leslie Scanlon - Staff Writer

'So, you ask, just what was that strange glowing object in the sky that skirmished with a Jefferson County police helicopter last Friday night?

The National Weather Service doesn't have a clue. The air traffic controllers at Standiford Field detected nothing unusual on their radar. The security staff at General Electric's Appliance Park - over which the apparent encounter took place - saw just the police helicopter. But a UFO investigator, while remaining non-committal about the Louisville case, said the description the police reported of a bright pear-shaped object that shot three baseball-sized fireballs at them shortly before midnight does match reports of UFO sightings from the 1940s and 1950s. Those reports, which have been carefully studied by government investigators, "sound an awful lot like the case you just reported to me," said Bill Pitts of Fort Springs, Ark., director of a UFO investigative group called Project Blue Book. Usually, only 10 to 20 percent of the thousands of UFO sightings reported each year are unexplainable, said Walter Andrus, international director of the Mutual UFO Network, a Texas-based group that investigates sightings. Most of the time, he said, investigators find that "something mundane" caused the observance - anything from unusually bright planets to weather balloons to falling fragments of rockets.

"I believe that the people saw something," said Bob Myers, a star enthusiast and former president of the defunct Stargazers of Louisville group. But, he added, "I don't necessarily believe that they saw some kind of space vehicle driven by some kind of alien being. Ninety-nine percent of the time there's an explanation."

Whatever did happen, a *Courier-Journal* story yesterday in which four police officers swore they had encountered a UFO provoked a spasm of interest. The police got calls from reporters, the TV tabloid show "Hard Copy," and about 75 citizens some of whom said they had seen UFOs too. Although no one can say for sure, people with scientific backgrounds said yesterday that the UFO probably was not:

* A plummeting meteorite. "It didn't seem to be moving consistently in one direction," said Alan Johnson, a professor of material science at the University of Louisville's Speed Scientific School. "An incoming meteorite usually streaks across the sky," he said, while this one "appeared to be dancing around."

* A lightning ball or fireball. This phenomenon sometimes occurs during intense electrical storms. But last Friday night, the snow stopped falling at 7:48 p.m., the temperatures were in the 20s, the solid cloud cover was beginning to scatter and Louisville experienced no thunder or lightning. "No way," said Rick Lasher, a spokesman for the Louisville office of the National Weather Service.

* A known aircraft. Although many can exceed the 100 mph at which the helicopter pilot said he was traveling when the UFO zoomed past him and instantly climbed hundreds of feet. John Dressman, a professor of mechanical engineering at the Speed School, said he's not familiar with any military or other aircraft that can climb that rapidly while moving forward. Dressman has one suspicion about what the pilots might have seen - reflections, created by a heavy blanket of snow and thick cloud cover. "I certainly would not question the credibility of

the officers - they seem very reliable officers," he said. But "there's a certain suspicion in my mind that the atmospheric conditions might have led to misconstruing things."

From about 1947 to 1969, the Air Force investigated UFO sightings in an effort known as Project Blue Book. They tracked "just hundreds and hundreds of sightings," said Maj. Dave Thurston, an Air Force spokesman in Washington. "None of them proved to have any basis in fact or to be any threat to national security. So we stopped the study." But in 1988, about 150 of the people who had been involved in researching UFOs for the military, intelligence or other federal agencies banded together to re-create Project Blue Book as a civilian agency. According to Pitts, the director, the sightings during the early decades - many of which were reported by astronomers, pilots, and astronauts - were so intriguing that "we think there's a definite possibility or probability that the better ones are extraterrestrial."

E.T.S IN KENTUCKY

Between 6 and 7 p.m., on July 28, 1880, many citizens in Louisville, were treated to a very peculiar sight in the form of a strange looking object as it flew above the treetops of that fair city. As it drew near, they were shocked and amazed that it looked to be a man sitting within and completely surrounded by some type of strange machinery. Witnesses reported that this man was frantically working said machinery with both his hands and feet, pushing and tugging at the many gears and levers that surrounded him and, all the while, peddling with his feet like a cyclist. The faster this figure peddled, witnesses noted, the more altitude the object gained. The slower he peddled the lower it flew and it was obvious to the onlookers present that the man was controlling the object with his movements. The entire apparatus continued on its way, disappearing into the sky as darkness fell.

Dispatches from Madisonville soon followed, describing an airborne object seen there as well. It was allegedly circular, sometimes changing shape to oval, with balls at either end. It passed out of sight heading south, leaving the citizenry quite alarmed and wondering what in the world the object could've been. Much was the same in Louisville, but the locals there hadn't long to wait for another visit. Nine days later, on Aug. 6, the phantom pilot was again observed over the city as he made his return voyage to whatever place these bizarre "men" call home.

One morning in 1973, a Russell County woman reportedly observed two three-foot-tall reddish-skinned humanoids near her house in Russell Springs. The entities were seen walking around the carport near the side of her house, and entering a small washtub-shaped craft sitting on the ground near the back yard. The strange looking vehicle then rose over the top of the house and disappeared. According to the Russell Springs Times Journal, October 24, 1973, the little men resembled small humans, aside from their red skin, but walked in a peculiar manner, as if on tiptoes. The ground was reportedly disturbed where the craft had been sitting.

STAR WARS IN KENTUCKY
Alien Attacks/Abductions

These allegedly "alien" entities have presented themselves to mankind in many guises, displaying diverse characteristics. Elusiveness isn't always one of them. Sometimes these entities are reported to actually initialize personal contact with witnesses, often of a sinister nature, though only rarely are instances of dire personal injury, or even death, reported in association with, or as a result of, these otherworldly visits. According to a controversial 1991 Roper Poll, 3.7 million Americans might have been abducted by aliens at some point in their lives.

One Kentucky incident involving UFOs and their occupants occurred in the winter of 1976, in Lincoln County, which would soon become one of the most oft-quoted cases of alleged alien abduction in the history of the phenomenon.

THE LIBERTY ABDUCTIONS

On Jan. 6, 1976, three friends, Mona Stafford, Louise Smith and Elaine Thomas, were traveling southwest down Route 78, heading home to Liberty in Casey County. They were returning from nearby Lancaster where Stafford had been treated to a late night supper in celebration of her 35th birthday. It was around 11:15 p.m. They were about a mile south of Stanford, the Lincoln County Seat, somewhere between the junctions of Highways

Louise Smith, Mona Stafford and Elaine Thomas, the three witnesses in the famous "Liberty Abduction" case

1194 and 198, when they noticed a strangely glowing red object hurtling through the eastern sky. Worse, it seemed to be speeding in their direction. This scared Stafford, who thought it might be an airplane in grave distress coming in for a crash landing. The three distraught witnesses could only watch as the light grew larger and brighter as it headed straight for the vehicle. Suddenly, the object shot rapidly down at an angle and positioned itself above the treetops to their right, traveling silently at pace with the car. All three described the object as disc-shaped with a row of round windows. Around each window, red lights blinked in a counter-clockwise direction. Below these were situated four small yellow lights which shone steadily.

At the top of the craft was a large, almost painfully luminous blue dome. Stafford later commented that it (the dome) was blinding as it reflected off the metal surface of the object which, she felt sure, was over 100 feet wide.

The sight of the thing immediately and completely unnerved the women and, much to their horror, the terrifying aerial anomaly suddenly shot like a streak toward the car, executed a half circle maneuver and flipped up onto its side, resting directly to the left of the vehicle where it flashed three blue lights onto the road. Then it shined another blue beam directly into the car, illuminating the interior as if it were daylight. Although she would later have no recollection of this part of the encounter, Smith, who was driving, then stopped the car and got out to stare at the object which had also stopped. Stafford later recalled that Smith had looked "petrified" when she leaned over the seat and pulled her back into the vehicle. She also noted that outside had become deathly silent. Even the wind had stopped. Inside the vehicle the blinding light was nearly unbearable. Their eyes began to water and swell. Their skin felt as if it was being burned as well followed by sudden pounding headaches. All three women began to cry.

Although conflicting reports exist, author Jerome Clark, in "The UFO Book: Encyclopedia of Extraterrestrials" (Visible Ink Press, 1998)' tells that, at this moment, the light from the strange craft blinked off and here the account goes from strangely bizarre to completely inexplicable. To their complete horror, the three women now found themselves traveling at over 85 miles an hour down a strange, completely straight road with no houses or street lights along either side. Worse still, the vehicle was not responding to Smith's attempts to control it. She took her foot completely off the gas pedal but it refused to slow down even a little. Crying for help, Smith was joined by Stafford, whose eyes were swelling so badly that she could hardly see. Both women grabbed the steering wheel in a futile attempt to bring the runaway car back under control. A light on the dashboard blinked on indicating that the engine had stalled, but even this failed to slow the car down. The vehicle began to lurch and jolt in a violent manner. Stafford later claimed that it felt like they were traveling over hurdles or speed bumps, much like riding in an airplane through pockets of violently turbulent air. All later agreed that it seemed they were being "pulled" down a long, straight, bumpy road which was entirely unfamiliar to them.

Suddenly, they found themselves apparently being pulled into the craft backwards. Then, after what seemed like no more than a second or two, the three were, once again, back in reality driving down the highway just South of Hustonville, eight miles from the location at which they first spotted the UFO. The car was responding normally and they were all strangely calm despite what they had just experienced.

They were all suffering from a terrible thirst and, upon reaching Smith's residence, all three women gulped down glass after glass of cold water. Smith took off her glasses and splashed some cold water onto her face whereupon the burning sensation her face and hands only intensified. Returning to the kitchen she glanced at the clock and was shocked to see that it read 1:25 a.m. The 50-minute trip had actually taken nearly an hour and a half. None of the women could account for the missing time. Smith's wristwatch was acting strangely as well, she informed the other two. Not only did it read 6 o'clock, but the minute hand was moving as if it were the second hand.

After trying unsuccessfully to reconstruct the evening's events, Stafford called the state police who politely informed her that they were not interested in the case. Meanwhile the burning sensations they all suffered were getting worse. Smith reportedly tried to approach her pet bird, a parakeet, only to have it react violently to her presence. Soon after Stafford and Thomas decided to go on home.The next morning they awoke in extreme physical discomfort with symptoms including raw skin, burning, watery eyes, blisters and headaches. Later Stafford, whose conjunctivitis seemed worse than her two friends', would see her doctor who prescribed eye-drops which did not help. Moreover, all three witnesses discovered that they were "marked." According to the Aerial Phenomenon Research Organization (APRO) Bulletin, vol. 25, # 4 of Oct.,1976, "... All three had a red mark on the backs of their necks, measuring about three inches long and one inch wide, with clearly defined edges, giving the appearance of a new burn before it blisters. Smith's and Thomas' marks were centrally located between the bases of their skulls and the top of the back, whereas Stafford's was located to the left, behind her ear. They could not account for the marks, which disappeared two days later."

In February, news of their experiences were leaked, without their consent, to the local media who ran a story on the women's claims including the missing time aspect. Another account was published in the Feb. 1 issue of The Kentucky Advocate. Almost immediately ufologists began pouring into Liberty for interviews but the women declined, stating that they wished no further publicity for themselves concerning the event.

One of the first investigators to be denied an interview was Mutual UFO Network's (MUFON) Jerry Black. But Black was persistent and finally, after many calls and the promise to bring another woman who had experienced missing time with him who understood what they were feeling and could offer some comfort, an interview was scheduled for Feb. 29. The group of MUFON investigators, accompanied by Leonard H. Stringfield, arrived and conducted the initial interview with the women. Stringfield was later quoted as saying, "The effects of the close encounter were still painfully apparent." All three women appeared drained and tired and complained of sudden weight loss. Stafford's eyes were still inflamed.

All three were still very upset over the nearly hour and a half that remained unaccounted for. Stringfield suggested that hypnosis was a useful tool in instances such as this, and could possibly be used to unblock the women's memories and overcome the unexplained amnesia.

On March 7, after much bickering about which UFO group had the "rights" to the investigation, a psychologist from the University of Wyoming, Dr. Leo Sprinkle, attempted hypnotic regression on Stafford. Sprinkle, a member of APRO, was unsuccessful in helping Stafford recall the missing time. She became hysterical when he attempted to expose her suppressed memories of that night.

Stringfield, much to later investigators' disapproval, then produced sketches of the more commonly reported "aliens" and, after viewing these, Stafford pointed to one drawing and said, 'This is it." He then asked if that was what she saw after the beam of light was shined into the car, to which she replied that she was unsure. She had a mental image of a similar creature, she said, but it faded and re-appeared like fog. At this point, partly due to criticism over Stringfield's "leading" of the witnesses during the proceedings, the investigation into the Liberty case ground to a halt.

Even though, admittedly, not under the best of circumstances, Stringfield's actions had yielded strong indications that an actual abduction had taken place, none of the prominent UFO groups were willing, or financially able to send qualified professionals back to Kentucky to continue the hypnotic regression treatments. They struggled for weeks trying to overcome the hurdle of financial shortfalls. It was Jerry Black who was finally able to offer a solution. Even though the investigators had all agree to keep the story out of the papers as much as possible until the women's health improved, Black was able to negotiate a deal with the National Enquirer which brought Sprinkle back to Liberty and even paid the three witnesses for their time.

They also brought with them Detective James Young, an experienced polygraph examiner for the Lexington Police Department. On July 23, Young administered the examination to all three witnesses. According to Young, the reports indicated that all were 100 percent sincere and believed they were telling the truth, This outcome surprised no one. All three women were devout Christians of good reputations and were highly regarded locally.

Eventually, each witness underwent separate hypnosis sessions and, while their stories were compatible regarding much of the subsequent details, no full account of the encounter could be constructed. Stafford recalled lying on a table in a dark, hot room, held motionless by a strange bright light which emanated a powerful energy while a mechanical eye-like device examined her body. Several diminutive figures, dressed in surgical garments and masks, observed the proceedings. She also remembered some type of web-like structure in front of her as she underwent the examinations, and being submerged in a hot, burning liquid. She felt pressure against her eyes and later claimed she felt sure that her eyes were actually removed from their sockets, placed for a short time against her cheeks, and then re-inserted back into the ocular cavities. She remembered seeing a woman lying on a table with a tube attached to her stomach, though she could not tell who the woman was, or even if it might have been herself.

Elaine Thomas also remembered leaving the car and being taken aboard the anomalous craft. She found herself in a large room with a window. Small humanoid creatures with gray skin and big, black eyes were present. They placed some sort of 'cocoon-like' device over her throat which tightened and choked her whenever she tried to speak or think. Then the entities placed a bullet shaped object over her left breast.

Though each of the women's memories would later return to a greater degree, Smith's were, at first, the vaguest of the three. Under hypnosis she also recalled a scalding liquid being poured onto her body as she lay helpless and paralyzed, undergoing some type of physical examination. The session was so unsettling to her that she declined the offer for a second one later that weekend.

On July 29 Stringfield phoned Smith to check on her health. His call found her bedridden - too ill to even go to work. She told him that something terrible had happened the night before. A voice had awakened her from a sound sleep, she said, and compelled her to drive alone to the site of the encounters. Once there, she parked the automobile and got out, feeling terribly frightened but unable to leave. She felt a tugging at her hands and suddenly, at around 3 a.m., she ran to her car and drove to nearby Stanford. During the drive she noticed that three of her rings, two from one hand and one from the other, were missing. She was sure they could not have fallen off as, on the rare occasions that she taken them off in the past, it was only with great effort and the assistance of a moistening agent that it could be accomplished. Earlier that morning she had returned to search for the rings, accompanied by a police officer, without success. Two months later, in September, two of the rings mysteriously reappeared near the doorway of her home.

In time, the women were able to recall even more of the events of the evening of Jan. 6. Stafford eventually remembered being separated from the other two women. She was led from the craft and onto a second ship, this one with three floors and a dome. The "aliens" that led her about wore dark hoods which covered their heads, had large, dark, frightful, eyes that were pointed towards the temples and hands which resembled "bird wings stretched out." She also claimed to have had another subsequent encounter with "alien" creatures.

After the abduction had left her an emotional and physical wreck, she moved in with her parents for awhile but on this particular evening she had decided to go back home to her trailer. She was lying on the couch, when a mysterious voice commanded her to turn around. She turned to see a figure around five feet tall and bathed in light standing just inside the kitchen. He was dressed in a shining robe and had hair and a beard of reddish gold. He looked, she said, just like some biblical character. Telepathically he commanded her to look into his eyes but she resisted, already trying to pick up the telephone. When he issued a second command she felt as though she had no will to fight and so obeyed the entity. Although she was uncertain about what happened next she did remember an odd remark the being made,

"Buree, the mind is still hungry." Then the figure simply vanished into thin air right before her eyes. No sense was ever made of the enigmatic statement.

The effects of the encounter and apparent abduction did not soon disappear from the three women's lives. All three claimed to experience varying degrees of psychic phenomena after the incident, which they invariably associated with their abductions. Elaine Thomas never completely gained her health and, just like her pet parakeet, died of unknown causes, three years later at age 52. Ironically, she was the only one of the three who claimed to have gained anything of a positive nature from the experience. She had asserted that the abduction had made her much more self-confidant and outgoing.

Corroborating evidence exists which seems to support the women's stories in the form of eyewitness accounts of strange aerial phenomena on the evening of June 6 independent of Stafford, Smith and Thomas. The Kentucky Advocate also mentioned that UFOs were reported from both Casey and Lincoln counties that night.

Within a couple of hundred yards of the abduction, one anonymous Stanford couple watched from the window of their home as a "large, luminous object," passed over the area. This occurred about 11:30 p.m. The object was described as brilliantly glowing and shaped like a light-bulb which disappeared traveling south. Other observers described the object as large and oval-shaped, traveling silently, with a row of luminous, reddish orange windows. Two teenagers out for a ride stated that they had given chase to a low-flying UFO after it had been observed hovering over the Angel Manufacturing Plant in Stanford. They chased the strange, disc-shaped craft all the way to Danville where they reported the incident to police.

Another report of significance came from the owner of the property where the three women's abduction allegedly took place. The farmer claimed that just down the road from his house, he had witnessed an unusually low-flying object which shot a white beam of light to the ground near what he took to be a stalled automobile.

Although over 30 years have passed since the Liberty incident took place, no one has been able to successfully debunk the women's claims and the Stanford abduction is still considered one of the best documented abduction cases in American UFO history.

KELLY'S LITTLE GREEN MEN

On Aug. 21, 1955, something extraordinary happened in western Kentucky. It was an event which was destined to become one of the most highly investigated and thoroughly documented cases in UFO history. Long before such encounters came to be called Close Encounters of the Third Kind, there was the incident in Kelly, hardly more than a wide spot in the side of the road in Christian County, seven miles north of Hopkinsville.

The encounter took place in a small, isolated farmhouse owned by the Sutton family. Eleven people were in the home at the time the incident took place: eight adults and three children, all members of the Sutton-Lankford family, and family friends Billy Ray Taylor and his wife. Around 7 p.m., while the rest of the adults were socializing around the kitchen table and playing cards, Taylor excused himself to go fetch a drink from the backyard well. Like many farmhouses of the time, the Sutton home had no indoor plumbing.

Taylor was gone only briefly when he ran back inside, slamming the front door behind him excitedly. When asked was the matter he told everyone that, as he was standing at the well, he had seen a flying saucer with flames "all the colors of the rainbow" shooting out the tail end of it as it passed overhead, stopped dead in the air and then dropped straight down into a gully on the neighboring property about 100 yards behind the house. No one took him seriously, of course. These were simple country folk and, to most of them, things of that nature simply didn't happen in rural Kentucky. Moreover, they were poor folk as well and, although they did have electricity in the house, no one owned a television, radio or telephone.

Elmer "Lucky" Sutton, the no-nonsense head of the household, thought Taylor was joking or, at most, had seen a falling star. After all, a meteor shower was supposed to be in progress that night. He knew Taylor hadn't been drinking, as alcohol was strictly forbidden in, or even near, the Sutton home. Glennie Lankford, Lucky's 50-year-old mother, would nail their hides to the barn door if she even heard anyone had been drinking.

They continued on at the kitchen table for about another hour. Then, around 8 p.m., the family dog started barking wildly outside. Lucky got up and looked out the window where he saw, to his astonishment, a glowing, round globe moving towards the house. This was, apparently, the source of the dog's extreme agitation. The assembled adults did what any Kentuckians would do: They grabbed their guns and headed outside, arriving just in time to see the dog dash, tail between its legs, under the house in an attempt to shield itself from the small creature that was standing in the yard holding its extremely thin arms above its head, almost in a gesture of surrender. It was the strangest, most terrifying sight the group had ever seen.

The creature was about three and a half feet tall, they said. With large, yellow glowing eyes and huge, pointed, "crinkly" ears. It had glow-in-the-dark skin that looked like silver or shining metal as it stood there beneath the glow of the outside light less than 20 feet away. They noted that it possessed neither a nose nor hair. It had a straight slit of a mouth which ran from ear to ear. As it got closer, they were horrified to see that its hands ended in cruel-looking claw-like talons. There was but one option. They opened fire. A hail of .22 caliber and 12-gauge bullets slammed into the "little man" from close range. Strangely, the thing merely flipped over backwards and ran off, apparently unhurt, into the darkened woods.

Completely daunted by such an unexpected reaction to lethal force, the two men hurried back inside to try and calm the women and children, who were already upset before the gunfire started. Their efforts were disrupted when the creature, or another like it, returned and was seen peering in one of the side windows. The men fired at once right through the window and, in a shower of glass, the little creature was seen to again flip over backwards and run away into the darkness. By now the women and children were crying and screamingly hysterically and the unexpected nightmare was spinning out of control.

Lucky and Taylor decided to go back outside to see if they could locate the body of one of the things they had shot. No one wanted to be left alone, of course, so Taylor, followed closely by Lucky and the rest of the Sutton family, slowly made his way through the house and stepped cautiously out onto the back porch. They could see nothing and all was quiet as they inched forward, guns at the ready. Taylor was about to step off the porch and into the backyard when, from behind him, Lucky and the rest saw a claw-like hand reach down from the tin roof overhead and grab a handful of the man's hair. He was then pulled back into the house by hysterical family members while Lucky continued down into the yard, turned, and opened fire on the little monster that was perched on the roof. The blast struck it squarely but, according to Sutton, the thing didn't fall normally to the ground, but seemed to float down almost casually. To his horror, Lucky noticed another such creature sitting on the limb of a nearby tree.

Inside, Glennie was tucking the children under the bed and Taylor, having composed himself somewhat, raced back outside to help Lucky shoot at the creature in the tree. When hit, this one, too, floated safely to the ground and ran away, only to be replaced by a third entity which ran out from the corner of the house and into the line of fire.

In all, the family claimed to have been attacked six separate times during a three-hour time period.

They could hear the things' claws scraping on the roof while others repeatedly peeped in the windows and, all the while, the western Kentucky night echoed with the sound of gunshots and the screams of children. By 11 p.m. they decided to abandon the farm and, leaving all their worldly belongings behind, they dashed outside and into the two vehicles parked in the driveway. They sped down Highway 41 toward Hopkinsville and the nearest police station where they told their incredible story.

Police Chief Russell Greenwell later described the witnesses as being genuinely terrified, telling one investigator, "Something scared those people. Something beyond reason. Nothing ordinary.'

Soon more than a dozen city, county and state police were combing the area but the diminutive invaders were apparently gone. Many spent shells were found littering the ground and interior of the Sutton home, affording mute testimony that the group had, indeed, fired off numerous rounds at something. At one point Chief Greenwell and a group of other men, while conducting a search of the grounds, reportedly saw a patch of luminous grass near the house which faded as the group approached. He also admitted that every man at the scene felt strangely uneasy while there. The idea that someone could have perpetrated a hoax against the well-armed family was immediately ruled out..

At length the investigators began to leave the scene and by 3 a.m. the Suttons were once again alone at the now-quieted farmhouse. Somewhat settled now they made ready for bed. But sleep was not to be had that night for

as soon as the lights were out, Ms. Lankford noticed a glow outside her window and saw one of the creature's taloned hands reaching up from below. Again, Lucky was forced to fire on the things which were seen, off and on, until just before dawn the following morning.

As the sun rose, the invasion of Kelly was over. But the invasion of reporters and investigators had just begun. Many looked for signs of alcohol but could find none. Local media and big city reporters came for the story. Most of them wrote sensationalistic pieces and one even claimed that the family was attacked by little green men. Many dismissed the event as the intoxicated hallucinations of backward, uneducated "hillbillies." Fed up with the resulting ridicule and slander, the farm was completely abandoned within 48 hours.

Even after the passage of more than 50 years, the testimony of this simple, unsophisticated family has never been contradicted. Investigators left Kelly with the conviction that all the witnesses were sincere in what they believed they saw. Many explanations have been put forth in attempts to explain what it was that frightened the family so badly that night, from escaped monkeys, to cats, to owls, but the witnesses have never retracted or altered the descriptions of the creatures and stand by their earlier statements. One of the most bizarre and baffling in the history of UFO encounters, the Kelly case remains unsolved.

The following article was published in the Dec. 30, 2002 edition of the *Kentucky New Era*, Hopkinsville, Kentucky.

Kelly Green Men?
Children of Witness to Alleged Alien Invasion Defend Father's 1955 Claim
New Era / Michele Cartlton

Geraldine Hawkins was only seven or eight years old the first time she heard the story of the Kelly Green Men. Although her father, Elmer "Lucky" Sutton, said he was one of the people who witnessed the alien invasion on Aug. 21, 1955, he didn't talk about it to Hawkins until the late 1960s when two writers contacted him for an interview.

"This was the first I'd ever heard of it," Hawkins said about the Kelly incident during an interview at her home in Princeton on Friday. "I remember it was a man and woman that came to the house. I had never heard anything about it. I remember sitting in the floor with my legs crossed listening to this story. It terrified me."

The sighting occurred at Kelly, a small town on U.S. 41 about eight miles north of Hopkinsville. "Lucky" Sutton, who was living in a small farmhouse on the Old Madisonville Road at Kelly, and several family members said a spaceship landed near the house that evening. It was carrying about a dozen little space creatures, they said.

"Lucky" Sutton and other family members said they had a gun battle with the creatures that lasted for hours.

Most of the Sutton family members who said they fought the aliens off with shotguns are deceased. However, Hawkins and her younger brother, Elmer Sutton Jr., of Trigg County, said their father shared his Kelly experience with them. Hawkins, 41, and Sutton, 35, are the children of "Lucky" Sutton and Glorine Powell, of Trigg County. Their father died on Dec. 5, 1995.

"He talked to me about it because I was one of the last ones to leave home," the younger Sutton said. "I prodded him about it a lot. A lot of times he wouldn't talk about it. If I'd catch him in the right mood, he'd sit down and talk for hours about it. When he did, I'd listen. To be honest with you, he knew some day he'd die. I guess he wanted one of us to know the truth."

According to the family, a visitor to the Sutton house, Billy Ray Taylor of Pennsylvania, had been in the back yard getting water from the well. He noticed a light streak across the sky and descend into the trees along a ravine about a quarter of a mile away.

A while later, "Lucky" Sutton's mother, Glennie Lankford, saw a creature with long arms and talon-like hands raised in the air approaching the back of the house.

"(Dad) said they appeared to have a human shape, but with some modifications that made them different," Sutton said. "He called them little green men. He called them green, but said they actually weren't green. He said they were silver, but they had a greenish silver glow to them. He said they were about 3-foot tall -- about the size of a 5-year-old. Their arms were double the length of humans' and had pointed ears. He said the eyes were in the same place as humans, but were more of an almond shape. The eyes had a luminous glow. He said they really didn't walk, just skimmed on top of the ground, but moved their legs."

"Lucky" Sutton and Taylor each armed themselves and fired several shots at the aliens, they later reported to police. The siege continued through the night, they said. None of the bullets seemed to affect the creatures.

"He told me he didn't know what in the world they had in mind, but he wasn't going to stand around to find out," Sutton said.

"He's just one of the kind of guys to see something like that and naturally think 'they're going to do something. I've got to protect my family.' I guess that's what he done. He bore arms and started laying into them. I'd have done the same thing. I'd have been aiming right between the eyes," he said.

"If they had hurt one they could have retaliated," Hawkins said.

"What else was he supposed to do? Go up and shake one of their hands?" Sutton asked.

The Suttons, Taylor, Lankford and a few children in the house that night said they piled into two cars and headed for the police station in Hopkinsville. City, county and state police, along with military personnel from then-Camp Campbell flocked to the Kelly homestead and stayed until about 2 a.m. They searched the house, the yard, surrounding fields and a wooded area, but reportedly found nothing.

The family claimed the creatures returned again about 3 a.m. and stayed until morning.

In the past 47 years, numerous media reports have circulated worldwide speculating about what happened in the community of Kelly.

Most recently, the local legend has attracted the attention of an independent production company in Glendale, Calif. A film crew from Barcon Productions came to Hopkinsville over the weekend to research the Kelly incident. Barcon has been filming eyewitness accounts for a film entitled "Monsters of the UFO" to be released next summer.

Contrary to some media reports, Hawkins insists that her father and other family members were not drinking on that night, nor did they fabricate the story. Although investigators at the scene failed to find the spot where the spaceship landed, she said her parents took her to the spot about 20 years later.

"The following weekend after those two (writers) had been there to talk to him, they took us out there to where it happened. I remember a big, round burned out place back there in the field. It was still there," Hawkins said.

Hawkins and Sutton said many of the reports referred to the Suttons as "a low-status group of people" and used their father and Taylor's employment with a carnival to discredit the family's story.

"They sensationalized the story because (Billy Ray and my father) worked at the carnival. That they were able to create this fiasco," Hawkins said. "He wouldn't have done that anyway. He wasn't that type of person. You could look at him and tell that something happened to them that night. They couldn't have made up something like that. They were just country folks. They wouldn't have thought to think up something like that so elaborate. They wouldn't have run to town terrified in the middle of the night."

Despite any speculations from outside sources, the siblings believe what their father told them about the Kelly incident.

"I could always tell when my dad was pulling my leg or not. He wasn't pulling a fast one," Sutton said.

"It was a serious thing to him. It happened to him. He said it happened to him. He said it wasn't funny. It was an experience he said he would never forget. It was fresh in his mind until the day he died. It was fresh in his mind like it happened yesterday. He never cracked a smile when he told the story because it happened to him and there wasn't nothing funny about it. He got pale and you could see it in his eyes. He was scared to death," he said.

Hawkins and Sutton agree that people should have more of an open mind to the unexplained phenomena.

"I think God didn't mean for us to understand everything. He doesn't want us to know everything," Hawkins said. "Man might want to know everything. I think there's some things out there that He doesn't want us to figure out and know what they are."

"We're here. We're breathing and living. Why can't there be something else out there,"

Sutton said, pointing to the sky.

"Back then I think it was harder," Hawkins added. "Now, in this day and age, people are more apt to believe stuff like that. A lot of people don't believe in this stuff. I do. I always have. I believe in ghosts, angels, UFOs. You name it, I believe it."

Hawkins and Sutton said they admired their father's work ethic and his strength in dealing with the media circus that followed his family's close encounter at Kelly.

"To me, in my mind, he was a hard-working kind of a man trying to raise a family who saw something out of the ordinary -- something people wouldn't believe," Sutton said. "He told the story and people called him a liar. I believe that was the hardest thing for him to swallow -- for people to call him a dog-faced liar and not believe it."

"I just want people to realize that they weren't crazy," Hawkins added. "They weren't just seeing things that night. Something really happened to that family."

THE STRANGE DEATH OF THOMAS MANTELL

As we have seen, not all UFO encounters are peaceful ones. Many witnesses suffer a high degree of emotional, or psychological trauma which often results in a wide range of physiological manifestations including insomnia, depression, weight loss and loss of concentration to name but a few. However, serious though these UFO related ailments are, these conditions pale in comparison to the price paid by a highly decorated citizen of the commonwealth back on Jan. 7, 1948. His name was Captain Thomas F. Mantell, Jr. and his UFO encounter cost him his life.

The tragic event began at 1:20 p.m. of that day when Godman Air Force Base field tower operator,. Sgt. Quinton Blackwell received a call from the installation's military police, who wanted to pass on an alert from the Kentucky Highway Patrol. They were getting reports of an unusual aerial object over Maysville,   some 80 miles to the east. Seeing nothing on radar, Blackwell then contacted Wright Field, Dayton, Ohio, who denied responsibility for any activity in that area. A few moments later the highway patrol called again. Now the UFO was being reported over Owensboro and Irvington. It was described as being huge, some 250 to 300 feet in diameter, circular and white with a red light near the bottom, moving in a southerly direction.

At 1:45 p.m., Blackwell decided to look for himself and was able to spot the anomaly. At that distance it appeared as merely a small, white, bright spot in the southern sky. Other officials present, including commanding officer Col. Guy Hix, also took a look and were further able to describe the object as umbrella-shaped with alternating red borders at the top and bottom. They stood monitoring the apparently motionless object for nearly an hour.

Then, at 2:30 p.m., four F-51 fighter planes approached Godman from the south, returning to Standiford Air Force Base.

From actual transcripts:

Godman Tower: "Godman Tower calling the flight of four ships northbound over Godman Field. Do you read? Over. Godman Tower calling the flight of four ships northbound over Godman Field. Do you read? Over..."

"Roger Godman Tower. This is National Guard 869, flight leader of the formation. Over."

This was Capt. Thomas Mantell, a member of the Kentucky Air National Guard and decorated WWII fighter pilot with over 2,000 hours flight time. Over 100 of those hours were spent in combat. This veteran pilot had fought in the skies of North Africa and Europe and had participated in the invasion of Normandy only four years earlier.

Godman Tower: "National Gaurd 869 from Godman Tower. We have an object south of Godman here that we are unable to identify, and we would like to know if you have gas enough, and, if so, could you take a look for us if you will."

Mantell: "Roger. I have the gas and I will take a look for you if you give me the correct heading."

At this point, one of the fighter planes, running low on fuel, requested and received permission to continue on to Standiford, leaving Mantell and the remaining two planes headed for the coordinates of the object sighted.

The planes climbed to 15,000 feet and, on reaching this altitude, radioed the control tower.

Mantell: "The object is directly ahead and above me now, moving at about half my speed. It appears to be a metallic object or, possibly, reflection of sun from a metallic object and it is of tremendous size...I'm still climbing...I'm trying to close in for a better look."

Mantell turned his Mustang fighter hard right and began to climb as the other two pilots scrambled to catch up. The flight reportedly chased after the object, which, according to Mantell's transmission, was traveling around 180 miles an hour. When they reached 22,000 ft. the other two radioed the flight leader that were abandoning the intercept. Regulations required that oxygen be used by pilots above 14,000 ft. and one of the planes' breathing apparatus was malfunctioning.

Mantell didn't acknowledge the message, and they left him still climbing into the sun at 22,500 feet. Three ten p.m. found Mantell alone in the air, chasing the unknown metallic object. According to some documentation, Mantell radioed that he was going up to 25,000 feet for 10 minutes. Then, if he was unable to intercept, he would terminate the chase. Officially, those were to be his last words. At 30,000 feet something terrible happened.

A moment or two later, W.C. Mays, of Franklin, Ky., heard a noise overhead that he said sounded like "a plane that was diving down, then pulling up." Mays looked up to see, far in the distant sky, that the cause of the noise was, indeed, an airplane but it seemed to be circling around and around. After a few circles, Mays said, the aircraft then went into a rotating power dive and made a terrific noise as it fell.

According to Mays, it appeared as though the plane exploded about half way to the ground, although he could see no fire. Years later another witness would claim that it exploded twice before impact. In any event, a woman named Carrie Phillips also heard an explosion and ran to her front window in time to see Mantell's plane crash down into a field only 250 yards from her home in Simpson County.

Mantell had become the first human being to give his life in pursuit of a UFO

When authorities arrived at 5 p.m. they immediately bagged Mantell's body and rushed it by ambulance to nearby Rooker Funeral Home. No one was allowed to view the corpse which soon led to speculation that there may not have been a body recovered from the wreckage at all. Nevertheless, a local fireman soon stepped forward to claim that he had pulled Mantell's partially decapitated body from the wreckage and had noted that his wristwatch had stopped at 3:18 p.m. The coroner confirmed that the watch had stopped at that time, which he judged to be the exact time of death. He released no statement regarding the condition of Mantell's remains.

The evening edition of the *Louisville Courier* read: "F-51 and Capt. Mantell Destroyed Chasing Flying Saucer!" and from there the story spread like wildfire across the country. The New York Times ran the story on the front page under the headline "Flier Dies Chasing Flying Saucer."

Not quite seven months after the term "flying saucer" was coined, the U.S. military was left with its first official extraterrestrial mess to try and clean up, cover up or sweep under the rug. Their immediate reaction was that Mantell had died from lack of oxygen (his plane had no oxygen equipment) while chasing the planet Venus! This insulted the intelligence of not only a decorated WWII veteran, but every other witness to the phenomenon that day as well, including the Godman tower operators and Col. Hix. That he might have blacked out from hypoxia was not in doubt, but the contention that men of such rank and experience could actually mistake Venus for a flying saucer seemed laughably ridiculous, especially when local weather reports made it clear that the planet would not have been visible to the extent reported that day. Responding to the outright rejection of the explanation by media and public opinion, the theory was revised, now positing that the object in question was nothing more than a weather balloon, in conjunction with Venus. And, although this explanation was greeted with as much criticism as the first, here the story stood for many years.

How did so many witnesses, including a WWII fighter pilot, mistake a military balloon for a metallic object of tremendous size traveling at 180 mph?

The mystery only deepened when, 50 years later, author Timothy Good uncovered pictures of the crash site which showed large portions of Mantell's aircraft, including the fuselage and wings, still intact after the crash, belying the official statement that it disintegrated on impact.

This was remarkable, considering the craft fell 30,000 feet. Good then interviewed crash investigator James Duesler, former captain in the U.S. Army Air Corps, who shot more holes in the official explanation.

Duesler wasn't called out to investigate the crash, he claimed, until after nearly 12 hours had passed. When he arrived, shortly after 3 a.m., the body had already been removed and Duesler was puzzled by what he saw. He was informed by others on the scene that nowhere on Mantell's body was the skin broken or penetrated, but every bone in his body appeared to have been broken and pulverized. Moreover, he noted that not one drop of blood could be found in the cockpit, a remarkable fact considering the fireman's subsequent claims of partial decapitation.

According to Duesler, due to the weight of the plane it should have nose dived into the ground, but this is not what he saw. The plane seemed to have "belly-flopped" into the clearing, leaving the surrounding trees undamaged and the fuselage largely intact.

"The damage pattern was not consistent with an aircraft of this type crashing into the ground," he was quoted as saying. "The official report said that Mantell had blacked out due to lack of oxygen. This may well have been the case, but the aircraft came down in a strange way."

Moreover, Deusler claimed that the wreckage was perforated with thousands of tiny holes which he could not explain using conventional reasoning. "I must admit that I found all this rather strange," he said.

Richard T Miller, who was working in the operations room at Scott Air Force Base, Belleville, Il., at the time of Mantell's death, reportedly made several statements regarding the crash. He was monitoring the transmissions between Mantell and Godman Tower that day and claimed to hear the pilot make a statement which never appeared in the official transcripts. According to Miller, Mantell clearly stated, " My God! I see people in this thing!"

At a briefing the next morning, investigators told him that Mantell had died pursuing an intelligently controlled unidentified flying object. That evening, Miller claimed, Air Technical Intelligence Center officers from Wright-Patterson AFB arrived and ordered all personnel to immediately turn over any and all materials relating to the crash. After this was done, they remarked that the investigation of the incident had already been completed.

"I was no longer a skeptic," Miller stated. "I had been up 'til that time. Now I wondered why the government had gone to all of the trouble to cover it up, to keep it away from the press and the public."

Eventually the government decided to admit that it was not an ordinary weather balloon Mantell had given his life trying to intercept, but a top-secret "sky hook" balloon. None of the witnesses recognized it for what it was, of course, because they had never seen one before. To the public each official release seemed just as, or even more, dubious than the last. They could foresee only one potential outcome of a confrontation between an F-51 Mustang and a weather balloon of any type, top-secret or otherwise, and it didn't involve the complete destruction of the fighter plane.

The account of the untimely death of the 25-year-old Kentucky native has been examined hundreds of times in as many publications by as many writer/investigators, but the mystery remains hotly debated even now. Many contend, as did British writer Harold T. Wilkins, that Mantell was shot from the sky by the UFO when he approached too closely. Some immensely strange and powerful "death ray" had been used as a show of force, perhaps, and a strong warning against any future attempts of the interception of these interplanetary vehicles. This theory, Wilkins claimed, explained both the condition of the crashed, perforated Mustang fighter plane and the alleged condition of the pilot's remains (which must have resembled little more than a shapeless mass), as well as the reason for the crash itself.

Vocal opponents of the UFO murder conspiracy have stood their ground. In the 1990s, independent UFO researchers succeeded where the United States government had failed for five decades. They discovered documentation revealing the fact that a weather balloon had been released from Camp Ripley, Minnesota, the morning before the incident took place, and at least two Kentucky witness testimonials described the balloon. Debunkers still refuse to consider that nearly the entire Ohio Valley was in the midst of a highly active UFO flap during this time period with sightings occurring in Kentucky, Ohio, Illinois. And Tennessee.

Maj. Donald E. Keyhoe, formerly of Project Blue Book, has stated that he highly doubts even the official explanation that Mantell passed out due to lack of oxygen, a position shared by many other researchers. Keyhoe claimed to have had a conversation with a fellow pilot who, wishing to remain anonymous, told him, "It looks like a cover up to me. I think Mantell did just what he said he would - close in on the thing. I think he either collided with it or, more likely, they knocked him out of the air."

In a book he later published about the UFO mystery, Keyhoe contended that the U.S. government was withholding important information regarding Mantell's death, and had chosen to cover-up the actual facts concerning the case. In fact, he felt that this one early Kentucky incident could possibly hold the key to the entire UFO phenomenon. The object seen by Mantell and so many others that day, he felt, must have been a gigantic space-ship, perhaps the largest ever to have entered Earth's atmosphere.

The Mantell incident remains unique in its infamy and is still regarded by some researchers as, perhaps, the single most important event in the history of 20th century ufology, with the Roswell incident and the Betty and Barney Hill abductions coming in at numbers two and three, respectively. Of interesting note to those who would scoff at such things is the time-line in which it happened. Not quite seven months after the phenomenon first burst into popular culture with Kenneth Arnold's June 24 sighting of nine silver discs over the Cascade mountains of the previous year, and less than six months before a shocked nation read headlines claiming that one of these mysterious discs had crashed and been retrieved just outside of Roswell, N.M., a statement which they quickly retracted. Coincidence? Some believers maintain that the Roswell craft was actually shot down by the U.S. Government in retaliation for Mantell's murder. In any event, the mysterious death of Thomas Mantell has become one of Kentucky's most enduring aerial mysteries and will continue to inspire generations of Forteans to come.

BLUEGRASS MEN IN BLACK

A personal friend of mine, T.W., whose character is impeccable, sent me this account of a peculiar bit of strangeness that happened back in the 1960s concerning the UFO phenomenon. It is presented here unedited or altered in any way.

"The year was 1966 and we lived about 45 miles from Lexington, Ky. We lived on a small farm. There was an old man and woman that lived across the road from me and I would go over and visit with them every day. The old man was in his 80s and walked on a cane, he could hardly even get around. One day when I went over to talk to him, he told me that a bright light had landed in his yard the night before. It woke him up and when he looked out his window.

It was sitting there in his yard and then it just flew off. I kinda laughed and then he told me to go out in the yard and look, that it had left a burned spot in his yard.

I walked out in the yard. He had a big front yard that I would mow every summer. Anyway, there was a big circle burned in the grass. It was about 20 to 25 feet in diameter, A perfect circle, with three little circles in the center, like where a tripod had set. I couldn't believe what I was seeing. I stared at it for a long time and then I went back and asked him if he had called anybody about it and he said no. We talked for a while and then I went home and told Mom and Dad about it.

I never really gave it much thought after that, after all I was only 10 years old, and flying saucers was the furthest thing from my mind. About three days later I was out in the front yard, when I saw this black Ford pull in their driveway. It was a '65 or '66 Ford with black and yellow official license tags. When it stopped, these two men got out of the car and they wore black suits and sunglasses. They knocked on his door and went inside. They were there for about an hour and then they just got in their car and drove off. They never once looked at the circle. As soon as they were gone, I ran over to their house and asked the old man if he had called someone about the flying saucer that had landed in his yard. That's when he told me that it wasn't a flying saucer and that he wasn't going to talk about it anymore, He told me to forget about it. Before those men came me and him would talk about it all the time. He never would talk about it again and I never brought it up again after that. He had a scared look on his face after they left.

I mowed his yard that summer and the grass didn't grow back until late the next summer. You could still see traces of the circle for a long time after that. The old man died about a year after that. This was in the spring of '66. I had never heard of the Men In Black until I was finally grown, about 25 years later or so. But whoever these guys were shut him up real fast.

Earlier that year before this happened, It was in the fall, my Dad and me was out in the back yard and this stuff was falling out of the sky that looked like long strands of spider webs. this stuff was everywhere and I asked Dad what it was and he said that it was spider webs blowing out of the trees. I told him that there sure must be a lot of spiders around. I picked some of the strands up and it felt silky, so I thought maybe he was right. The funny thing was there wasn't any wind blowing that day and this stuff was everywhere, strands eight to 10 feet long and longer. I just thought it was strange and never really thought no more about it until many years later, when I heard about other people that had seen the same thing. I never once thought about getting a camera and taking pictures of the circle and webs. I don't think we even owned a camera back then.'

KENTUCKY SKYFALLS

'Skystones'
Dried Flesh
Fiery Rains
Cookies, Fish and Coins

As you may have gathered by now, some very strange things have been seen in the skies above Kentucky. Many citizens of the commonwealth, myself among them, have looked into the sky and stared in wonder, and sometimes terror, at what they've seen there. But UFOs, otherworldly scenery and phantom beasts are not the only phenomena associated with the Bluegrass skies. Not only are many of the objects which have been seen flying through the heavens above Kentucky a mystery, but so are many of the objects which have, apparently, fallen from them.

Sometimes things just fall from the sky.

It is a simple truth. And just as true, but not so simple, is the fact that sometimes these things really have no business at all being up in the sky in the first place. Things like frogs, fish, rocks, blood, coins, fiery rain - the list is amazingly endless and no one can say with any degree of certainty just where these items originate from - other than the sky.

They do fall, nonetheless, leaving people from all walks of life to shake their heads and ponder how it could be that things of such an anomalous nature could possibly fit into the current scientific understanding of the heavens and how they work. Some academic scholar from one discipline or another usually puts forth an hypothesis or two to explain skyfalls but, more often than not, the only thing these theories end up doing is insulting the collective intelligences of everyone involved, including the general public.

Skyfalls simply defy all logical attempts at explanation. They fit into no established or accepted patterns of meteorological formula. And yet they still fall - seemingly at random and within highly localized areas. Sometimes they fall from a single small - often discolored - cloud. Other times from a clear, cloudless sky. They fall to the ground where they lie in silent mockery of every scientific meteorological dogma that ever existed.

Skyfalls were first brought to public attention by Charles Fort, a turn of the 20th century writer who spent the latter years of his life frequenting the great libraries of the world, going through endless stacks of scientific journals and old newspapers, in search of items he considered to be out of the ordinary or not in conjunction with current scientific teachings. He took tens of thousands of hastily scribbled notes and, eventually, turned them into three wildly popular books. The effect of his writings on the general public was so profound that from then on, all items of an anomalous nature were lumped together under the banner of "Forteana." Tens of thousands of people interested in the subject matter and influenced by

Fort's satirical disdain for scientific dogma became known as Forteans. The label stuck, even after Fort's death in 1932, and is still used to this day.

Fort, who documented thousands of alleged anomalies from around the globe, also catalogued several from the Bluegrass State. Of these, two were of reported skyfalls.

On April 19, 1919, two stones fell from the Cumberland County skies, landing in Cumberland Falls. They were not large, as rocks go, and, although any stone that fell from the sky today would be called a meteor and then forgotten, what made these rocks different from ordinary meteoric material was that they were two entirely different types of stones and were, apparently, cemented together by some type of mortar. From whence this anomaly came, of course, none could say. Nothing else was seen in the sky at the time and nothing else, save the stones, fell from it. The eventual fate of the sky stones was not recorded.

One of the most bizarre and thoroughly investigated skyfalls in history happened on March 3, 1876, in Bath County. There, within a highly localized area of Olympic Springs, a substance was observed falling from the sky, which, on examination, looked like strips of dried flesh. Resembling beef, this matter fell already neatly cut into square strips, or flakes, from two to five inches in diameter. Several witnesses claimed to have personally seen the meat fall out of a cloudless sky and cover an area of land some 100 yards long by 50 yards wide.

Newspaper men flocked to the area to report on the sensationally strange "Kentucky Phenomena," as it came to be called, and, as these Kentucky incidents often do, the report left the nation's entire scientific community in an uproar. Impossible! they cried. Inconceivable! They were quick to gain various samples of the so-called meat for independent analysis which were, in turn, given to several specialists from differing academic fields. Not one could agree, independently of the others, on the identity of the substance. All of them, it seemed, had produced dissimilar test results.

Some, like scientist Leopold Brandeis writing in the pages of the Sanitarian, were of the opinion that the substance was nothing more than nostoc, a simple blue-green fungal algae, in seemingly perfect disregard for the matter's reported physical appearance resembling dried flesh. Prof. Lawrence Smith, of Kentucky reported in the New York Times, March 12, 1878 edition, that, after a careful examination of the specimens gathered from the Kentucky event, he was able to identify it as the dried spawn of some creature, most likely a frog. How such an immense concentration of frog ejaculate could come to fall from a clear blue sky Smith refused to speculate.

Others of high repute held that the fall was some cleverly conceived hoax or that it never occurred at all, completely dismissing the testimony of the eyewitnesses to the event. Others explained that the nostoc was, no doubt, already present on the ground and obviously swollen from recent rains to such a degree that it suddenly became noticeable and was falsely presumed to have fallen with the rain. Never mind that it was seen to fall from a clear, cloudless sky and that at no time did anyone mention a rainstorm in association with the event.

Local residents shook their heads in disbelief that established men of science could so nonchalantly be reduced to little more than babbling idiots spouting incompetent theories.

President of the Newark Scientific Association, Dr. A. Meade Edwards, wrote that he was, at first, confidant of Brandeis' initial identification of the mystery substance but, when he called on another doctor, a Dr. Hamilton, to examine a sample, Hamilton steadfastly declared it to be lung tissue, though no mention was made by him as to whether he thought the tissue belonged to a human or an animal. Hamilton then sent for what was left of Brandeis' specimens which he had misidentified as nostoc and, after careful examination, found that these were also entirely comprised of lung tissue as well. All other available specimens were then requested. These he was able to identify as masses of cartilage and muscular fibers. They were, in his analysis, exactly what they appeared to be. Meat.

Hamilton went so far as to offer his own explanation, of sorts, regarding how the material could have fallen from the sky. He claimed that it could have been vomited up (or down, depending on your point of view) by a large flock of vultures passing overhead. These nauseous scavengers, he went on to explain, were apparently so high up as to render them invisible to the naked eye. How many sick birds it would take to disgorge such a tremendous quantity of vomit as to cover an area some 300 feet by 150 feet he did not say. Nor could he elaborate upon the principles of any force which could make such a large flock of birds all empty their stomachs at the same time.

In the *Monthly Weather Review*, a Prof. McAtee listed the fallen material as a "gelatinous substance supposed to be the dried spawn of fish or some batrachian" and suddenly the mystery fibers became, at least "scientifically," some sort of dried jelly which boasted no resemblance whatever to meat of any kind. Tiring of all the official squabbling over the nature of the substance, one stout-hearted fellow reportedly took a sample and bit off a plug which tasted, he claimed, like venison.

On March 21, 1898, Mt. Vernon in Rockcastle County, reported the fall of "sulfur rain." The raindrops reportedly burst into flame upon hitting the ground and smelled strongly of sulfur. This mysterious, hellish, precipitation fell on other parts of Rockcastle County as well, according to the Monthly Weather Review for March of that year. Apparently, the scientific community had an uncharacteristically small amount to say on the matter and burning rain still remains a total enigma to this day.

Some things that fall from the sky can be downright useful. Especially if one has a good supply of fresh milk handy. It was reported from Louisville on May 16, 1965, that Stanley Morris, while sitting in his living room chair one morning, heard a tremendously loud crash that seemed to come from behind his home. Puzzled and alarmed, Morris sprang from his chair and dashed into the backyard where, to his complete amazement, he found the roof of his garage was entirely covered with bags of cookies. Furthermore, he noticed that the neighbors to either side of his property had undergone the same calamity. Bags and bags of cookies. Cookies everywhere. On closer examination they were found to be contained in bags which were entirely devoid of markings, or writing, of any type. This might have been a bad situation had not the mysterious cookies turned out to be perfectly edible. And luckily, the milkman was due any minute.

Not so lighthearted was another strange meteorological event which happened in that city back in 1911. The morning of March 7 of that year began rather dismally in Louisville with an overcast sky and steady drizzling rain which continued unabated for around 30 minutes. Then hail stones began to fall. Then, at around 8 a.m. the hailstorm reportedly gave way to a singular wall of darkness which enveloped the area.

The darkness was, reportedly, so ominous and intense that it immediately spread terror and panic throughout the entire city. Many alarmed residents were sure that the end of the world had come at last. When it finally lifted a short while later everyone was stunned. One is led to wonder just how dark it would have to be to make grown men and women flee in terror from it and what could possibly have caused such an extraordinary blackness to envelope the entire city in such a manner. Whatever the cause, the phenomenon was apparently of a transitory nature for it has not been reported again since - much to the relief, I'm sure, of citizens everywhere.

Another meteorological incident happened to my own family back in the summer of 1975 which may be worth noting here. We were living in Spottsville on Mound Ridge Road, the same location in Henderson County where my older brother and I had seen the remarkable sky vision related at the beginning of this chapter.

One Saturday morning we awoke and, after breakfast, began the day as we usually did, by going immediately outside to play. A strong thunderstorm had swept over the area late the previous night and the rainfall had filled all the roadside ditches with water. The standing pools on the ground immediately attracted out rapt attention, as muddy water puddles often do to children. We were about to commence the beloved rock-skipping and puddle-wading rituals of childhood when we noticed that something unusual was going on. The shallow water was moving. To our delight we found that all the puddles were filled with small fish. And not the typical guppy-type fish that are so commonly seen in fresh water ditches either. These were goldfish and angel fish with black striping and long, flowing dorsal and tail fins, as well as a small, colorful minnow type fish with which we were unfamiliar. All tropical fish! Every ditch and puddle on the property was teeming with them and they must've easily numbered in the thousands.

We filled every bowl and jar we could find with water to contain our newfound pets, much to our mother's dismay, and, between six kids, we must have owned more goldfish that day than any other family in Kentucky.

Our parents had never before seen the like and were at a loss to explain how the fish could've gotten into the ditches and puddles. The area was not prone to flooding at all. They concluded that, as impossible as it might sound, they must have fallen down during the rainstorm. We children, of course, could care less where they came from and scarcely gave it a thought, so delighted were we at their appearance. Alas, our childish happiness was to be short lived for, in captivity, the fish only lived a mere seven days before going belly-up - probably due to malnutrition - in their jars. On the eighth day after our discovery I took the last remaining goldfish and released it into a small pond near the house which completely dried up a week later due to lack of rain.

The event was never repeated during the many thunderstorms at that location which were still to come.

Fort coined a word to describe the sudden appearance, seemingly from out of nowhere, of anomalous objects like these - teleportation. It is an apt term, if not a well-understood one, to anyone who has witnessed such phenomena.

In 2004, a friend and I were visiting in my home in Henderson one morning. We were both avid boxing fans and, while we were discussing the finer points of a recent professional bout, something extraordinary happened which neither of us could even begin to explain. A coin fell down, apparently from the kitchen ceiling, bounced on the floor and rolled to my friend's feet. His mouth dropped open. "What the hell? Did you see that?"

"Of course I did," I said. I was sitting scarcely three feet away. He looked up in amazement, as if trying to find some source from which money might fall from my ceiling. I picked up the coin. It was an ordinary quarter, dated 1984. "Where in the hell did it come from?" he asked. I followed his gaze upward. "No idea," I said, as I shoved the coin into my pocket. "Wonder if there's any hundred dollar bills up there?"

IV. KENTUCKY'S MYSTERIOUS DIMINUTIVES

SMALLFOOT
The Mysterious Creatures of Summershade

South Central, Kentucky

Summershade is a small Kentucky town nestled amid the hills and hollows of what lowlanders like myself would call hill country. It is located in Metcalf County and the scenery there is strikingly beautiful and much different from the marshy lowlands of western Kentucky. Mountains, valleys and stone-bottomed creeks dominate a landscape that is covered with seemingly endless expanses of thick, virgin forests. Within these forests, and scattered upon the sides of the stony mountains and creek banks there, can be found entrances to countless darkened caves which open into murky caverns containing passages which lead deep underground, connecting to the largest known cave system in the world, nearby Mammoth caves. Who can say where all these tunnels lead and what might be found within them? Perhaps even an unknown species or two might live in such immense subterranean networks as these and utilize them as convenient and highly effective escape routes when needed.

In 1995, my brother, Robert, moved to Summershade. His property consisted of roughly 75 acres on two parallel ridges covered with thick growths of pine and fir. A small, rocky stream ran near the house, separating it from the barn and completing the picturesque scene. All was well for a few months. Then he noticed that some of his chickens were starting to disappear. He could find no trace of them, nor any spoor left behind by any nocturnal visitors to his hen house. They were just gone. He thought little of it, even though our family had found out the hard way back in Spottsville some 20 years earlier what a steady disappearance of barnyard fowl might mean.

Chickens were, after all, usually the primary targets of any and all roaming predators, being easy prey items, especially when cooped. Aside from the chickens, none of the larger livestock seemed bothered and nothing else on the property was disturbed. Nonetheless, as the weeks went by, the chickens continued to vanish and Robert remained bewildered as to why. It was not until after two family friends, Tim S. And Chris W. (real names on file), had come for a lengthy visit that the unidentified chicken thieves were finally described.

When his friends announced that they were intending to stay for several weeks, Robert graciously offered them the use of a good-sized camper to sleep in. They took the camper about 100 yards from the house and parked it beside a heavily wooded area so as not to disturb anyone or be more bothersome than was necessary. When they retired of an evening they would drive to a dirt access road and walk a few steps to the camper. Later, the bedraggled pair told my brother that several times, as they returned to the camper, their headlights had illuminated what appeared to be "little, hairy creatures." These things were only two to three feet tall, they claimed, and were covered from head to toe with dark brown hair. They shied away when the light hit them and ran swiftly out of view, alternating between bipedal and quadrupedal locomotion. Moreover, each time they were seen, they appeared to travel in groups of from two to four individuals.

One night, as the two were readying for sleep, they heard a strange noise, a "chattering" sound, coming from the darkness outside. They looked out very quietly, and were alarmed to see a considerable group of these creatures in the woods just outside the door. Worse yet, they seemed to be stealthily approaching the camper, darting from tree to tree. Despite this, every so often one or two of them would let out another "monkey-like" grunt. Chris immediately grabbed the handgun Robert had given them for protection. He would've started shooting, he said, if Tim hadn't stopped him. He feared that such an act might anger the creatures. Maybe even enough to make them swarm the camper all at once. Then what? They certainly couldn't shoot them all. They noted that the diminutive critters were covered in dirt and dried mud, as if they were freshly returned from a digging endeavor on one of the many nearby creek banks. They were relieved when they decided to step outside with their flashlights and again the creatures made a swift retreat from the lights but, even so, neither could sleep a wink after the episode. They hadn't wanted to say anything about it at first. But now things were getting serious.

The adults of the household could tell that both the boys were telling the truth and did not disbelieve their story. They had absolutely no reason to make up such a tale. Besides, Robert himself had seen a somewhat similar creature, up close and in broad daylight, back in Spottsville when he was ten years old - and that one had been around ten feet tall! Surely, if that was, indeed, what they were dealing with now, the three- foot variety couldn't be all that scary. Especially not with such an array of firearms available. Nearly the entire family were avid hunters. How much trouble could the creatures be? Robert completely failed to take into account the overwhelming advantages that even smaller animals may afford themselves by traveling in groups. But he would become rudely awakened to this fact one evening not long after.

As it happened, one night Robert and the two boys, now accompanied by Chris' father, James, found themselves outside after dark trying to locate one of the horses that had escaped the fence. All four were armed with handguns of varying calibers. It was best not to take any unwarranted chances. Especially in karst country, a region made up of porous limestone containing deep fissures and sinkholes and characterized by underground caves and streams, No telling what could be hiding in the caves.

The two adults carried powerful flashlights in addition to their weapons. As they searched a forested area near where the camper had sat, the group became aware that they were not alone in the woods. They could see small, dark figures moving swiftly and noiselessly through the trees around them. The two boys pointed wildly at the things in silent vindication. The men shined their lights to and fro and drew their weapons. The boys followed suit. Whenever the light beams would hit one of the beings it immediately shrank back into the night and out of sight, running at first on its hind legs before dropping down to all four, then rising once again. The creatures exhibited no eyes-shine, they noted, and these, too, appeared to be covered in mud. Robert also related how, when standing, the creatures' front legs looked somewhat longer than the back ones.

The worst of it, he later told me, apart from seeing the weird little boogers in the first place, was that they were intent on advancing toward the group of witnesses, maneuvering their way in on all sides in an apparent attempt to surround them. Only this time, the creatures were operating in complete silence. What these things had in mind as an end result, fortunately, was never discovered for, when one of the things became bold enough to approach within a few inches of James, the alarmed quartet opted for a hasty departure from the area. James later told me that one of the creatures had rushed in from behind him and ran straight up into a tree without slowing down at all. The force of the movement was such that he could feel the wind on his neck. They all considered themselves lucky that they had somehow managed to make it back to the safety of the house without firing a single shot.

I subsequently interviewed each of the witnesses and they all agreed on every detail and each strongly attested to the fact that they weren't particularly interested in going outside after sundown because of it. I walked much of the area in question but could find no evidence in the form of physical traces of the reported creatures nor apparent signs of digging on any of the nearby creek banks. By the time I was able to make it to the site things had quieted down, it seemed. In the ensuing months Robert informed me that every single chicken that he owned, not surprisingly, had disappeared.

Business and personal reasons kept me from returning to that part of the state for many months. Then, in May, 1998, another sighting took place. This one by Robert's son, DJ, and one of his friends, a neighbor from down the road.

My mother had recently returned from Yuma, Arizona, and decided to move a trailer onto the property next to Robert's house. She had immediately purchased three dairy cows to put out to graze with the horses. The two youths were busy entertaining themselves in the back yard on the day in question, when they noticed that one of the cows had separated from the other two and was running around in the field. On closer inspection they saw that it was being chased by one of the strange, hairy creatures. This one was slightly larger than the ones previously seen by his father -around four or five feet tall. It also looked quite dirty, they told me, before describing the same curious ambulatory gait as the other witnesses. The only reason the thing didn't catch the cow, both boys claimed, was because it had accidentally run into an old barbed wire fence and stumbled to the ground. After this, the creature seemed to give up the chase entirely. Moreover, the two claimed to have witnessed a footprint left behind by this thing before a subsequent thunderstorm obliterated any and all traces of evidence which may have existed at the time. They described it as looking like the print of a man, except for the toes, which appeared to be split-hoofed.

The fact that one of these unknown creatures was, evidently, confidant enough in his own abilities to single handedly attempt to bring down a full-grown heifer says much about the animals' apparently aggressive natures. Not mentioning, of course, the fact that a pack of them had already tried to surround four armed men. The pattern here seems to suggest a mostly nocturnal animal. That they were all covered in dirt or mud in every sighting appears to give credence to the supposition that they might utilize, on a regular basis, the intricate and extensive cave systems that exist in the area. They would almost certainly be omnivorous, taking full advantage of every available food source. Could these mysterious creatures actually live in the area, as described, yet still remain unknown to modern science? The answer is yes.

South central Kentucky, like the rest of the state, is no stranger to reports of hirsute, ape-like humanoids both small and large. Sober witnesses have been describing such things, from all parts of Kentucky, for generations. According to Loren Coleman's "Mysterious America" (Faber&Faber,1983), in nearby Monroe County there exists a location called Monkey Cave Hollow. The name was given by early settlers and referred to the strange tribe of "monkeys" which inhabited the area, living in caves and foraging for roots and berries. According to Coleman, these critters were hunted to their apparent extinction, with the last of them reportedly shot and killed around the turn of the 20th century. I humbly submit the strong possibility that at least some of them got away.

The region seems to be a favored haunt of these mysterious monkeys. Bordered on three sides by the state's largest lakes; Barren River Lake, Dale Hollow and Lake Cumberland, the land between and around these bodies of water remains largely virgin and unspoiled. At present writing I have been to the area several times and gazed upon the many mountains, valleys, forests, rivers and streams. More than enough resources to adequately sustain and conceal large numbers of creatures such as these. With room to spare. I've explored some of the regions stream

beds and forests and marveled at the natural beauty to be found there. In some of the caves, one can put his ear to the ground and listen to the swift water running through the darkness far below. Much of this regions' wilderness areas are so remote that they are frequented by very few people- if any. I have no doubt that scores of the area's caves eventually interface with the aforementioned Mammoth Cave system in nearby Edmonson County, which remains a unique enigma in itself and still holds many secrets that have yet to see the light of day. One of them, I'm certain, must be the existence of small, monkey-like, nocturnal humanoids.

LEPRECHAUNS IN KENTUCKY?

All of Kentucky's diminutive unknowns, however, do not appear to belong in the "Hairy Dwarves'" sections of books such as this one. Nor can they be collectively categorized as looking like little monsters, long of canine and claw and bent on some evil, destructive or frightening purpose. Some have been described as looking, apart from their miniature dimensions and strange fashion sense, relatively normal -even human.

Most non-European societies hold the very idea of "Little People," of any description, whimsical at best. The rational mind cares little that beings such as these have been seen and reported by humans, in one context or another, since the beginning of history and, as a phenomenon, it is one shared by nearly every culture in the known world. The "wee folk" have been encountered by witnesses from all walks of life and are not restricted, it seems, to Eastern and Northern European locales. Evidence does suggest that a race, or races, of intelligent, diminutive, human-like beings may have existed at one time, or may still exist, in the continental United States - even within the boundaries of the Bluegrass State.

I first became interested in the possibility many years ago in my youth as I wandered along the ridges overlooking the Ohio and Green rivers in western Kentucky. My brothers and I spent many an idle day hunting for Indian artifacts in the cultivated fields of Henderson County. I was

just a kid when I found my first pygmy flint, a leather punch that was only a quarter of an inch in length. Several years later, and a few miles away, my brother and I found another. This one was a tiny projectile point made from quartz. It was smaller than the fingernails of our little fingers. On first inspection both appeared to be of American Indian origin, only far too small to have been of any use to, or even constructed by, normal-sized hands. When examined under a magnifying lens the percussion and pressure flaking was executed so exquisitely, and yet were so minuscule, that I could scarcely imagine the miniature tools that would be required to make them. Or the tiny hands that held the tools. I have also beheld, on two separate occasions, very small human-looking footprints in the middle of well plowed fields that were under four inches in length, or about the size of a newborn infant's.

While I had often heard rumors of anomalous artifacts and archeological discoveries which occasionally surfaced in the U.S., I had, at that point, never once heard or read of anyone claiming to have actually seen one of these intriguing entities within the state of Kentucky. Then, in 1998, While perusing the June, '98 issue of Fate magazine, I learned of a woman from Glascow in Barren County who claimed just that. After reading the article, I decided to contact the woman, Sharon Joy Rogers, in hope of ascertaining her sincerity and gathering more information than the meager paragraph had allowed. I immediately acquired her phone number from information assistance and called her. I found Rogers to be a very pleasant, cordial woman. Her tone was one of casual sincerity and, during the course of the interview, I became convinced that she was an extremely honest and intelligent individual who had, indeed, witnessed something singularly remarkable outside her home just as she claimed.

Yes, it was true, she told me. She had seen what could only be described as a little person, not three feet tall, wearing a tan and brown outfit complete with a short cape and pointed hat as it casually sauntered from around the corner of a neighboring house and disappeared behind a bush. It went behind the bush, she said, but never came out. She was quite certain that it was not just some child in a costume, but a fully grown, yet tiny, man. It looked to her, she informed me, just like an illustration of an elf in she had seen in a previous publication. The sighting had taken place at dusk one evening of the preceding year. She had always been a nature lover, she claimed, but had never before seen anything of this nature. Unlike the vast majority of other eyewitnesses to the unexplained, this brave woman chose to come forward and share her story, regardless of any possible forthcoming repercussions, in hopes that it might serve to benefit and inspire others just as it did herself.

We talked at length about a variety of subjects during which time I was able to gather the full details concerning the sighting incident and, as she thoughtfully answered each question I had for her, gain insight into her character and emotional state of mind.

The sighting took place in 1997 during the brief interim of twilight just between dusk and full darkness. In late autumn of that year, Rogers had been standing outside her home when she happened to glance across the street towards an old house which had stood vacant for some time.

Was she compelled by some force, like a sixth sense to look in that direction at that exact moment? Did the magic of twilight somehow aid or enable her to see that which most of us normally cannot? Regardless, she stood there and watched as this entity stepped out from around the corner of the old house. Even though the figure stood slightly less than three feet tall and could weigh no more than forty or fifty pounds, in Rogers' estimation, she could tell immediately that it was an adult with normal proportions in accordance with its height. She was not frightened at all, she claimed, but rather surprised and amazed at the sight.

She had seen pictures of elves and wood sprites before and this one seemed to fit that image perfectly. The little fellow's outfit allegedly looked as if it had been plucked straight out of the Middle Ages. Tight fitting hose or breeches adorned the lower half of the figure, with linen leggings that wound up to his knees. A thigh-length shirt, or coat, covered his arms and torso, accentuated by a short cape which hung at waist level. Topping of the medieval ensemble was a small, pointed, or peaked, hat resting atop his head.

Everything about him, including his shoulder-length curly hair, was in shades of browns and tans. She hadn't noticed if the being had worn gloves or boots, and she did not see a pair of pointed ears sprouting from beneath the little cap. It was a wonder she had noticed any particulars at all, she told me, as she was so surprised at what she was seeing. She rubbed her eyes for a second and blinked but the man was still there. As the elfish figure strolled towards a short bush that grew next to the house, Rogers, who had lived in the neighborhood for four years and was quite familiar with all the homes there, thought to herself there couldn't possibly be enough room between the bush and the home to allow the beings' passage. But he seemed to have no trouble at all, she said, and walked right through. Once behind the bush, the fellow stopped. The limbs of the shrub were bare, having already shed its leaves but, although the vacant house could clearly be seen through the empty branches, Rogers suddenly realized that she could no longer see the little man at all. It was as if he had simply disappeared. She had waited for some time, she confided, for him to come out from behind the bush. He never did.

In contrast to many experiences involving unknown entities where the witness is left feeling shaken, frightened, confused or worse, Rogers said she in no way felt threatened during the sighting and views it as a pleasant, uplifting experience. A recent widow of devout faith, she considered herself a highly spiritual person. She harbored a sympathetic passion, she revealed, for all things concerning nature and its animals and prides herself in the fact that she always strives to do her part to help all God's creatures and not contribute to the alarming rate at which nature is being exploited and destroyed by mankind. She never turned away any stray or hungry animals, even though she barely subsided on a meager pension. She had a little garden which she tended with pride and much care.

Rogers said she felt sure that the being she saw on that autumn evening was real and somehow connected to nature and its care or protection. And, while he had never made eye contact with her, she believed that this elemental entity had been aware of her presence and had allowed himself to be seen by her. Perhaps he had sensed her ecological passion and, as a reward, allowed the woman a glimpse of another such being, a kindred spirit, if you will, albeit one from another existence or plane of reality that is, at present, outside of man's understanding.

It is also interesting to note that, when asked if she had ever experienced something before which she could not explain, Rogers admitted to having lived in two different haunted houses in the past. one in the Ozarks and the other in Ohio County, near the banks of the Green River.

I still applaud Rogers' willingness to come forward, in spite of possible negative public reaction, and share her encounter with the unknown. This takes a certain degree of bravery and strength of personal character that is mostly lacking in today's modern world. I am grateful to her for providing us all with yet another example of Kentucky's unique, enigmatic and diverse natural mysteries.

As a side note, the location which this sighting took place was Huntsman Street. Perfectly appropriate, as it turns out.

Many, of course, will dismiss the preceding narrative as nothing more than a flight of fancy. But I'm not so sure. In December, 2006, I interviewed a Bigfoot witness from

Hebbardsville, in Henderson County who claimed that he had seen the creatures many times over a period of years in the vicinity of an ancient Cherokee petroglyphic burial site (see Bigfoot and the Great Hill) Moreover, he informed me that the big hairy ones weren't the only special creatures that lived on that hill. They shared it with the "Little People," a race of small yet powerful spirit entities who were fond of music and dance. I asked if he'd ever seen one. Yes, he replied. Twice.

He described them as appearing uncannily similar to the Rogers account, right down to their little pointed hats. But only around two feet tall. I met the man, recorded his report and photographically documented the burial site. Having been able to spend some time with this witness, I can confidently state that he was intelligent, articulate and sincere in everything he shared. He told me these little beings were called the "Joui-stee," and that they were spiritual helpers of the pure of heart.

According to tradition, these miniature beings had fed the runaway Cherokees who had escaped the infamous Trail of Tears. They could be quite mischievous as well, and anyone trespassing in their domain with less than noble purposes were at risk of their trickery. His last sighting, he claimed, was in 2005, after his morning meditation and prayers. He had opened his eyes and seen a Joui-stee watching him from behind a tree. It was dressed in a green shirt, pants and pointed hat. It ran away upon his approach and he noted, even though it, "scooted out of there at a good clip," that it wore Indian-style moccasins instead of pointed shoes. Everything else about the little man, it looked to him, resembled nothing so much as the classical descriptions and portrayals of Leprechauns.

How are we to take such incredible stories and fantastic claims? Could beings of this nature actually exist? You decide.

The following is another true account of human interaction with the Little People as presented by Fortean extraordinaire, Stephen Wagner, on his immensely entertaining website, **About: Paranormal Phenomena.com** (http://paranormal.about.com).

Reprinted with permission:

CANOE TRIP INTO THE UNKNOWN
A leisurely canoe trip takes a turn into the unknown

When Steve W. set off on an adventure with just a canoe and a head full of summer dreams, he never expected that it would take him on the most fantastic journey of his life. Around the bend on that scenic river, the 50-year-old man discovered, was the dwelling place of creatures that he once regarded as belonging only to the world of storybooks and magic. But now, with his own eyes, he saw that they were real. This is Steve W.'s true story:

"On June 24, 2003, I went canoeing in western Kentucky on the Rough River. I had just wanted to get away for a little rest and relaxation, away from my normally hectic life. I put my canoe in at a nice little portage near the Falls of Rough, just downstream of the falls, which is not too far from Rough River State Park. The current was very fast because of all the recent rainfall. It was really just a typical canoe ride down a very pleasant and scenic river.

I had a very funny, queasy, nervous feeling, though. I was inexplicably anxious for some reason. Although I could not define why, I felt like I had something to fear - and I sensed death. Taking these sensations seriously, I was extremely cautious on the river because I didn't want the death to be mine. After several miles, I paddled the canoe to the riverbank and tied off to a tree. I got out to stretch and to explore the area. I climbed the bank and looked for a smooth, dry spot to pitch my tent. After deciding to camp near the water so I could keep a good eye on the canoe, I went on a little hike. I climbed up the hill and around the bend to a little creek that flowed back into Rough River. Looking down eight or 10 feet into the creek, I spotted what looked like the top of a clay jar. I instantly recalled a dream in which I found some ancient pots.

This recollection sent my imagination running wild with the thought that I might have found some old archaeological artifact. I started down the bank toward the creek. The bank was extremely slippery with mud and down I went, sliding all the way. My backside and hands were caked with gooey mud, but I stopped just short of the water and very close to the old earthenware pot. It was more like a clay crock and I quickly realized that it probably wasn't very old and that the bottom was probably broken as well. I poked at it and noticed there were little handprints on it. I figured a raccoon had already searched it, but upon looking more closely saw that these prints were not like a raccoon's; they were more like little human hand prints, about an inch wide.

As soon as that thought entered my mind I dismissed it as preposterous. I started pulling on the jar, but it was stuck really well in the mud with suction holding it down like glue. I figured, well I'm all dirty anyway; I'll just get a stick and pry this thing loose. After working on it for a while, it finally budged. But when it did, I heard something.

I heard what sounded like little kids laughing. It was coming from down the creek several yards away on the bank somewhere. When I at last managed to pull the crock jar out of the mud, something screamed! It sounded like a little girl - really high-pitched and loud! Man, I was scared. Who or what could it be?

Not knowing exactly what to do, I grabbed the jar and began to scramble up that muddy bank. Glancing back, I saw something move down near the creek. Now I was freaking out! I made it back up the bank and set the stoneware jug down. It was just a cylinder about 14 inches tall and 12 inches in diameter. It had a little rim about an inch down from the top. It was dark brown on the outside and light brown on the inside. It guessed it weighed about five pounds. And, yes, it did have little handprints on it - that wasn't my imagination

I sat at the top of the bank for a moment looking at the jar, trying to reason away the hand prints. It's no big deal, I finally decided, compared to that scream and those voices. Leaving the jar for the moment, I walked along the creek a ways and stopped every once in a while to peek through the bushes and see if anybody was there. That's when I got the shock of my life!

When I looked over that bank I saw two little people standing about 10 inches tall. As incredible as that sounds, I'm not kidding! They had pale skin, little brown leather pants held up by suspenders, no shirts and little pointy hats made of what looked like leather. They had leather foot coverings that went up past the ankle. Their hair was a reddish color and their eyes blue. Their hands were only about an inch wide!

They knew I was watching, but they continued their task: they were pulling some kind of wooden stump down that muddy creek bank with long leather ropes or strings. These little men were surprisingly clean, I remember thinking, for the work they were doing. Then I heard a thump back where I first went in the creek. I looked back and there were three more of them - men just like the first two - and they had pushed that crock jar back down the bank. They were all laughing - high-pitched laughter, like a bunch of kids. Then I heard a loud snap... and they were all gone. Their footprints were plainly visible in the mud, but they were gone along with the crock jar and the wooden stump. They had vanished in a split second

My heart was racing and I struggled to catch my breath. I was feeling pretty insane! How am I going to tell anyone about this? Yet that's exactly what I decided to do. I walked almost two miles back to the old mill by the falls where I started. (The stream was too fast to try to paddle the canoe back upstream.) I had my cell phone with me, but it was just one of those emergency ones that I was going to use to call my girlfriend when I was ready to come home and she could come get me and the canoe.

At the falls, I spotted a man in a pickup truck, whom I assumed worked for the golf course they were building there. I told him I needed a witness to what I had just seen. I didn't expect him to believe me just from my story, but I thought perhaps I could get him to at least come look. He told me to quit smokin' that stuff.

I practically pleaded with him to get someone else and we'd go down there together and I would show them. He flatly refused, saying I was crazy and that he wasn't going anywhere with me.

Nearby was a cable TV repair truck; the repairman told me get away from him, too. I suspected that the guy in the pickup called the repairman on a CB radio or cell phone and told him he thought I was crazy. Between what I had seen and the reactions of these two guys, I was starting to feel a bit paranoid. I started to think: they'll call the police and have me arrested, and I sure don't need that.

I gave up on those two and decided to walk back downstream to the ditch where it all happened. I just had to look again. When I got there - I cannot explain it - it wasn't the same. There were no footprints, no sign of the little people at all. Where I slid down the bank was as clean as a whistle - no skid marks. The mud looked completely undisturbed. I was and still am absolutely positive that was the exact spot where it all took place. But there was no sign of anything.

I loaded up my gear in the canoe and got the hell out of there. About 20 miles downstream I camped out in a hay field. That night as I lay in my tent, all of the strangeness and impossibility went through my mind of the strangest camping trip I ever had. I just could not get those little people out of my mind. They knew I was watching them, but for a little while they didn't care and then they vanished. In my mind I can still hear them like little kids on a playground, laughing, screaming, playing.

Was it real? Am I crazy? They were real. When I told my girlfriend the whole story, she just laughed and told me of the time she had seen a little green man under the lilac bush at her grandmother's house when she was little. She had no problem with it. Well, it's a big deal to me because I have to live with knowing what I experienced. It was just too strange! Little people indeed!"

Leprechauns and fairies? Hairy, split-hoofed miniature predators? Here in Kentucky? Are all these people lying and, if so, why? Even without the anecdotal support of eyewitnesses, the pygmy flints and tiny footprints I've personally witnessed leads me to believe that there may be something going on here. And then a report surfaces which simply defies categorization and credulity, something so utterly bizarre that is a complete exercise in futility to try and make any sense of it at all.

THE LITTLE MONSTER

Seeing is believing, right? Or are some things seen by the naked eye just too fantastic and, therefore, beyond belief? Christopher M. Walker wholly believes that he and a group of friends witnessed such a sight just before midnight on July 4, 1990 when he was 14 years old.

Chris, now 31, is a no-nonsense type of fellow. A family man with a wife and two children, he has worked in the construction industry for nearly two decades. He's not the type to lie or make up stories. Like his family, I believed him when he related to me the strange events of that Independence Day evening 17 years ago.

He and his buddies, he told me, had been sitting on a stack of old skids behind a factory building located on the east side of Henderson that night. One of them had a pilfered pack of smokes and passed it around. The mischievous quintet was sitting there, as kids are often wont to do, telling jokes and lies and smoking cigarettes. All of them knew they were too young to be doing it, one of them was only 10 years old, but doing what wasn't allowed was a way to be cool. Still, the 10-year-old was in Chris' care and, if they had gotten caught that night, he said, there would've been hell to pay. All around them were dumpsters and many stacks of old skids from the factory. Chris was busily engaged in the seemingly endless endeavor to be cooler than his other teenage buddies, tougher, braver, when all their boasts were cut short by a loud banging sound.

They turned to look and saw, about 30 feet away, a wooden crate sitting atop a rusted old dumpster. The crate was moving each time the noise rang out and the youths realized, with much astonishment, that whatever was making the noise was inside the crate and trying to beat its way out. The crate started to rock back and forth, back and forth until it finally toppled from the edge of the dumpster and fell to the ground with a crash. What happened next, he soberly informed me, was the most frightening moment in his young life.

Slowly rising from the wooden debris was a dwarf-like creature covered from head to toe, with the exception of its face and hands, with short, dark hair of uniform length. The street lamp down at the corner illuminated the thing, and reflected red in the creature's eyes. Fully erect it stood only around three and a half feet tall. It looked around, frantically turning this way and that as if disoriented or lost. The boys stared wide-eyed at the thing, glued to the spot by a numbing fear. The creature had pointed ears, like a pigs, red eyes, and a flat, wide nose. It had a mangy look about it. Some of the hair on its body was thin or bald and the skin beneath was dark brown while on its bare face and hands the skin seemed a lighter shade. The group watched as the thing continued to look around bewilderedly for about 10 seconds. Then, when the reality of what they were seeing actually sank in, their paralysis broke and they all fled the scene with much haste, running all the way back to Chris' house nearly half a mile away without stopping.

Of course, no one believed them when they told their story.

When I spoke to Chris in 2006 about the encounter, I was able to gather more details about the entity's appearance. It was muscular, he said and it had the overall bodily proportions of a midget. Although the arms were of normal length it had short, bowed legs. They couldn't see its feet. Moreover, it looked like it had been wearing clothing of some sort which was threadbare and torn, hanging off its arms and legs in short ragged strips. When the group fled they dared not look back, he said, for fear that it might be giving chase.

The next year, 1991, Chris was surprised by an impromptu visit from another friend who was not involved in, or even knew of, the aforementioned experience. Something seemed wrong with him to the point that Chris had blatantly asked what the matter was. The youth was not willing to tell, at first, for fear of ridicule but, at length, he told an odd story. He said that as he was driving over the Washington Street Bridge, which spanned Canoe Creek near Lincoln Avenue, he heard what sounded like a woman screaming in pain. Then suddenly, a small, dark, hair covered little "thing" ran out from under the bridge on two legs, and up into the mouth of a large drainage tunnel. He said it stopped then and turned around toward the passing vehicle, letting out another high-pitched scream. It had red eyes and pointed ears.

That these incidents actually happened I have no doubt. What the hirsute little creature might have been, and how it could have possibly managed to become sealed inside the crate to begin with will forever remain a most baffling mystery.

V. BIGFOOT IN KENTUCKY

APEMEN AMONG US
Bigfoot in Kentucky

Do gigantic, apelike bipedal hominids, completely unrecognized and unexplained by modern anthropology, inhabit the marshy bottom lands, untamed forests and lonely mountainsides of Kentucky? The answer is unequivocally - YES! Reports of these "wildmen," by whatever regional nom de plume they may have been called, seem as old as the Kentucky hills themselves. The Bluegrass State is an amazing hotbed of Bigfoot activity which has been almost entirely overlooked by the Fortean community at large. Nevertheless, incredible incidents involving these apemen have quietly been taking place in the commonwealth for as long as there have been people here to record them. The question, then, is not whether or not these hirsute giants exist here - for they surely do - but what are they? Are they flesh and blood animals or are they merely part of the human experience, manifestations of some primitive, Jungian wildman archetype? This question has been hotly debated for decades with no clear, definitive answer expected any time soon. Whatever the origins of these oversized anomalies may turn out to be in the end, one thing is apparently clear regarding Bigfoot in Kentucky: they are here. And they aren't going anywhere.

Due to time and space limitations what follows below represents only a small portion of the reported incidents involving Bigfoot activity within Kentucky boundaries. So prolific are the number of Kentucky incidents regarding these creatures that I have truly come to believe that every single county in the Bluegrass State has played, or is still playing, host to these mysterious, hirsute, apemen. It would indeed take a large volume, much larger than this one, to adequately examine all of the reports involving the appearance of the commonwealth Bigfoot. So we will look at a few of them in no particular order but, before we begin, a few words of gratitude are in order. In late 2005, my web partner, Bigfoot investigator Charlie Raymond, and I started a website devoted to chronicling all credible encounters of the Bigfoot phenomenon in the Bluegrass State. It would serve to give the citizens of Kentuck, we felt, an outlet for reporting experiences and interactions with these strange hairy bipeds and, indeed, just about every other mystery animal imaginable, without fear of public ridicule and the negative repercussions usually associated with the public disclosure of beastman sightings.

It was an ambitious undertaking to be sure, but immediately successful as the reports began to roll in. To date, more than 125 sightings from over half of Kentucky's counties have been posted and I have no doubt that, as time goes by, all of the commonwealth's 120 counties will be represented there. A special thank you must go out to the entire population of Kentucky for making kentuckybigfoot.com the number one website concerning the Bluegrass Bigfoot phenomenon. Now, let's look at a few of the reports:

In 1993, a huge creature some eight feet tall and covered with long brown hair was seen emerging from a large cedar thicket in Lawrenceburg in Anderson County. The witnesses, deer hunters who were also father and son, bolted for the safety of their truck when the monster stepped suddenly back into the woods. They could hear it following them, they claimed, and wasted no time exiting the area of Bods Mill Road. Deer hunters are often prime witnesses to Bigfoot activity in any given state. They are usually in the thickest parts of the woods well before daylight, sitting silently in tree-stands 15 to 20 feet above the forest floor, well camouflaged right down to their scents, awaiting their unwary prey. Although some of them might not admit it to just anyone, more than a few brave Kentucky hunters have been scared out of the woods on occasion. But, as any one of them will surely tell you, sometimes what you can't see is more frightening than what you can.

Submitted to kentuckybigfoot.com on Jan. 18, 2007

1. Your first name: Aaron (full name on file)
2. Which county: Anderson County
3. Estimated date: Dec. 5, 2006
4. Estimated time: 6 a.m.
5. City or nearest city: Lawrenceburg
6. Length of time of the encounter: 10 minutes
7. Number of witnesses: 1
8. Describe the encounter: (edited for grammatical errors)

'I was going deer hunting and it was early. Before dawn. It was a little foggy and the temperature was changing to colder. I walked to the opening near my deer stand when I heard footsteps behind me. I then heard what sounded like screaming - real low-pitched sounding - almost a growl. I got to the stand and climbed up. For about 10 minutes it (whatever this thing was) circled the tree I was in and made these sounds. I would have shot at it but I never could see it because of the dense fog. I don't think it was any animal I know of. I stayed there until about 10 a.m. then left. On the trail back I noticed there were branches broken off about chest high and I felt like someone was watching me the whole way.'

9. Describe the creature with detail: 'I did not see it but I heard and smelled it. There was a terrible skunk smell and the loud growling.'

The follow-up to this report was done by Bigfoot researcher and kentuckybigfoot.com co-founder Charlie Raymond, who had this to say about it:

"The witness had never heard of any sightings in Anderson County until researching and finding this website. He did not see any footprints in the area because it was very grassy. During the summer he camped in the same area and smelled the same smell and heard what sounded like footsteps late at night around the campsite. He was so frightened that he would not look outside his tent. This was on the same farm near Wildcat Road. He doesn't feel safe going back there without a gun at any time of day. This farm is owned by his father-in-law and he's very strict about people coming on the property, otherwise he would invite researchers to come out and investigate. He seemed very sincere, credible and eager to learn more about Bigfoot. He would love to help find one, not to shoot one, but to help us learn more."

In January of 1993, at about 2:30 a.m., two motorists saw an eight-foot-tall, hairy, man-like creature while driving about 20 miles outside of Mayfield in Ballard County. According to them, the thing had long, shiny, dark hair covering its whole body. Despite this fact, they both noticed that it had very distinctive, or pronounced, muscle definition on its arms and legs. The face was human-like, they said, especially the eyes. It turned its head and watched them as their vehicle passed only two or three feet away.

The following Barren County report was submitted on Jan. 15, 2007

1. Your first name: Chris (full name on file)
2. Which county: Barren County
3. Estimated date: Jan. 3, 2007
4. Estimated time: 4 a.m.
5. City or nearest city: Cave City
6. Length of time of the encounter: 10 min.
7. How many witnesses: 1
8. Describe the encounter:

'I was looking everything over to make sure that I got all my deer hunting things when suddenly I heard this loud screaming. So I remained in my deer stand. Then I smelled this awful smell like something was dead. It was then that I caught sight of this thing walking out of the corner of my eye. It was around 25 yards (away) from me.'

9. Describe the creature with detail: 'Brown-reddish hair. Around seven to eight feet tall.'
10. Additional info: 'When I heard the scream, everything got silent.'

It is interesting to note that, time and again, witnesses state that when Bigfoot is near all the other fauna, right down to the insects, suddenly become quiet and an eerie silence falls like a shroud over the entire area. Again investigator Raymond follows up and adds these comments:

"The witness returned my phone call and spoke with me at great length. He sounds very credible and sincere. He is 20 years old and has been hunting for approximately six years. On January 3 at 4 a.m. on a rainy morning, he went to retrieve his deer stand, which was 15 feet up a tree in Lazy Acre Estates. As he began removing the straps, he was startled by a high-pitched scream. It was then that he sat in the stand and remained very quiet, surveying the area. A rotten stench began to fill the air so incredibly strong that he felt nauseous. Then, approximately 25 yards away, he saw a dark, hairy creature walking from left to right in front of his stand. It was walking upright swinging its arms much more dramatically than a human would. Its hands swung down around knee level. It had broad shoulders and a bulky body.

The witness could not make out any facial details nor could he approximate hair length. He said the creature paused a moment directly in front of his location then proceeded to walk quietly 40 or 50 yards away from his tree stand. The witness has heard similar screams five or six times over the past two years while hunting on this private property, located near Mammoth Cave."

Picture the scene:
A woman sits in the front room of her quaint country home sewing on a dress she plans to wear to church this coming Sunday. The back door is open and sunshine pours in. All is quiet in this peaceful setting. Until a five-year-old boy bursts in through the back screen door, panic-stricken and crying. The door slams as he runs and jumps into the woman's lap and clings tightly to her neck. What in the world? the woman thinks as the boy's tears run down his face.

"Mommy," he sobs. "Mommy, It's the hairy man. It's the hairy man! Don't let it get me!"

This is not a scene from some Hollywood Sasquatch movie. The incident allegedly took place on Wilson Ridge in Casey County, in May of 1957. For the rest of that hot, long summer, the child would not leave his mother's side and would panic, crying and screaming in terror, every time they tried to take him outdoors. He was even too terrified to make it to and from the car without breaking down. Even as an adult, he refuses to speak about the incident to anyone - including his own family.

What in the world could he have seen to have scared the lad so? Perhaps it was the same "hairy man" which scared two other Casey County children four years earlier. The children came upon the creature, described as being large and covered with dark brown hair, lighter on the chest area, giving it the appearance of a gray vest, while it was apparently digging in the ground using two sticks as tools. The thing's finger- and toenails, they said, were long, thick, uneven and squared. The youths fled when the monster began to approach them, growling and baring its large, square teeth. This incident reportedly took place only a half mile from the mysterious Green River, a name which pops up in the reports again and again.

Bigfoot was seen in Trimble County in 1962. Farmer Owen Pike described a creature about six feet tall and covered in dark hair that attacked his dogs and fled on two legs. Other sightings of the creature also allegedly occurred there and the year became known for the "monster scare."

Also in the 1960s, a tall, hairy "thing" was allegedly seen peering into the window of a home on US 127 near Liberty. The window reportedly belonged to a teenage girl. It was two stories off the ground.

Also in Casey County during the 1960s, the vicinity of Goose Creek was said to be the haunt of some fierce "varmint" which no coon dog in the county could tree. In fact, just one whiff of the varmint's scent, it was said, would send the bravest coon dog running in the other direction every time.

Goose Creek, a tributary of the Green River, was also the location in which a retired Kentucky State Trooper reportedly heard a nighttime "Yowler" in 1965. A year earlier in Grant County, a seven-foot-tall, dark-colored monster with shiny eyes was seen at a local trash dump just off US 36. The incident sparked a monster hunt craze that had the local farmers crying foul. Two out-of-town teens were accidentally shot during the fervor (not fatally). On a single night local police chased away 14 carloads of armed monster- hunting teenagers. After officials announced that they planned to hand out citations to all non locals in the area after dark, the monster hunts ceased. Sightings of the creature, on the other hand, did not.

In the late 1950s two teenage boys spotted what they later realized was a Bigfoot in Cary, Bell County, near the mouth of an old coalmine. They described it as eight or nine feet tall and apelike with gray or white hair.

Also in Bell County, this time years later, in 1966, hairy monsters were encountered on Bugger Mountain near Brown's Creek in Hen Holler. Moreover, Bell County was the reported scene of a 2004 incident involving a Bigfoot being struck by an automobile (see: Atypical Reports).

According to the *Kentucky Post*, members of the Jones family encountered a shorter version of the creature, perhaps a young male, one night in March of 1980. The incident took place in Big Bone Lick, birthplace of paleontology. The creature was reportedly only four or five feet tall, weighing an estimated 300 lbs. with broad shoulders and a flat face. It was bold enough to approach the family's mobile home, shaking the door and causing much alarm. When the thing attempted to overturn the trailer it was fired on by the man of the house - to no effect. It simply ran away on all fours and made its escape by leaping into the nearby Ohio River and swimming north. Police investigations revealed nothing save for the fact that the area has a history of monster activity. The Jones family alone claims to have had several more run-ins with the creature on the property.

In Ashland, in Boyd County, a mother and son witnessed an extremely tall creature with long, stringy hair as it crossed a road one night in 1998. According to the mother, its stride was so immense that the monster crossed the road - a distance of at least 20 feet - easily in only two steps. Ashland is an extremely active area for hairy monsters it seems. Seven years earlier, in 1991, a similar creature, also described with long, stringy hair, chased two witnesses to their car as they were investigating a local "haunted" bridge. It ran on all fours as well, but when it stood up, they claimed it was at least 16 feet tall! Another late night sighting of Bigfoot crossing the road was made in Murray in Calloway County, in 1968. The two witnesses were Dr. Richard Young and Charles Denton.

Online submission, Feb. 12, 2007

1. Your first name: Joshua Sparks
2. Which county? Boyd
3. Estimated date: October, 2006
4. Estimated time: 8 p.m.
5. Length of time of the encounter: five minutes
6. How many witnesses? 2
7. Describe your encounter:

'My son and I were walking in the woods off the country road known as Greenfield Road which connects to Shopes Creek and Hurricane Hollow. We had recently discovered some tree breaks and tee pees in that area. As we walked, my son, who is five, pointed and said, "Daddy, there's Bigfoot." I said, "where?" and he pointed to a location about 50 yards above us on a ridge. There was a Bigfoot creature standing at the top of this ridge. It acknowledged that we were there with a grunt. It then proceeded to break in half a small tree and began hitting a larger tree with a stick. We stood there frozen and not wanting to leave because we live for this. It then began walking toward us and it let out a loud moan/scream and grunted. I felt then that we had worn out our presence and I took my son and slowly walked away. We were there maybe five minutes at the most. Every time I see a Bigfoot I just freeze up and can't help but admire their enormous size and yet see the gentleness they portray.'

8. Describe the creature with detail: 'At least seven and a half feet tall; approximately 350 to 400 pounds. Covered in black hair. It was dark and my flashlight didn't grant me the ability to see its face. It did have a distinct odor to it. An outdoor odor.'

On Sept. 15, 1975 Bigfoot was seen in Breathitt County. The creature was claimed to be around eight feet tall with a slightly human-looking, hair-covered face. It fled into the woods when the witness stepped outside to investigate. This thing's mournful vocalizations have allegedly been heard by area residents on many occasions over the years and are said to sound "like something from the pits of hell." Breathitt, like many other Kentucky counties, has a history of reported monster activity.

Over in Hazard, in November, 2001, a large, hairy critter was seen crossing the road one night in front of startled motorists. Seventeen years earlier, in January, 1984, small, barefoot, childlike footprints were discovered crossing a frozen creek in Jackson. No human children were reported missing from the area.

Christian County played host to hairy monsters in the 1970s, an extremely active decade for Kentucky anomalies. As many as five witnesses observed, on three separate evenings, a six-foot-tall Bigfoot-like creature with broad shoulders and glowing green eyes lurking around some old abandoned houses. In March, 1979, an eight-foot version was seen, again on several different occasions, by motorists traveling along the Pennyrile Parkway.

In Maysville, Fleming County, a Bigfoot reportedly chased a woman around her car at a local shopping center in Sept. of 1980. One month later, according to the Fleming County Gazette, a back porch freezer in Fairview was raided by a large, white-haired monster that ran off on two legs when chased, carrying pilfered food items in its hands. A frozen chicken, two loaves of bread and a package of hotdogs appeared to be the motive for the break-in. Trace evidence was reportedly left behind in the form of long white hairs on the freezer, footprints and a trail of frozen goods. The chicken was found shortly thereafter - still frozen and partially eaten. The witness was sure that no animal could have opened his freezer door, a feat which would require hands.

Daviess County, in the western part of the state, has a long history of monster activity as well, According to the Owensboro Messenger Inquirer in 1978, residents of the 2800 block of Fairview Drive reported that they had witnessed a huge dark colored "monster" on several occasions, apparently observing them from the safety of the nearby woods. It was eight to 10 feet tall, they claimed, and four to five feet wide at the shoulders. A truly massive creature, it usually appeared in the evening hours and was said to smell like rotting corpses, or death. Tracks were found which measured 14 to 16 inches long and six to seven inches wide. Evidently, the authorities were unable to offer any help so a neighborhood posse was formed to rid the area of the gigantic, malodorous menace. They were well armed, of course. The hunt for the beast was successful and they came upon it by the banks of an old pond where they reportedly fired at it repeatedly with .45 caliber rifles at close range. Miraculously unscathed, the thing ran away leaving no blood trail at all, only an odd wet spot where the beast had stood.

Website Submission, July 9, 2006

1. First name: Josh (full name on file)

2. Which county? Daviess
3. Estimated date: July 2, 2006
4. Estimated time: 3:36 p.m.
5. City or nearest city: Owensboro
6. Length of time of the encounter: 15 minutes
7. Number of witnesses: 1
8. Describe your encounter: (edited for errors)

'I was on the northwest end of Bon Harbor Hills where a lot of coal mines used to be and some entrances (to these) are still open in places deep in the woods. Me and my dad were checking out a dam that my uncle was enlarging next to a small pond. My dad had walked back down to a vegetable garden my uncle and his son were growing, so he didn't experience it. I could feel a presence looming over me up the ridge about 100 feet away. I stepped into the woods and immediately knew I was out of bounds, literally. I was right next to a teepee-type structure that I had read about as being possible Bigfoot boundary markers. I began studying it when - WHAM!!! Out of nowhere this five- to seven-pound rock grazes my ear and knocks the tee-pee over. I was frozen where I stood. I looked in the direction from where the rock came from. I didn't see it at first but then I saw about a seven- to nine-foot-tall large shadow jump from behind a big oak tree at the top of the ridge. It took off going down the other side of the ridge and I took off in the other direction back to my vehicle.'

9. Describe the creature with detail: 'Very large. About seven to nine feet.'

10. Additional info: 'Lots of ridges in area and deep ravines. Also, there are a few coalmine entrances still open in the area. A few months prior a very loud scream emanated from a nearby ravine followed by a horde of forest animals fleeing the area. FAST.'

Kentucky Bigfoot investigator Charlie Raymond interviewed the 17-year-old witness and found him credible. He added that the witness claimed to have conducted a search for trace evidence and found some large impressions which he felt were possible footprints of the creature. He informed Raymond of his intentions to acquire photographs of any forthcoming discoveries of footprints or teepee stick constructions.

A woman experienced a late-night sighting of Bigfoot near the Uniontown boat dock on Dike Road in Union County in November, 1996. The creature walked unhurriedly across the road in front of her vehicle and disappeared into the tree line which ran there along the Ohio River. She described it as around 10 feet tall with long arms and covered with long, wooly hair. It was broad-shouldered, narrower at the waist and had a gorilla-like head with no neck. Her husband and son, both commercial fisherman, had heard this creature many times as it splashed about in the shallow waters just off the shore of a large island in the river. The area has a long history of monster activity. Interestingly, it is also the site of the largest concentration of desecrated Native American burial mounds in the world and the largest known burial site in Kentucky. Over 800 graves belonging to the Angel Medina culture were desecrated and looted at this location in the late 1980s. The crime garnered national attention and, consequently, massive protestations from Native Americans across the U.S. Hundreds of representatives soon descended, en mass, on the area to hold rituals and sing sacred chants as they re-interred their ancestors back into what they considered sacred land.

In the late 1990s, I was able to gain access into the area, known locally as the Slack Farm,

(Left) The Slack Farm in Union County as it looked after the largest Native American desecration in U.S. history

(Above) The Slack Farm as it looks today. This area has been the scene of many strange events, including cattle mutilations, UFO sightings and Bigfoot reports. Local folklore holds that the forested hill in the background, and all of the surrounding bottomland, is home to huge hairy beasts that locals simply call "gorillas".
(Photo by Kaleigh Duncan)

and have a look around this magical place. Some stealth was required. Since the grave desecrations of the previous decade, which resulted in the nation's first lengthy prison terms for Indian grave looters, the area was highly restricted and trespassers were promised immediate jail terms as well. This was not the first time, nor the last, that I would find myself risking much just to stand on one piece of ground for a little while. Nonetheless, my wife and I were able to spend several quiet, uninterrupted hours there completely unnoticed as we walked the far end of the ridge which sat below a very large, forested hill. This hill, like so many others in the commonwealth, was reputedly home to large, hairy, manlike animals known locally as "gorillas." As we walked close to a small creek at the base of the hill, we unexpectedly came upon the carcasses of around 10 hogs. They were ripped to pieces and strewn over the entire lower end of the ridge. They appeared to be fresh, despite the curious absence of blood, and none of the meat looked as if it had been eaten. After this, an extremely uncomfortable feeling came over both of us, almost like we were being watched, and we decided it would be best to leave. I have no doubt at all that gorillas exist in the area.

On July 23, 2005 at 8:30 p.m., a man hiking around a large lake in Warren County saw a Bigfoot chasing a deer across a game trail. He yelled out in fear which caused the beast to stop and look at him. Then it ran back into the woods in the direction from which it came. It was very large and walked and ran on two legs, like a man, the witness claimed. It had a muscular body covered with brown hair. He also described it as having human-like eyes and a bad smell.

In Trigg County in 1996, two mussel poachers saw a Bigfoot while sitting in their car at the edge of Lake Barkley. It disappeared into the woods when the headlights were turned on. Vocalizations were then heard and a large, heavy log was thrown forcibly against the car. The next day, they returned to the site and examined the log which, they claimed, was so heavy that both of them together could not lift it.

In Powell County in August of 1978, a 10-year-old vacationer running an errand noticed a strong, disagreeable odor while walking down a dirt road in National Bridge State Park, part of the area known as the Daniel Boone National Forest. He then noticed a huge five-toed footprint in the middle of the road. Looking along the path he saw what he had first mistook for a small tree suddenly walking quickly away. He described this "tree'" as very tall and covered with dark, greasy looking, shiny hair. It had very long arms which swung as it walked away on two legs like a man. The boy ran back to camp and led his father and his uncle to the location where they observed the giant track as well and found that it was 20 inches long. Later that night the entire family was awakened in their tents by a loud noise which sounded like a huge boulder rolling down the hill and plunging into a nearby lake. The next morning more large footprints were found around camp as well as an overturned picnic table. Talk at the nearby lodge centered around an RV which had allegedly been overturned during the previous night with the sleeping owners still inside.

More recently, in Powell County comes another report of a Bigfoot near water. Early one morning in April of 2004, a lone traveler, walking home along the banks of the Red River near Stanton, got quite an unexpected surprise. It was about 2:30 a.m. when he walked into an awful smell, then heard a large splash in the water and turned to see a large, manlike shape as it stood on two legs in the river. He described the thing as having broad shoulders, a long, almost conical-shaped head and long, shaggy hair like an Irish setter's.

An apeman was seen near Russellville, Logan County, in 1972 by a local deer hunter who described it as seven to eight feet tall, approximately 500 pounds, with a short neck and arms that hung nearly to its knees. It put in another appearance in 1991, this time near Lewisburg. It fled when one gun-toting witness gave chase, allegedly breaking branches off trees up to a height of eight feet.

In August of 1998, a seven-foot-tall, hairy, red-eyed Bigfoot was reportedly seen on several different occasions by residents of Blackburn Church Road in Shady Grove, Crittenden County. On Bear Mountain, in Estill County in 1993, a witness was actually able to view through binoculars a large, manlike creature covered in reddish hair busying itself by beating a rock against the side of a log. Described as around seven feet tall, with a conical head, ape-like face with large dark eyes, no neck and dark gray skin, the creature was at least two and a half feet wide and covered with short, thick hair everywhere except around its eyes and nose. The thing suddenly stood up, the witness claimed, hunching over with its arms by its knees as if somehow realizing that it was being observed and faced the witness, waving its head from side to side in a strange manner. It then fled into the woods.

One Graves County witness, alerted by the sound of breaking limbs one night in 1998 in Mayfield, saw a large, hairy, black Bigfoot with small glowing red eyes. Again, the terrified witness fled when the creature started to approach, but then, who can blame him?

Website submission on Nov. 6, 2006

1. Your first name: Mena
2. Which county? Powell
3. Estimated date: Monday, Nov. 6
4. Estimated time: 12-4 a.m.
5. What city, or nearest city: Red River Gorge
6. Length of time the encounter lasted: couple hours
7. How many witnesses: 2
8. Describe your encounter:

'Me and my fiancée believe we encountered something like a Bigfoot. It started with feeling like we were being watched and then that night when we went to sleep, we thought we heard raccoons playing with the foil we left out, when we peeked our heads out nothing was there and the foil was all intact, so we went back to lie down. I couldn't sleep so I stayed awake. a few minutes later I heard a man's footsteps or what I thought was a man's footsteps messing around in the leaves at that time my fiancee woke up 'cause he heard it too. He again peeked outside and nothing was there, so a couple hours later we wake up and start cooking breakfast.

It was still very dark, like 3 a.m., when my fiancee was stirring up the fire he saw two eyes peer out of the brush. They were red. When he went to look at it again they were gone. He also smelled a rancid ferret-ike smell. We figured we had enough moonlight to start packing and we were both really freaked out, so we packed up in the moonlight and started down the path and we both felt like we were being followed. We got halfway to the parking area and we heard someone walking below us except it was a really good drop and no paths below and it was 4 a.m., and we were the only ones camping, so we figured, oh good. People.

We were relieved till we started getting to the parking area, and all of a sudden I heard something jump behind me and start running. I walked faster and then right next to me above the bushes something was charging or trying to scare us, so at that time we pretty much ran and it chased us the whole way. It seemed like it was trying to run up the hill to cut us off. We got to the parking lot and it stopped. We never saw an animal or what the thing was.'

9. Describe the creature with detail: 'Smells like ferret. Red eyes. Medium size. I heard it running on two feet and then four.'

10. Additional info: 'A strange growl sound. The area was one of the main hiking paths. About a mile or so in there was a rock and you climb it and then you see a huge flat cliff rock and you walk back into it more and you'll see the camping spot.'

Charlie was able to contact the witnesses who assured him the eyes were at a distance of about chest level from the ground. Both witnesses were pretty shaken up. There was a full moon that night although the skies were heavily clouded. When asked if they either smelled or heard anything the boyfriend replied, "Smell. At one point Mena went to sleep and I was rounding up for the evening when I smelt something very odd. I grew up around the woods, and I know what various animals and the woods is suppose to smell like. This was not one of them. It did smell similar to a ferret, but for me to be able to smell a ferret it would have to be really close to smell as strong as I did.

I immediately jumped up as soon as I smelled it, and there was nothing there. If it was another animal, the amount of smell that I smelt, the animal would have to be very close, and I seen nothing, making me feel like it was a large animal. Sounds. When we did go to bed, we left our tin foil from cooking in the fire pit. Once we had quieted down in bed, we heard footsteps leading up to the camp and then messing around with the tin foil. Then the footsteps were walking around the tent and I even heard something brush up against the tent. We were too terrified to look. After whatever it was had left, I looked out and of course nothing was there. We also footsteps on the way out, but not voices. I thought to myself great, there are humans out here, too. So I remember that making me feel better. The footsteps seemed to be about 200 feet up the path from us. We could hear so well because it was absolutely silent, really weird for 5 o'clock in the morning. Usually birds are up at this time.

We got to the place where we heard the steps from and something came up from the gorge running past Mena, scaring her half to death. We both ran. When we got back to the car we realized that despite the footsteps we heard, we did not see anyone at all, and any campers that would be out there would be in the sack, not out in the middle of the woods by themselves."

In Greenup County, near US 23 on Jan. 4, 2001, a nighttime encounter took place with a large eight-foot- tall, 450-pound hairy beast that made strange grunting noises. Witness quote: "When it saw me I was completely terrified."

Trace evidence was left behind in the form of large footprints which were photographed. In Harlan County in September, 1980, a hairy giant was seen crossing rural Hwy. 1137. The witness claimed it had long, ape-like arms, human-looking hands and a large chest. The head was described as being long and wider at the bottom with a stiff tuft of hair on top. The hair which covered the thing was light colored, long and "nappy."

One evening around 9 p.m. in November, 1995, campers in White Plains, Hopkins County, were disturbed by loud, unexplainable moaning sounds which came from a thickly forested area known as Lonesome Woods. An eight-foot-tall, hunched-over, hairy monster was seen drinking from a nearby stream. Witnesses claimed that it made an incredibly loud exit as it ran away on two legs over a ridge, and sounded like "a truck driving over the branches."

Five years later, in the summer of 2000, near Morton's Gap, a couple out fishing one night was startled by loud snapping noises in the nearby trees. Scared, they hurried back to their truck only to see a large Bigfoot creature attacking the vehicle. It hit the truck three times, they said, then it ran back into the darkened trees.

Terrified, the two eventually made it back to the safety of the vehicle when they heard the creature let out a high-pitched, blood-curdling scream. It was posited that this might be the same monster that was featured in a 1979 account in a local newspaper about a three-day flurry of sightings in the Hopkins County area.

Jefferson County also has a long history of monster sightings. A night time "Yowler" was heard many times over the course of the summer of 1971 at Pleasure Ridge Park.

In 1977, a couple on a late night date, stargazing by the railroad tracks at Old Taylorsville Road, saw a hairy creature standing about 100 feet behind their parked vehicle. It was described as resembling the Bigfoot from the movie Harry and the Hendersons, only ferocious-looking instead of docile. Four months later one of the witnesses claimed to see it again.

In southern Jefferson County, in the summer of 1987, four teens found themselves running for their lives as something big came crashing through the woods in their direction. The incident was initiated when a disturbing, high-pitched vocalization was heard and one of the youths yelled back. Thankfully, they all escaped.

On Sept. 10, 1998, a couple jogging in the Jefferson County National Forest encountered a seven- or eight-foot-tall, 400-pound creature covered with brown fur, which they at first took to be a bear until they saw that it was walking just like a human. Frightened, the two fled screaming to their car.

Hairy upright monsters have been sighted cavorting around since at least 1959 in Kenton County, where passing motorists saw one on a bridge in Covington. Such activity shows no sign of slowing down yet, it would seem.

Website Submission on Nov. 17, 2006

1. Your first name: Chris
2. Which county? Kenton
3. Estimated date? Nov. 14, 2006
4. Estimated time? 11:30 p.m.
5. What city, or nearest city? Ft. Thomas
6. Length of time the encounter lasted: less than a minute
7. How many witnesses? one eyewitness, two heard sounds
8. Please describe your encounter:

'My companion, Liz, and I were sitting on her porch smoking cigarettes and talking. There are dense woods behind her house and about 20 yards of lawn between the porch and the woods. The porch light was on and it cast a fair amount of light onto the lawn. We could easily see the tree line but not past the first line of trees. Shortly after we sat down, we were startled by the loud crack of a limb or branch. We thought it odd but wrote it off to the natural falling of a limb. After that, because we were then aware of the sounds from the trees, we noticed some rustling and the sound of someone moving around.

I yelled, "hey, whatcha doing back there?" thinking that it was kids trying to spy on us. It continued and then we heard another limb break further back in the woods (not as loud as the first). I grabbed a flashlight and walked back to the woods with the intention of looking like a tough guy and yelling at whoever was back there. When I reached the woods, I stood at the tree line and shined the flashlight in and yelled, "hey!"

It was then that I saw walking away about 40 feet in front of me what I thought was a small bear, four or five feet tall, walking on two legs. I got really excited and shouted "Hey!" to try to get it to turn around but it didn't. I freaked out and ran back to Liz and we went inside because I wasn't enough of a tough guy to keep smoking cigs outside.'

9. Describe the creature with detail: 'Looked like a small bear. About four or five feet tall

and walked on two legs. It was covered with hair and had a thick body. I couldn't see much else because it was dark.'

In a follow up interview the witness stated, "The hair was either black or brown and looked shaggy but I couldn't determine length. It looked like it covered the entire body. No sounds. The only sounds we heard were the breaking of the branches and some rustling that sounded like footsteps. As far as the head and body go, it just looked like a bear or a short stocky person standing up and walking. The stride made it look like it was hobbling a bit. As it was walking away, all I could see was the shaggy hair, not really any visible shape to the head. No smell. No footprints that I could find but I didn't look real hard. There are a bunch of leaves back there which is why we could hear it walking and rustling around. It was definitely weird though. Good luck with the research. I'll be keeping my eyes peeled towards those woods."

Website Submission June 23, 2006

1. Your first name: Rick
2. Which county? Kenton
3. Estimated date? June 7, 2006
4. Estimated time? 11:30 p.m.
5. What city, or nearest city? Independence
6. Length of time the encounter lasted: minutes
7. How many witnesses? 2
8. Please describe your encounter:

'I was driving on KY 536 and a seven-foot-tall, shaggy-looking creature walked out of the woods in front of my truck and another truck heading the opposite direction, put it's hand on the hood of my truck and kept walking into the woods on the other side of the road.'

9. Describe the creature with detail: 'Approximately seven foot, shaggy, hairy, walking upright.'

10. Additional Info: 'My dog was in the truck and started acting strange before the creature even walked out..'

Follow-up report: Witness sounds very credible and sincere. He added: 'I was going about 20 mph, accelerating off a turn going uphill. I had to slam on my brakes. I didn't find any prints on my hood, but it did stick its hand out and appeared to look at me but I couldn't make out any features. The truck in the oncoming lane hit its brights and I couldn't see much then. Just a big hairy upright thing crossing the road.'

In Lawrence County, near Blaine, In 2004, a husband and wife were out ginseng hunting early one summer morning when they began hearing the sounds of snapping trees and brush in the woods close to them. The husband looked up to see a large hair-covered creature watching him from the trees. It was covered in long, reddish-brown hair and had a man-like face with large, dark eyes and huge shoulders about four feet broad. It stood six or seven feet tall, they claimed, and had a muscular build. It smelled like a cross between a skunk and a wet dog. The man described the head as being somewhat pointed toward the back. Its face looked like a bearded man's with hair thinner around the eyes and forehead.

It had a wide mouth with thick, dark lips. The area has history of creature sightings. The couple claimed that two of their dogs had come up missing earlier in the year. Their bodies were later found ripped apart with organs missing. In 2004, something threw a large, football-sized rock at the husband as he was deer hunting behind his house.

Another man told him that while driving south on Route 201 he saw a large, hairy creature run across the road on two legs. He refused to hunt in the area after that. One week later, the wife claimed that around dusk, the dogs started going crazy. She stepped into the back yard and saw a different, lighter colored creature standing about 75 feet away. Moreover, the husband also claimed that four years earlier, while hunting in the company of his father and brother, the group heard what sounded like two Chinese men talking from one hill to another, then the sound of a large tree falling. They quickly left the area.

A Kentucky Bigfoot illustration by the author, drawn from witness descriptions

Trace evidence in the form of many trees twisted in two about the height of a man from the ground was later found in abundance.

Lawrence County also played host to Bigfoot in the late 1980s, this time in Louisa, when a seven-foot-tall, white example reportedly approached a car driven by terrified coon hunters late one night on Route 23. According to the hunters, the monster had long hair and walked in a peculiar manner - with its arms sticking out in front of it. The witnesses fled the scene before it got too close.

Website Submission on June 10, 2006:

1. Your first name: Phyllis
2. Which county? Lee
3. Estimated date? 1957
4. Estimated time? 11 p.m.
5. What city, or nearest city? Beattyville
6. Length of time the encounter lasted: 20 Minutes (approximately)?
7. How many witnesses? 3
8. Please describe your encounter:

'I was a passenger in a truck along with my grandmother and uncle, traveling up White Ash Hill. The road was dirt and mud in those days. It was raining and muddy. My uncle was having a hard time getting up the hill to where we intended to leave the truck and travel on foot, as usual, to the top of the hill. Something very large and frightening would run across in front of our truck and throw branches from the holly thicket on one side of the road. This continued for 20 to 30 minutes until my uncle finally managed to back down the hill.

Upon checking the next morning, the road was a muddy mess but you could certainly tell that something had gotten mad and stomped around. (Broken) branches were everywhere.'

9. Describe the creature with detail: 'Large, dark color. Guess to be nine to ten feet tall and very angry. It was hard to see more. I was a child and very frightened. My uncle and grandmother refused to tell anyone. They thought they would not be believed!'

10. Additional Info: Road running between river and railroad track through underpass up White Ash Hill down river from Beattyville before Bellpoint.

Website Submission June 4, 2006:

1. Your first name(s) Justin, Neil, and Aaron
2. Which county? Letcher?
3. Estimated date? June 4, 2006
4. Estimated time? 1 a.m.
5. What city, or nearest city? Ermine?
6. Length of time the encounter lasted: minute or two?
7. How many witnesses? 3
8. Please describe your encounter:

'We were up on the mountain camping out for the night. Then all of a sudden, we heard something running down a big long field of grass. We all heard it so we ran down closer to see what the hell it was. Then after we got closer to it we seen it walking down the road. It was running like no man could run. It also was screeching and making a lot of banging noises in the distance.'

9. Describe the creature with detail: It was a big brownish-black creature that was very large in size. It was probably seven to eight feet tall. It was running very fast through the field like no man could run.'

10. Additional Info: The area was in an open field right next to the woods. It was screeching and making a lot of noises in the distance.'

Website submission May 25, 2006:

1. Your first name: Clyde
2. Which county? Martin
3. Estimated date? May 24, 2006

4. Estimated time? 3 a.m.
5. What city, or nearest city? Inez
6. Length of time the encounter lasted: 10 minutes?
7. How many witnesses? 4
8. Please describe your encounter:

'Me and a few of my male companions were gathered around a campfire. .One of my friends had passed out due to drinking and we had carried him inside of the tent. Several hours later we heard groaning sounds coming from the direction of the tent. We thought nothing of it. Little did we know something had been watching us. The groaning went on for hours until we finally checked our drunk friend. He was silent and the groaning continued. I peered behind the tent in the direction I thought the sounds were coming from, and there it was. About 15 feet from us appeared an apelike creature sleeping, It was rolling around as if it were trying to find a spot to get comfortable.

I was quiet for several minutes and then I called to one of my friends to check this out. He came to see what the fuss was about and when he saw the apelike creature he screamed in fear. The creature raised its head, looking startled. It rose from the ground it appeared to be about seven or eight feet tall. It took off hastily.'

9. Describe the creature with detail: 'Somewhere between seven and eight feet tall, Brownish hair that appeared to be about two to three inches thick around its body. I couldn't see very much in detail. These are the only facts I can give from what I've seen.'

10. Additional Info: 'A mildly wooded area, behind the 4-wheeler trails, on a hill behind my house.'

Website submission Jan. 19, 2007:

1. Your first name: Jeremiah
2. Which county? Mason
3. Estimated date? late 2002 or early 2003
4. Estimated time? 11 p.m.
5. What city, or nearest city? Maysville
6. Length of time the encounter lasted: 10 ½ minutes
7. How many witnesses? 4
8. Please describe your encounter:

'On the first encounter, I left my house around 10:30 p.m. to go pick up a friend from his house in Germantown. I was traveling north with three other friends in the vehicle on Clyde T. Barbour Highway. I had turned left onto KY 435 and drove to my friend's house in Germantown. I picked him up and decided to go the same way that I had went to pick him up. There was three people in the backseat and someone in the front of my car. We had turned the car around, a right turn, traveling at around 20 mph.

As I turned the corner there is a two-story farmhouse on my right and on the same side, about 30 feet to the side of the house, was a very small garden with tall weeds on the side of the road. On the other side is a drop anywhere from 10 to 15 feet. As I drove, I caught a glimpse of what appeared to be a large dog on the side of the road, so I slowed the car to let it run

A Kentucky Bigfoot illustration by the author, drawn from witness descriptions

across the road without me hitting it. I turned on my brights to scare it from its position as I slowed to around five to eight mph.

It moved slightly as someone in the backseat asked, "What is that?" I then replied, "I think it might be a dog." The eyes glowed red from the high-beams and moved a little to it's right. This so-called dog had a blackish fur on the shoulder area. As I pulled closer, I stopped the car, put it in reverse, and turned the car to face the animal.

My lights now fully caught the animal still hiding in the weeds which were around three feet in height. I pushed the horn and it stood on two legs at a height of around six to seven feet tall. All of my friends then started screaming questions asking, "What the hell is that?" As everyone in the car was screaming I had already put the car into drive and peeled the tires to get away. One of my friends then turned in his seat looking through the back window as I looked through the rearview mirror seeing in the moonlight this animal run into the field towards the forest.

The second encounter was on Clyde T. Barbour Highway going southbound towards home. Me and my brother were making our way home from Aberdeen, Ohio. I was driving and it was a clear night with the moon out bright, I was driving around 55 or 60 mph up the highway hill. I had just passed KY 435 and the same spot from the last encounter when I scanned the highway in a daze and looked up at the hill where they had used dynamite when they were building the highway to blow the hillside out for the pavement

I looked at the hillside at the limestone and caught a glimpse of a rather tall animal with blackish fur running with my car. I pointed at the beast which had apparently been running on two legs and asked my brother, "What is that?" As we moved on, still watching the animal, it jumped from the hill and landed in some trees and disappeared.'

9. Describe the creature with detail: 'Tall around 6 ½ to seven feet. It stood and walked/ran on two legs with arms reaching its pelvis. Black fur and red eyes in bright headlights. Large body possibly 3 ½ feet wide, with stringy hair longer on the shoulders that looked like it was wet.'

10. Additional Info: 'I heard nothing from the car engine and the radio and my friends talking.'

A rather well-publicized Bigfoot account appeared in the Oct. 12, 1980 edition of *The Chicago Sun-Times*. It concerned Charles Fulton and his family, who claimed that, while watching television one night in October, they heard a commotion out on the front porch apparently involving one of Fulton's roosters. When he looked out, sure enough - there was the rooster in the hand of a seven-foot-tall, 400-pound, manlike creature with long white hair and (by some accounts) glowing pink eyes.

Upon being seen it threw the rooster against the side of the house and headed around back. Fulton grabbed a .22 pistol and promptly gave chase, despite the bizarre appearance of the intruder. He was able, he later claimed, to fire on the creature twice to no effect as the monster made its escape in a "slow motion" kind of run, exhibiting large strides but, strangely, moving at low speed. He felt sure that he could catch up to it but, even more strangely, the faster Fulton ran the further away the creature appeared. "It was like a dream," he said. Thankfully, the rooster escaped with no serious injuries.

Dog Slaughter, McCreary County, Cumberland Falls State Park - Daniel Boone National Forest- 1984
As told by actual witness, Mr. W.:

'The year was probably 1984. Me and a buddy decided to go camping for a night or two on the Cumberland River in the Daniel Boone National Forest. It was in August and it was very hot that day. This place is called Dog Slaughter and it is very secluded. It is quite a ways below the Cumberland Falls State Park and the only way to get to it is to backpack in or by canoe. It is really rough terrain and it is rough going.

I'm just guessing, but we estimated at least three miles or so to the nearest main road and then you have to travel a ways to get to where there are people. We had been going backpacking there for about five years or so and it is really beautiful country. The fishing is real good too. A year or two before I stopped and asked a park ranger or game warden if we could pack a gun in there and he said he wouldn't be back in that place without one. Anyway, we got in there that afternoon just before dark, we wasn't going to stay that long so we didn't take a lot of food. We had a lantern, tent and fishing poles. My buddy also brought a portable Coleman stove, which he almost left behind because it was so rough carrying it in there, much less trying to pack it out.

We got to our camping spot and dark was coming fast, though the sun was still up. It doesn't take it long to get dark back in those mountains. As we walked upon this sand bar we were looking around and that's when we found huge footprints in the sand and they looked like somebody had walked around the sand bar barefooted. But these tracks were really big. We followed them and they walked right into the river and across a little cove and then up a huge logjam. There was just the one set of prints. What was really odd was where the tracks started, there was a brand new shiny fish stringer still tied up with about eight really nice white perch on it. Somebody had walked all the way into this rough place and caught these nice fish and just left them there to rot, and they had already started to decompose. This was really strange, but we never really gave it much more thought.

We set the tent up in front of this huge boulder, next to the river. My buddy got the stove going and we started cooking some beans and pork shoulder. We lit the lantern when it got dark and we didn't bother with building a fire. We was going to wait until the next day to gather fire wood because this place is full of copperhead snakes and we didn't want to get bit gathering wood after dark with no light. After we ate, we talked for a while and then got in the tent to sleep. We were so tired we were going to get up early and fish.

The crickets and frogs were really making quite a racket on that riverbank until they all stopped and it got really quiet. That's when we heard something jump off of the big rock behind our tent. When it hit the ground, it grunted. Then we heard a twig or stick break. That's when this thing started growling, coming towards us. The growl was so big and loud it filled that whole river bottom up with its growl. I looked at my buddy and said do you hear that? By then we were both getting worried. It was between us and the way out. No matter, we still couldn't have gotten out of there because we were so far back in the mountains and the way out was all uphill now.

My buddy said, "what are we going to do?" and I told him that I wasn't going to stay in this tent with whatever it was coming towards us. I didn't have a gun, just a hunting knife and hatchet. But, thankfully, my friend had brought his .22 rifle. So he stuck it out of the tent door and shot off about five rounds. I guess this scared it off, because it didn't come on into camp. It just stayed out in the woods growling until just about daylight.

We never did see what it was. But after reality set in and we realized where we were at, I was starting to get worried. I had already made up my mind to jump in the river and take my chances there. That's the only time in my life I've had the hair stand up on my neck from fear. There are black bear in there, but if this had been a bear we would have never kept it out of camp because of the pork shoulder we were cooking. Besides I've heard and saw bears before out in the wild and this was no bear. It sounded big and mean and it meant business. When daylight finally did arrive we thought we saw something big and black walking on the rocks way up the river, but by then we were both so sleepy we couldn't make out what it was, though it didn't look like it walked on four legs, but we couldn't be sure. We didn't stay another night, not really because we were scared, but because we were so tired and didn't really want to go to sleep and have it come back and besides that a bad storm was coming and we barely made it out of there before it hit.

I don't know to this day what it was we heard or what those footprints were, but we talk about it still every time we get together. I've been going camping on the Cumberland River for years and that's the first time anything like that has happened back in that wild place. Though a couple of time before this, when we would go back in there, we would notice this strange smell on a rock that stuck out over a little stream that runs out of the mountains into the river. The rock is covered with moss and is a nice rock to lay on and relax. The last couple of times though, this rock smells like a monkey's cage, like something that really smells bad has been laying on it. I never could figure out those footprints, because anybody that knows Cumberland River at all knows it's not safe to walk around with boots on much less barefooted because of the copperheads, they're thick in that place. I wear a size ten shoe and the footprints made two of mine. The Cumberland River is a great place for varmints to hide. I never will forget it as long as I live!'

Again, it is that which we cannot see, perhaps, which scares us the most. I conducted several telephone interviews with Mr. W. and we spoke of the incidents at length. He sounded very sincere and credible and he still wondered, after more than 20 years, about the source of the terrifying vocalizations and gigantic, human-like footprints they had seen that day on the Cumberland River. Whatever it was had scared the two men half to death and made the hair stand up on their arms and the back of their necks. It was the only time in his life, he told me, that he had reacted with such fear at something he could not even see. They didn't want to see it. They just wished it would go away. If it had continued on into camp he was more than ready to throw himself into the river in order to escape the area.

He related to me how his friend was an extremely rough and tumble sort. Not afraid of anything and always in fights and scuffles with other people. Fearless, he said, until that night. The large, black figure they had seen during their retreat the following morning looked as if it walked on two legs like a man, and they wasted no time in fleeing the scene. That was one fishing trip, he told me, that neither of them would ever forget. The name of the area in which the event took place, Dog Slaughter, might hold some clue as to the history of Bigfoot activity there, as it is widely reported that these creatures possess an extreme dislike for dogs.

More recently, in the same county in 2003, Pine Knot was the scene of another nighttime sighting by a motorist driving down Hwy 92 between McCreary and Whitley counties. According to the witness, he saw what he at first took to be a deer approaching the road. Fearing it might run out in front of his vehicle the man slowed down and, on closer inspection of the animal, he is surprised to see a seven-foot-tall, gray- colored Bigfoot with large, red eyes. The creature then began to act as if it was angry. The motorist spared no gas in fleeing the scene. The creature was later described as being of medium build with an athletically muscular frame, large, domed head and a hairy face.

From The Bardstown Newspaper, Nov. 2, 1978
(Thanks to Rick Carter for forwarding this)

Nelson County - October 1965
The Whortlechort

The hills and hollows of Nelson County, where this incident took place, are normally peaceful spots where farmers nestle tobacco and corn against the ridges, and cattle graze the gentle slopes rising from the creek beds. Coon hunters pick their way through the wood and step lightly across fences here and the crisp autumn nights are usually filled with nothing more fearsome than screech owls, or an occasional fox. It was on such a night in October 1965 that two brothers saw something which they've never forgotten. One says he doesn't tell the incident to many people any more. "They just laugh and call you crazy," he says, "but our eyes didn't fool us." And neither of them will deny it ever happened.

While their father and mother attended a school fall festival that evening, the boys had been instructed to go the their grandmother's farm and find a cow which was expected to have a calf. It was not quite dark, and they had taken the pickup truck to the back field as far as we could drive, he remembered. They parked the truck and headed up a fence row to a clump of trees where the cattle usually bedded at night.

"As we moved up the fence row, we spotted something in sort of a hunched position. There were a lot of buck bushes growing around the field and we couldn't see too well. We didn't think it was a cow, but we didn't know what else it could be," he said.

About 100 feet away from the object, their dog started barking uncontrollably, then the animal backed off and would not follow the boys any closer. They were no more than 50 feet away from it now. All of a sudden, the creature raised up two legs and began running away from them. It stopped under an arch formed by two trees and for a moment faced its pursuers. The brown hair-covered body stretched seven to eight feet tall. The brothers aimed their flashlights at it once and caught a glowing red reflection from its eyes.

"We couldn't have watched it for more than a few seconds, then we both ran off scared to death. I turned once to see if was chasing us and I saw the creature put its hand on a fence post and just flip over into the next field." The next day when their father went out to the field to check their wild story, he found a path through a field of uncut oats in the exact spot where the boys claimed their "monster" jumped the fence.

They never saw the creature again, though once that same year, their mother and sisters heard an unusual noise in the barn. That summer another unexplained incident happened. In a certain corner of their garden something would eat the corn as fast as it came on the stalk. In 1965 few people had ever heard of "Bigfoot," but several years later when one of the boys was in college, he accidentally ran across the account of several Bigfoot sightings in the northwest.

"We called it a Whortlechort, I read everything I can about them (Bigfoot) now, and almost every account that I've read seems to match up with ours," he said. Through his reading he has also learned that Bigfoot are believed to be vegetarians and very shy of people and other animals "I don't think I'm scared of it, but I never go up in that field at night without thinking an awful lot abut what I saw." I believe God created the world through evolution, and maybe what I saw is the "missing link" between man and apes."

From witness interview, 1997:

Chad Askins and one of his friends had parked his vehicle near a creek bed on an old abandoned farm in Ohio County just about dusk one evening in 1988. They were there to relax for a bit and sip a cold one or two before heading back to their homes after a long day of hunting. The men were parked facing the creek bank, which sloped upwards a few feet in front of them before dropping down the other side into the creek bed, which was not in view. They had only been there a few short minutes when a large, dark shape rose up from the other side of the bank, as if whatever it was had been stooping down in the creek.

Askins saw the thing immediately as it rose to its full height and observed that, although it was roughly human in shape, it was of tremendous size and covered with dark colored hair. Both men could hardly believe their eyes as the thing took two long, slow strides to their right, then stopped and turned in their direction. It did not turn its head, Askins said, which seemed to be mounted directly onto this thing's shoulders with no visible neck, but turned its entire body from the waist up. The sun was just setting behind the monster which turned it into little more than a stark silhouette, but they could see that it had extremely broad shoulders and was "very thick" through the middle.

They could not see any facial features nor could they see the creature's lower extremities, which were blocked from view by the slope of the creek bank in front of them, but they stated that it had a human- shaped head with long hair and thick, muscular arms. Chad felt sure that it must have been over ten feet tall.

It just stood there calmly, he said, completely unafraid as it watched the two men in the descending darkness. The feeling was not mutual, however, and Chad and his friend men wasted no time in exiting the area.

I asked Chad why the encounter had such a frightening effect on the two, since the creature had made no threatening move towards them. He replied that, to him, the scariest thing was the monster's sheer size and the fact that it looked immensely powerful, like it could break a man completely in two with no great effort. Also was the fact that it seemed entirely unafraid of them, making not a single move to flee their presence as most wild animals would.

Further questioning left me with the strong impression that he knew very little about the Bigfoot phenomenon - other than the fact that he was convinced that this was the identity of the animal they saw. When asked to compare what he saw to the subject of the famous Patterson/Gimlin film of the late 1960s Askins was entirely unaware that such a film even existed and seemed very anxious to view the footage if he could. This witness struck me as being completely honest and intelligent and his sincerity while recounting the event was obvious.

Few places can compare to Henderson County when it comes to anomalous activity.

From witness interview on Jan. 20, 2006:

On the evening of July 14, 2005, 22-year-old Adam Candler was driving down Green River Rd. No. 2, just off T.S. Charner Road in Spottsville, when he noticed a large, dark object stooping down in a roadside ditch. When Candler's vehicle approached to within a few yards, the object suddenly stood up and ran on two legs into a nearby field. It was seven to eight feet tall, Candler said, and looked like a man with slightly longer arms and covered all over with black hair.

Due to the passage of several months since the sighting took place, a subsequent field investigation into the area to look for possible substantiating evidence would, most likely, yield little if anything. The witness stated that two other members of his family and one of his friends have seen this creature, known locally as The Spottsville Monster in the same general area. Investigation is ongoing and attempts to

contact these other witnesses are currently in progress.

Back in the early 1980s, 10-year-old Billy G. (Full name on file), while playing alone in the woods in Corydon, Henderson County, was interrupted by a huge ape-like creature with long arms as it walked across a nearby field toward him. Its body was muscular and completely covered in dark hair. Billy was so scared that he froze for a few seconds before finally managing to squat down behind some trees until the thing walked past him. He later told me that what struck him most was the immense thickness of this thing's legs - like tree trunks. When it had disappeared into the distance he ran all the way back to his house and never played alone in the area again.

In the Geneva river bottoms, a deer hunter witnessed an eight-foot-tall creature covered with black frizzy hair walk beneath his tree stand just before dawn one morning in the early 1990s. It walked right past him, within a few feet of his location, apparently unaware of his presence. He claimed that it made absolutely no sound as it passed beneath him. Scared to death, he waited until dawn and got the hell out of there. When asked for a description of the thing he replied that it looked like a giant, hairy negro. He refused to hunt in the area after the incident.

Another report from this same area and time period involves a carload of teens out joy-riding late one night. They parked the car next to an isolated area called the Grassy Pond, a large, secluded lake, and got out to stretch their legs. They were standing there talking when a terrible scream came from the other side of the lake, followed by the sound of something huge jumping into the water. They could clearly hear that whatever it was, it was swimming with overhand strokes like a human swimmer. As it was approaching very rapidly, they were inclined to leave the scene in a very hasty manner.

More recently, in October of 2005, a worker at the Geneva Store on Hwy. 136 became upset and quit her job when, on arriving there at 5 a.m., saw something very tall and hairy standing behind the dumpster beside the store. She stood frozen with fear as the thing stared at her, then took off through a nearby field. The thought of arriving at work again by herself after that was out of the question. Oddly, a dead body was found in this field back in the early 1970s. It was a local man who had apparently died of blunt force trauma to the head. The case remains unsolved.

Astute readers may have noticed that Henderson County, in western Kentucky, is the only county in the commonwealth which appears in every chapter of this book. Henderson is truly a magical and mysterious place. I was born and raised there along the banks of the Ohio and Green rivers and there I've been fortunate enough to witness a variety of astounding sights and experiences relating to the unexplained. This is not, in my opinion, because I am special in some way, or an anomalies magnet, but merely because I've lived nearly my entire life in and around the places in which these enigmas tend to appear, or manifest themselves. Large, hairy wildmen certainly are no strangers to my home county. Indeed, it appears that they have made for themselves a permanent home here.

I've personally spoken to witnesses of Henderson County monster activity from as far back as 1935 but I'm sure they stretch much further back in time, though poorly reported or documented; nor are they strangers to me. Again, this is mainly due to the bottomland locations in which I lived. Watershed areas, I've come to understand, are like Bigfoot roadways which they use mainly under cover of darkness. In 1971, when I was five years old, my family lived in Reed, also in Henderson County, at a place we called the Booth's Farm on Collins Road. One night, as we sat watching TV, my older sister glanced out the kitchen window and saw a "monster" looking back at her. She screamed. Very loudly. My father, shotgun in hand, rushed out with my mother behind him and fired two shots at a tall brown figure as it was running down a dirt road which led to the back fields.

When dad asked my sister what it looked like she said, "Frankenstein," but it was known thereafter as "The Brown Man." This location, as it turns out, is a very active one regarding monster activity with sightings dating back to the 1960s and continuing on to the present.

In 1968 another, or possibly the same, creature was seen there by the previous family by the name of Driskell and giant five-toed footprints were found. We were forced to move after my mother saw a red-colored UFO land out behind one of the barns late one evening.

After a brief stay in the city, we moved to Spottsville in 1975, where my family endured a terrifying 11-month ordeal with a group of large, hairy, bipedal monsters (see The Spottsville Monster section) with a penchant for causing terror and killing livestock. We spent the next 10 years living in the city away from the easy country life but returned to Reed in 1985.

All hell broke loose here as this stately old two-story home on Carlinsburg Road was haunted on the inside as well as out. While UFOs routinely buzzed overhead and black panthers roamed the woods beyond the yard, Bigfoot put in a few appearances as well. My former brother-in-law, while driving down Ohio River Road No. 2 in broad daylight, saw what he at first took to be a deer standing alongside the road. Then it stood up on two legs and ran off into the thick brush. It was six or seven feet tall, he said, covered in brown hair and very fast.

A similarly described beast, this one with glowing green eyes, approached my four-year-old daughter, her mother, and my sister one evening as they were gathering clothes off the line. The two women were so frightened that they ran off and left the child standing at the clothesline. My sister rushed back, grabbed her under one arm, and rushed into the house where they immediately closed and locked all the doors and windows. Unfortunately, I happened to be away that night practicing for an upcoming musical engagement.

On one occasion, around midnight, the entire family was awakened by a thunderous crashing sound that thoroughly shook the entire house. It was so loud that we actually thought that someone had lost control of their vehicle and crashed it into the house. It was strange that the three dogs we had didn't bark a single time. We looked out the windows but saw nothing. Heard nothing. There was no vehicle. My father insisted that no one go outside until morning when we found the garage door ripped off its metal tracks and lying on the garage floor.

While artifact hunting alone in the bottoms one day, I came across a trail of immense footprints crossing a muddy field. The mud was a foot deep so I could make no positive identification of them but the creature that made them walked on two feet and had an extremely lengthy stride which I was completely unable to match.

On another occasion my stepmother was out in the barn checking on one of the dogs that was being kept there when the dog suddenly began howling in misery. Seconds later something "growling and making the weirdest noises" entered the open bottom level of the barn beneath her feet. The sound made by whatever this thing was moving around the barn and coming her way. She was terrified beyond words, which was totally out of character for her. So much so that she actually climbed into the pen with the dog and hid her face as this thing approached. She remained this way until the thing eventually wandered away. Even though she didn't see it, she said, she could tell that whatever it was walked on two legs. In 1989, after repeated sightings of black panthers, she'd had enough and moved out.

In 1999, while driving down Hwy. 60 one afternoon in Baskett, Ky., I happened to look over to a bean field on my left and was surprised to see two large, hairy creatures standing in the beans about 10 feet from the top edge of the field. Both were brownish-gray in color and were positioned with their backs toward me. One was squatting down, apparently doing something to the ground or digging around in the beans - which were tall enough to obscure whatever its hands were doing. Both these creatures were very big, at least six or seven feet tall and, since the highway was full of afternoon traffic coming home from work, I'm sure that other motorists must've seen these things as well. If this is so, however, it seems that none of them felt particularly inclined to come forward.

It is interesting to note that all these locations are within 10 miles of each other and are routinely the locations in which all manner of mysterious Kentucky phenomena are experienced. These places also have a few things in common, chiefly being that they are all within a stone's throw of either the Green or Ohio rivers and they are littered with the burial mounds left centuries ago by the Native Americans. Make of that what you will.

The above entries barely begin to scratch the surface when it comes to the entire body of public knowledge concerning reported Bigfoot activity within Kentucky boundaries. An entire volume is planned by this author to more properly examine the many Bigfoot reports which continue to come in by the handfuls. Until then, we can at least rest assured that these hairy monsters are real.

And, if history is any indication, they are here to stay.

Even the ancient people of Kentucky were aware there were giants among us.
This rock art of giant human-like footprints was found in Powell County

THE HEBBARDSVILLE HILLBILLIES

After nearly a year of gathering information and acquiring contacts I was finally able to investigate rumors that large, hair-covered, bi-pedal monsters were still being seen in

Hebbardsville, Henderson County, just across the mysterious Green River from Reed and Spottsville - about which I have written so much. I learned that, in early winter 2004, two stargazers were parked on Negro Hill, located on Pleasant Hill Road, overlooking the Green River bottomlands, when they spotted two figures in the field below them pulling up old cornstalks and apparently eating the roots.

The creatures were large, apelike and hirsute, one having brown hair and the other white. Returning to the scene the following morning, signs of the beings' presence, in the form of uprooted corn and tracks, were reportedly found. The creatures were dubbed "The Hebbardsville Hillbillies" by the locals and the press. I also learned that there was an old abandoned house in the area where something had reportedly constructed a mighty strange bed out of grass and sticks. Although I was warned by a local journalist that a fugitive from justice had been apprehended in this same house a couple years previously, and it was possible that this man had made the bedding himself, I was determined to see it personally and decide for myself the nature of its construction, if it still existed. However, since the source of the information did not reveal the identities of the alleged witnesses, finding any information at all regarding the incident proved to be a daunting task in itself.

As luck would have it, I ran into an old acquaintance of mine, Greg Tackett, one-time Hebbardsville resident, who claimed to know the story and locations well and agreed to lead me to them at my convenience. I had also recently been in contact with an old Cherokee gentleman, M.F., who wishes to remain anonymous (real name on file), who claimed to have seen these creatures countless times in the Hebbardsville area since the 1960s and could

Negro Hill in Henderson County, a site consider sacred by the Cherokee Indians and a place of recurring Bigfoot activity.

provide much detail about their appearance and behavior. Among other claims. I decided to try and kill two birds with one stone, so to speak, and both explore the 2004 sighting location and interview this fellow in the same weekend.

Saturday, Dec 16, 2006 was mild. I had made an appointment to meet Greg and explore the locations mentioned in the Hillbilly sighting, including the house where the strange bedding was found. I pulled into his drive at mile marker number five just as he was pulling out. He is a plumber by trade and had received an urgent service call. He apologized and asked to postpone the adventure until the following day, which was fine by me. I had scheduled an interview with M.F. for 2 p.m. that Sunday to record his testimony, do a sketch of the creatures he claimed to have witnessed so many times and photograph the tooth and the location on which it was found, if possible.

I told Greg that I would return around 11 a.m. the following day. He promised to be ready. Instead of returning home, I decided to go ahead and drive the 15 or 20 miles to Hebbardsville, and do some reconnoitering of the Pleasant Hill area. Moreover, Greg had informed me that the lady who ran a small country store in Hebbardsville had a copy of the original newspaper article concerning the Hebbardsville Hillbillies in her possession. According to him, she had this article displayed on the front counter for many months for everyone to see and had only fairly recently taken it down. She was a very nice, friendly woman, he informed me, and was sure that she would show it to me if asked. I had never seen or been able to read the original article. Due to work schedules and time constraints I had as yet been unable to conduct a microfiche search at the local library.

Twenty minutes later, I parked my truck beside the store and walked in. Several people, mostly local farmers, were milling about the store or eating lunch at the tables in back. A young mother and her two children were standing at the counter behind which two older ladies were busying themselves frying burgers and ringing up customers. I grabbed a coke and got in line. When I approached the counter I smiled and ordered a cheeseburger with pickle, onions and mustard. "The burger'll be a few minutes," she said.

"That's all right," I replied. "I've got time."

As she took my money I asked if she was the owner. She replied affirmatively with what sounded like a little suspicion in her voice and I got the feeling that this would not go well for me. Nevertheless, I informed her that I was a local writer, come to investigate the Hillbilly sightings.

"Do you know anything about that?" I asked. "Sure don't." she replied. "Don't know nothin' about that."

"Really? A friend of mine told me you had a write-up from the newspaper. Said you had it taped to this very counter for a long time. That true? Do you have the article?"

"Sure don't." she nervously replied and I could tell immediately that this "nice, friendly" woman was lying to me. Usually people love to talk and, more often than not, will if given half a chance, and there's no better place in the world than a small town country store if tales are what you're looking for. Unless you're an outsider. Though I was born and had spent nearly my entire life right there in Henderson County, she had never seen me before and viewed me with obvious distrust. I couldn't really blame her for it either. It was just the way of things here.

"Look, all I know is that happened years and years ago on Pleasant Hill Road. And there ain't been nothin' like that goin' on 'round here lately."

I noticed a couple of "good ole' boys" eyeing me from the back of the store. The next couple of minutes passed uncomfortably and quietly. Then I took my lunch, thanked her and walked out.

I found Pleasant Hill Road to be hilly and heavily wooded, especially as I drove closer to the river. Bisecting the area was a large swath of land that a local logging/mining company had reduced to pasture by removing the trees and mining for coal, turning great tracts of this virgin wilderness into bleak, treeless meadowland. Despite this, there was still hill after rolling hill of densely forested woodland to be seen with small, gently running creaks which snaked their way through every few yards it seemed. Even the tracts of second growth timber were fairly dense.

I drove to the end of the road and pulled into the lot of the old African American church that stood on the ridge overlooking the Green River. Gazing out the windshield at the lowlands of Ash Flats I ate my lunch. I was disappointed at my inability at getting the

The Hebbardsville Hillbilly, illustrated by the author and drawn from witness accounts

store owner to speak with me regarding the Hillbilly sightings, or even to let me see the newspaper article, but I still had high hopes that my luck would improve by the following day. The sun was high and bright and I was loath to go home but I knew that there was little I could do without my guide, other than wander around aimlessly in the woods, so I started the truck and headed out.

Sunday the 17th was slightly overcast as I got into my 4 wheel drive and headed east again. It was already unseasonably warm, with forecasted temps reaching into the 70s. True to his word, Greg was ready and eager for the undertaking and I owe him a huge debt of gratitude for agreeing to help on this venture.

Shortly afterward we headed out, pointing the truck toward the steadily climbing sun and the Hebbardsville river bottoms. We would have to take the long way around, Greg said, and come up to the hill from below, through the field where the initial sightings had occurred. The location of the old house site, said to be situated back in the woods at the end of Book Lane, was owned by the logging/mining company and allowed no trespassers. If we were caught on this land, chances were good that it would not end well for us. However, we both felt that some things were worth risking in the quest for answers to mysteries of this nature.

We found the lane and drove on but the dirt road soon turned into a muddy ruin two feet

The location at Hebbardsville where witnesses have routinely spotted a creature eating routes and grass. According to witnesses, this creek is a primary route of travel for the monsters.

deep, and we realized that the only way to continue was on foot. I stopped the vehicle in the middle of the road. It was a very isolated location and there was no chance of passers by spotting the truck from the main road. We were both confidant that we could get in and out without being noticed. A short while later I was standing in the field where the two creatures were seen feeding on the corn stalk roots. I looked up at the old church, situated high on the wooded ridge above me and took a few pictures.

We walked for another hour through the mud but, when we approached the intended spot, there was nothing to see but level ground, the old house which contained the nest had fallen victim to the area's logging activities. I had arrived months too late to see and photograph the alleged Bigfoot nesting site. Though I was disappointed it was just as well. My camera had inexplicably malfunctioned as we approached an outlying shed and I was unable to take pictures for a time, although nothing unusual was noted by either of us. We made the return trip as rapidly as possible. The day was wearing on and I had other business to attend to in in the tiny town of Hebbardsville.

BIGFOOT AND THE CHEROKEE HILL

(Note: The names of the locations in this report have been intentionally altered)

After learning from a local paranormal investigator friend of mine about an old Cherokee fellow who also claimed to be a Hebbardsville, Bigfoot witness, a phone interview was arranged and conducted in November 2006. The information proved correct. Not only did the witness describe repeated, often at will, sightings of groups of these hairy creatures since his childhood, he also claimed to be in possession of what he was convinced was an actual tooth from one of these creatures. Moreover, he could describe, in great detail, the physiological features, general attitudes and predictable behavior of these mysterious "Hillbillies" known to the rest of the world as Bigfoot.

After several more phone interviews a meeting was arranged and, under the promise of strict anonymity, M.F. agreed to allow me to photograph the alleged Bigfoot tooth for possible identification. M. F. Lived only a short drive from the Hebbardsville area, only a twenty minute drive from my own doorstep. And so it was that, after my initial investigation of the Pleasant Hill site, I drove Greg back home, turned around and continued on to M.F.'s home.

My heart sank at the sight of the closed and locked gate in front of the house. No one was home. He had warned me that he and his wife were taking a trip out of town that particular weekend, but

Bigfoot witness holds what he believes is an actual tooth from one of the Bigfoot creatures. Witness found the tooth at the foot of an ancient Cherokee burial site in Hebbardsville.

expected to be back home the previous night. Evidently they had not made it. I had tried phoning him that morning and his answering machine had picked up. I had hoped, in vain as it turned out, that he would be back before our 2 p.m. appointment. I waited for a few moments, then turned around and drove away, feeling somewhat defeated and tired from the morning's excursion.

I arrived back home around 3 p.m. and kicked off my shoes, wincing at the dime-sized blister the rubber boot had left on my right heel. I was sore and nearly exhausted from all the walking I'd done After reviewing the digital photos of the Pleasant Hill sighting area, I decided a short nap would be in order, so I turned on the rotating fan and lay down on the sofa. No sooner had I closed my eyes when the phone rang. It was M.F. He explained that his wife had took ill on their trip, forcing them to stay away an extra night. They had only just arrived back home. He was still willing to meet with me, he said, if I didn't mind driving back out to Hebbardsville. I looked at the clock. It was well after 3 already with less than two hours of daylight left. I told him I was on my way.

I found the gentleman to be pleasant, friendly, down-to-earth and obviously intelligent. He immediately pulled the tooth out of his pocket. It did resemble a human canine, or eyetooth, only about three times as large. I examined it and noted the obvious authenticity and great antiquity of the object, taking several photographs. It was complete with most of the root system still intact. The outer edges were very slightly serrated, almost imperceptibly, which I found most unusual. M.F. viewed the tooth as a scared object, he had told me during one of our previous phone conversations, and he would not consent to DNA testing because to do this would mean that at least a partial destruction of the tooth would occur. Nor would he allow the tooth to depart from his possession for any length of time. As a matter of fact, he had informed me, he didn't really care at all to try and prove the existence of these creatures to anyone. They had always been a fact of life to his people.

Evidence of his Cherokee heritage was displayed about his yard, flower beds and doorsteps, and worn proudly around his neck. The creatures we call Bigfoot were the "Old People of the Forest," he told me, and their reality caused no controversy except to the whites. It would be amusing if not for the fact that, in their ignorance, the logging and mining of the white man was causing the rapid desecration and destruction of the Bigfoot's habitat, land considered sacred by the Indians since the beginning of history.

"Can you show me where they lived?" I asked. There was daylight left. He asked me if I cared to take a ride.

M. F.'s story was an interesting one. He had first been exposed to the creatures while growing up in the Spottsville-Reed areas, although at least two earlier generations of his family had their own tales of sightings and strange happenings. He remembered his great-grandfather recounting how he had run outside one night after he'd heard some kind of commotion to see one of the "Old People" carrying off two of his full-grown sows, one under each arm, like they were piglets. It swiftly made its escape even though the pigs weighed about 200 pounds each!

Around the time of the "Spottsville Monster" events of 1975, his brother was finding strangely mutilated dead cattle. He had lost six head that year. Literally. All six carcasses were found with their heads torn off and missing. They only found one head, he claimed, and it was stripped to the bone and missing the lower mandible. None of the other meat on the carcasses was consumed or even disturbed. When the family moved across the Green River to Hebbardsville the sightings continued. In fact, he claimed that from the late 1960s until the early to mid-'70s hardly, any weekend went by when he and a car load of friends didn't park near the intersection of Ash Flats and Old Bell roads and observe groups of these creatures, ranging in number from four individuals up to as many as 15 or better, engaged in the act of eating bitter roots and grass

He said there were countless sightings by dozens of different individuals. "Were they hairy Indians?" I asked. No, he said. They were not Indians of any type. They had black skin and an average height of eight to ten feet tall, although he had seen one awhile back that was at least a twelve-footer. Their eyes were dark brown with no visible whites or irises. They were bearded, had thin lips, a weak chin and a flat, wide nose like individuals of African descent. They had normal-looking hands of a large size with pale-colored palms, but their feet had an opposing toe sticking out at an angle away from the other four toes, like an ape's or chimp's.

They had extremely long arms, which hung down past their knees, and could run on all fours 35 to 40 mph. The females also possessed beards, though shorter ones than the males. They were of more stocky build, had furry breasts and carried their young beneath them clinging to their bellies. He described the males as being covered with short, straight, usually dark hair, with longer areas of about six inches at the beard, backs of the head and genital areas.

"Pull over here," he said as we approached a medium-sized muddy creek at the Old Bell/Ash Flats location. This was the place, he told me, that he and scores of friends had watched the creatures feeding countless times. According to him, they didn't seem to mind being watched unless someone got out of the car. Then they would all rush into the creek and be gone in an instant. They traveled the creeks, he claimed. The water would wash away the tracks and they were excellent swimmers.

After photographing the location, I asked him if he could take me to the place where he found the tooth. He said nothing for several seconds as he carefully considered the request. I was beginning to think that I had overstepped my bounds, as it were, when he looked up. He would take me there, he answered, if I promised never to disclose the location. It was a sacred place, he explained. A burial place of the Cherokee people and home to other powerful legendary beings as well as the "Old People." I agreed and we got back into the truck.

We traveled a short distance from the Ash Flats area and stopped. "Follow me," he said, and started up a thickly forested ridge. Although he was nearly 60 years old, he ascended the steep terrain as nimbly as a jack rabbit and, after a short but vigorous trek, we crested another large hill and stopped.

"Look freely," he said. "Take pictures, but nothing else".

I looked around. We stood at the rim of a forested ridge which wound around the area like a dark circle, forming an impressive natural amphitheater. The bottom of the "bowl" formation was mostly clear and somehow comfortable-looking. All around me were graves, stacked in layers. Some ancient beyond reckoning. Many were marked with stones onto which Cherokee petroglyphs and letters were carved. I had hunted Indian artifacts nearly all my life but had never seen a single stone in Henderson county bearing intact Native American images or writing. Now I was surrounded by them.

"This place is called "The Great Hill" by my people," M.F. said.

The Great Hill. Here were buried the bodies of the famous Cherokee chieftain, Double Head, his daughter, Corn Blossom and countless others. I snapped pictures, one after another, while the sunlight faded much too swiftly. Daniel Boone, pioneer hero of old, had written of this place. Twice he was taken prisoner by the Shawnee just across the Green River. Twice his freedom was bartered for and obtained by the friendly Cherokee. Two heavily weathered stones still bore his name and short messages, carved by Boone's own hand during his stay there over 200 years ago. Still other stones were carven with images of corn stalks, deer and sun. Three stones displayed the likenesses of strange faces. No one knew who most of the graves belonged to. This was the final resting place of the Great Chiefs of antiquity whose names were lost forever. Stone circles were present.

Raking back the dead leaves revealed a wealth of stone artifacts still lying where their makers had placed them many

Daniel Boone Rock -- one of two stones bearing inscriptions by Daniel Boone. This one was found on the "Great Hill" Cherokee burial site

(Above) The gravestone of Cherokee chief Double Head and (Below) the burial place of his daughter, Corn Blossom.

generations ago. This was also the sacred home of other mythical beings from tribal lore, he told me. They were called 'The Little People,' tiny humanoids standing only two feet tall who could be either friendly or malignant, depending on the contents of one's heart.

During heavy rains some of the graves would wash out, I was informed, and he had needed to re-inter some of the bones on occasion. He had found the tooth several years ago here, in 2004, at the foot of the hill, washed up by the rushing water. No other creature native to this area had teeth like it, he felt sure. The claim was intriguing but not unprecedented. There are many 19th and early 20th century reports of the unearthing of giant human, or humanlike, skeletal remains in the Bluegrass State. Most were said to have been taken from Indian burial grounds but not all. M. F.'s own mother had told him how she had witnessed the excavation of one such skeleton in Beals back in the 1920s. Workmen had unearthed the skeleton while trying to bridge a creek. She said it was measured and found to be 12 feet tall!

As with all the old reports, the remains fell into the hands of private collectors and out of common knowledge. Admittedly, this was the first time that I had been able to personally view an alleged tooth from one of these giants.

"The whites don't know about this place," he said. "If they were to find out..."

He didn't need to finish the statement. I knew exactly what would happen if the location was ever made public. Hordes of relict hunters would descend upon the location and have it stripped clean, all 15 acres of it, within a week.

"Can you keep this secret, Bart?" he asked.

I looked squarely into his old, intelligent eyes. "You can trust me," I said.

Smiling good-naturedly, he replied, "I know."

As the last feeble rays of the sun disappeared and we were left standing in the darkness surrounded by trees and ancient graves, I knew it was time to take my leave. I vowed to return again soon, however, for better pictures and more conversation if he'd have me. "Any time," was his reply. I had made a new friend, it seemed, one who struck me as being perhaps the most knowledgeable person regarding Bigfoot that I had ever met. I had obtained both the story and the pictures that I sought. And much more.

I took many photographs of this extraordinary location, both out of my own fascination regarding the history of the site and the significance of the fact that the giant tooth had been found there, and I am indebted to M.F. for the opportunity to do so. With his help I was also able to sketch a facial study of these particular humanoid's features for all to view. I would like to express my sincere gratitude to this man for agreeing to speak with me, sharing some secrets and showing me such an interesting and historically significant location, one unlike any other that I have ever seen.

ATYPICAL KENTUCKY BIGFOOT REPORTS

An ever-growing number of incidents involving human interaction with Bigfoot, or Bigfoot-like creatures, contain atypical elements which cannot be pigeon-holed into the flesh and blood, unknown primate' paradigm. Some of these atypical Beastmen have been seen performing amazing physical feats which no natural animal of any species could hope to duplicate. Many researchers, investigators and writers choose to dismiss or ignore reports of this nature but, since I have experienced some of these atypical Bigfoot traits personally, I am not one of them. In some cases, these atypical types have been known to walk without leaving prints - even in mud or snow - leap incredible distances and even seem totally impervious to high caliber bullets. Time and again, the witness reportedly fires on these things at close range with no visible effects.

They have been reported to exhibit powers of mental telepathy, even mind control, and, much like UFOs and even ghosts, they have been known to vanish right before a startled witness' eyes. These types of monsters often appear before, during or after extended periods of elevated paranormal activities, or "flaps." Although uncommon it is not unheard of for multiple phenomena to manifest in the same general area, much to the chagrin of the locals. Coincidence? What are the odds of two different unexplained phenomena, if unrelated, showing up in the same general area at the same general time? Pretty remote, I'd guess. And, even the most biased researcher must admit, it is damned peculiar when Bigfoot is noted in the same location in which UFOs and ghosts have also made recent appearances.

From a 1997 witness interview:

1. Subject of sighting: Possible Bigfoot
2. Date, time and location of sighting: Summer of 1975. Afternoon. Pritchett Farm, just off Old Henderson Road, Henderson County
3. Approximate distance between witness and subject: 100 to 150 yards
4. Describe in detail animal witnessed: Light brown, hairy being. Large ?body and shoulders. Thick neck and big head

5. Did the animal walk or run on two legs four, or both? Stood on two legs. Seemed to wobble as it stood

6. Approximate height of animal?: Seven to eight feet tall

7. Approximate weight of animal: 350 pounds

8. Did you notice any strange smells during the sighting? If yes, describe: No. Not at this sighting

9. Did the animal seem threatening at any time? No

10. Were you frightened by the encounter? Yes. Very.

11. Did you try to communicate with the animal? No

12. Did the animal try to communicate with you in any way? Yes

13. Describe the animal's skin, or hair, color and texture: Light tan hair. Thinner hair on face

14. Did the animal act aggressively at any time? No

15. Was the animal frightened of you? No

16. Did the animal leave any physical evidence at the scene such as footprints, hair, etc.? No

17. Do you, or anyone you know, possess any evidence, photographic or otherwise, to support your sighting? No

18. Describe in detail what happened during the sighting and how it ended: 'A friend and I were riding my motorcycle. We stopped under a tree and my friend started going, "look!" I didn't see anything so I told him to point. I looked where he was pointing and there it stood looking right at us. It made some movement like wobbling. We were both scared so we got back on the bike and left as fast as possible.'

19. Has this animal, or others like it, been seen in the area before or since? Yes

20. Do you feel that the animal could be encountered again in the area? Yes

21. Describe, as best you can, the animals head and face: Seemed to have a human-type face. Large head.

22. Describe the anima's limbs, hands and feet: Did not see. Only saw from chest up.

23. Did the sighting take place during the day or night? Day

24. Describe the weather and/or visibility conditions at time of sighting: Excellent

25. Do you feel that the animal you saw was a natural, though unknown, animal, or a supernatural entity? Explain reasons for this belief: Supernatural powers. I had a feeling that it was trying to communicate (telepathically) at that time. A very bad feeling. Very frightening.

Witness Information:
Full name of witness: John C. D. (full name on file)
Age: 37
Birth date: Dec. 23, 1961
Sex: Male.
Occupation: Construction

1. Were you suffering from any form of mental illness at time of sighting? No

2. Were you under the influence of any hallucinatory drugs or alcohol at time of sighting? No

3. Have you ever witnessed any unusual animal sightings before or since? If yes explain: 'Yes. I think I saw this thing in and around my house. I have witnessed a black panther, or very large cat, in the area. Also, Just before the sighting, me and my entire family saw a large, flying

orange ball of light in the sky.'

4. Have you or any member of your family experienced any type of unexplained phenomena in the past? If yes explain: "Yes. My whole family has experiences thought to be caused by this creature such as being watched and some of them think that it doesn't have to be in a visible form to be there.'

5. Does the area in which the incident took place, to your knowledge, have a history of unexplained phenomena? Yes

6. What is your religious preference? (optional) Raised Christian

7. Do you have any personal theories about a possible explanation for the phenomena that you observed? If yes, explain: No

AFFIDAVIT: I, John C. D. do hereby attest soberly and sincerely that the above document is an honest and truthful account of a strange event to which I have been a witness. All of the descriptions contained therein are accurate and without deception of any type, accidental or deliberate. I give this information freely and without clause, waiving all rights and without regard concerning monetary gains or any other benefits, for the sole reason of sharing this truthful event with others. The aforementioned event did, in actuality, take place and was not the result of any psychopathological delusion or hallucination of any order. I stand by and bear witness to the integrity of the report and the descriptions I have set down in writing therein. I release this information to the author/investigator to use in any way he deems worthy, and to the public in hopes that it will contribute to a greater understanding concerning phenomena of this nature.

Signed: John C. D.

Date: June 10, 1997

When I interviewed John about his sightings, I was immediately put at ease by his casual, down-to-earth demeanor. We talked for awhile then other members of his family began to arrive and join in the conversation. They all had their own stories to tell about creatures that were obviously not of the physical world, but somewhere else entirely. The whole affair had begun after the entire family observed a small orange sphere as it cavorted in the skies over the family farm. Of the lot, the sister's experiences were the most unusual. She claimed that there were two creatures which frequented the property. One of them "good," and one of them "bad."

The good one was covered in white hair. The evil one had dark brown hair. On one evening, she claimed, the good had actually saved her life after the bad one "walked right through the wall like a ghost" and into her bedroom, intent on doing her harm. The white creature had shielded her body with its own while the evil beast fumed and tried to get at her. Eventually it left.

The mother had a frightening look at one of the things as it walked up the driveway towards the house late one evening. She thought it was her husband walking up the drive at first, she told me. It was dark and all she could see was a silhouette. As it got closer, she knew it wasn't him.

It was a tall, hairy monster wearing an old, beat-up hat and a tattered shirt. As it stood at the door, she grabbed the kids and shoved them under the bed. It soon walked off into the night, but the incident frightened them all very badly.

I could see the fear on her face when she recounted the tale. The entire family felt that these things were supernatural in nature. Possibly even demonic. They were convinced that the beasts had the ability to become invisible to the human eye. Ridiculous?

A STRANGE KENTUCKY ENCOUNTER

There is a place in Smith Mills, Henderson County, called Burbank's Lake. It is also known locally as Spook Hill. As you might guess by the name, down through the years this particular spot has garnered a reputation for being haunted. I believe it to be a "window" location, as many inexplicable experiences have taken place in this area, including various cryptid sightings such as Bigfoot, water monsters, giant birds and black panthers. UFO activity is not uncommon in this area, and there are many ghost stories associated with Spook Hill as well. Lending to this aura of mystery, no doubt, is the fact that there are two very old cemeteries, long since reclaimed by the forest, to be found at the hilltop.

Also situated there, between the main cemetery and the slave cemetery, are three ancient lakes. One is fairly big and deep and all were rumored for as long as I could remember to contain monster bass. The male members of my family have always been avid fishermen so, one day in the summer of 1987, we decided to go and fish there. This was totally against our dad's better judgment. He had lived near the area when he was younger and had been personally warned by Mr. Burbank never to let dark catch him on the property. He never said why. Also, my older half brother, Harold, had told us a scary story about a time when he and a brother-in-law had gone night fishing there in a boat a few years before. He claimed that every time the two tried to land the boat and come ashore to leave, the woods would erupt with the sound of breaking branches and heavy footsteps, forcing them to shove back out into the lake.

"It sounded like a herd of elephants was trompin' around in there," he said. Every attempt to leave the lake was met by this resistance, which frightened them both, and they were forced to spend the entire night in the boat out in the middle of the lake. Only when dawn broke were the two allowed to leave, which they did in all haste, never to return. This intrigued me to no end, green as I was back then, but the lure of trophy bass enticed us all.

We arrived at the lake in the early afternoon and headed through the trees down to the water. We had been able to procure a one-man bass boat with a small trolling motor from a friend. It could hold two people but just barely. As there were six of us, four brothers and two friends, this meant that four would be confined to fishing from the banks.

We found the place to be absolutely teeming with water moccasins and not one of us had brought a weapon of any type, only fishing poles. Since everyone wanted to fish the other side of the lake, we opted to be ferried across one by one rather than walk through the tall grass, trying to avoid a possible snake bite. It took forever for the little motor to chug everyone across the lake. By the time we made it to the other side it was already late afternoon. The sun was making a rapid disappearance behind the trees. We fished awhile without much luck. I remember catching one largemouth that weighed a couple of pounds and, before we knew it, darkness was fast approaching.

My older brother, who had been hogging the bass boat with a family friend, finally sputtered in to shore and began taking everyone back across, one at a time. This took around 30 to 40 minutes round trip, with five trips to be made.

Complete darkness fell with just myself and one of my younger brothers remaining on the far side of the lake. We had half a gallon of kerosene and had earlier gathered what wood we could find, which was mostly wet, since it had rained a couple of days previously, and used it to build a small fire. We were sitting there bemoaning so much trouble for nothing when the sound of breaking branches and heavy footsteps erupted from the woods in front of us. It was a terrifyingly loud commotion and we jumped up in fright. I have never before or since, been so terrified by any type of sound. It was, looking back, totally unlike me to react in such a manner. Perhaps it was because, at the first limb fractured, we both knew immediately what was out there in the darkness of those haunted woods. Worse, the sounds soon began to come from behind us and to our right as well, and they were getting closer.

We heard no grunts. No growls. No breathing. Just the heavy footfalls and the terrific explosions of cracking tree limbs all around us. We thought we were both going to die that night, without a doubt, and I still count myself lucky to have made it out of there alive.

We could see nothing as it was quite dark. There was no moon and heavy cloud cover. When the sounds got quite close, I threw some kerosene into the fire, determined to at least see what was about to eat us. The fuel ignited and the fire flared up, illuminating an area of about 25 feet in all directions. We saw nothing. The light would only last for a few seconds then it would subside and plunge our surroundings back into utter darkness. When this happened, the sounds would start up and approach us again. Over and over I threw the fuel into the shrinking fire, washing the woods in sudden firelight. When I did this all the sounds immediately stopped. We never did see a thing. Not even a single eye-shine. The kerosene didn't last too long.

We had been yelling and making a good-sized noise of our own, to no avail. It seemed that only the light was holding our would-be attackers at bay. But the fire was fading fast. Soon it was reduced to a tiny flame at one end of a small, wet branch and the noises were closing in once again. The smaller the light became the closer the ungodly racket approached. I grabbed the burning twig and held it up in front of me as we walked backwards down toward the water's edge. I told my brother to get ready to swim for his life. The noises followed us down to the lake, amazingly, even though this area had very few trees! It sounded like invisible branches were being broken by invisible beings. Lucky for us, just as we were about to get wet, we heard the sound of our brother on the boat shouting his approach. We yelled for him to hurry. When he reached us we were in a state of agitation, to say the least. He wanted to know who was next. Well, to put it simply, we found out a one-man boat can actually carry three people in an emergency.

ROADKILL

Bell County, Kentucky
Date: First week of December, 2004
Time: Shortly after 9 p.m.
Location: US 461, between Somerset and Mount Vernon

'My friend and I left Somerset and were looking for US 461. I missed the turn as the road was pitch black. - no street lights and hardly any houses for light. I decided to do a U-turn since there was no one around, to go back to the road. I started pulling over to the shoulder and saw a dead cat. The very next instant I saw what I can only describe as a huge boulder with hair! There was no way to avoid impact but impact did not happen. Instead, my car went up and over. Instantly after my car came to a stop, a gagging smell filled the car. It was not the smell of hitting a rotten animal. It was a combination of smells but very nauseating.

My friend and I became very ill in the days afterward. She was a month in recovering from the cough and lung congestion. We did not stay to inspect anything because of the smell. It was absolutely horrific.

What I saw was whiteish, all one color. There were no visible legs, arms, head, feet or anything. There was only a very large ball of fur.

I pulled over at the first gas station and there was hair hanging off my tailpipe. The smell of the car filled up the parking lot and was very embarrassing. My car sustained seven hundred dollars worth of damage to the underneath and my husband fixed everything. I believe I hit a Bigfoot. No doubt in my mind. I know two people that have witnessed, on two separate occasions, a Bigfoot balled up by the side of the road and a bike trail, respectively.'

I have spoken to this witness, Mrs. Angela Barth, many times via email and always found her to be very pleasant and honest and a delight to talk to. I was shocked to learn that the most bizarre aspect of this experience was not running over a possible Bigfoot, but something else entirely. She was, in fact, keeping something about the encounter to herself. Withholding something which she thought was too unbelievable to tell anyone. Luckily, my unequaled southern charm and rugged good looks soon won her over. She wrote:

'Only a very few people know about this. Having read what you and your family endured I know you will be interested.

Two years ago in December, I was coming back from the hospital in Somerset,. My daughter had back surgery and we was leaving about 9 p.m. I was driving this pitch black road to get to I-75. I missed my turn and thus had to turn around. I was going to make a U-turn and started to leave the road onto the shoulder to negotiate the turn. I saw a dead cat and then a HUGE furry ball. I mean it was huge. It was too late. I hit it. If you have ever had an accident you know the absolutely helpless feeling of being unable to prevent it and then just go with it.

After I came to a stop the stench filled my car. It was nauseating beyond belief. Not rotten, just NASTY. My friend started gagging and begged me to hurry up and leave. I didn't even know if the car would start! It did and I made the turn. I cannot tell you how bad the car smelled and continued to smell.

We went to the nearest gas station to check the damage. I was so embarrassed because my car was stinking so badly you could smell it all over the parking lot. I looked under the car and there was hair hanging off my tail pipe. Gads, it all stunk so bad.

Nothing remarkable so far? I looked at the clock and we had left the hospital an hour and a half before. It was ten thirty and we had only gone about thirteen miles since leaving that hospital! We didn't do one thing but leave the hospital, miss the road we needed by a few hundred feet, hit something, and then turn around!

Now, not being able to account for that much time is unnerving. We tried every way to figure it out. We both got serious lung congestion after this and I was sick for a week or more. My friend was sick for a month or longer until someone contacted a person I will call "K." and he told her some herbs to take to detoxify her body.

My car had seven hundred dollars worth of damage to the exhaust system and whatever that is that holds the wheels on underneath. My husband could not understand how I could not see something so big before I hit it! I saw the cat, but not the big, furry, ball.

This was hands-down my strangest experience.'

Barth was responsive to further questioning and even added some new insight.

'In the seconds before impact I saw the dead kitty and then the big furry ball. It was whitish, rather like a polar bear. All one color. I saw absolutely nothing but the ball. No legs, arms, head,. It looked like a huge ball of hair. It was as high as the hood, ball-shaped. I had no idea at the time what it was, none. I didn't even think about it, which I now find very unusual.

I didn't actually turn around to see anything. I was in the process of leaving the road to make a U-turn when I hit it. I merely finished the U-turn after the smell started and found the car actually would start! I do recall wondering if the car was too messed to even run but I didn't care. I .just wanted to get away from the smell. I wasn't concerned one iota what was out there! We weren't scared. Actually, we were laughing hysterically. It was just weird. Neither of us looked to see what I hit or even thought about it!

We didn't suspect anything was strange at all until we noticed all the time was missing. We thought the smell was a bit excessive, but that was all. It was a calm kind of. thing. I cannot describe it. Ninety unaccounted for minutes and we were both calm upon discovering it.

I have no idea when we realized it was most probably a Sasquatch we hit. We certainly didn't even entertain the thought at first. It was on the way home. I clearly recall we were near Lexington when it suddenly hit us both what had happened. I can't explain most of it, but I mean it to be matter of fact. What happened, happened.

The hair was there. I didn't care at the time. It did not occur to me about what it could have been and I didn't know about the missing time at the time I looked under the car. I pulled over at the very first gas station to see if major stuff was leaking out. I was gagging just to be near my car! I looked at the clock after I got back in the car and made the discovery. You see, it took awhile for the whole thing to sink in. I cannot explain it at all. Of course hair was hanging off my tailpipe wasn't unexpected because I had just hit something big and hairy! Maybe that is woman's logic. I don't know. I just know it didn't matter to me at all. I was three hundred miles from home with the real possibility my car was all jacked up!

Actually, my car WAS all jacked up. I forgot to mention the oil leak it got in the first letter. I couldn't drive it after that until my husband fixed it! Geez, he was so aggravated with me. I was so thankful to have made it home.

Blood? I don't recall any. I don't recall if the hair was still there either. I finally told him what had happened. I waited a few days because I just did not know how to tell him what happened and it didn't go over very well! I saw the little cat but not something as big as the front end of the car! That is precisely right. He or anyone else would have done the same in the exact same scenario. It was how it was, not just something special for me.

No, I don't think I killed it. I hit it is all. I think it got really furious and skunked us! Probably cussed us good for ninety minutes! I'd say it is more like it needed help and time to get it! I think the cat was a snack it had just caught and maybe put down when my car was coming. My daughter saw one in a ball on the side of the road several years ago. My daughter-in-law saw one in a ball when she was a kid. It was hiding on the side of a bicycle trail all balled up! I think they ball up when they want to get on the down low! If you crouched down, tucked your head down and got into the best ball you can with your body? That is precisely what we saw.

I have no explanation for the time loss. Guess that is the purpose for it! I cannot explain seeing that cat and not seeing the big fur ball. Here is another description. A huge snowball all rolled up - with hair! No limbs at all, none like a deer or cow would be all askew in death on the highway. It was around sixty that December day and there was not one lick of snow and had been none. I wish it had been a snowball I hit!'

Many things can be learned about phenomena such as these when one learns to ask the right questions. It turns out Barth and her entire family has a long history of brushes with the unexplained, from Bigfoot to UFOs and even spectral, or ghostly, encounters which spans two different states and several decades. I assured her that I had spoken to many people such as herself, people who seem to have multiple experiences with unknown phenomena. And that I was one of them myself. As such, I could not so readily disregard statements about these atypical creatures which depicted them as being even further out of the ordinary than they would seem at first glance.

Barth claims that, although it does bother her sometimes, she has learned to live with the knowledge that there are 90 unaccounted for minutes gone from her life.

She feels that, whatever happened during those lost moments, she wasn't harmed in any way so "no harm, no foul." Neither she nor her friend has any plans at the moment to try and find out what happened that night via hypnotic regression. In any event, I'm very grateful to this witness for her willingness to speak candidly with me about her experiences.

Incredibly, Barth isn't the only citizen of the Bluegrass State who claims to have had a close encounter with one of these creatures while driving a vehicle. In his book "The Locals" (Hancock House, 2003), my friend Thom Powell writes:

"I was contacted by a rural family from Horse Cave in Hart County who described to me a curious one-car accident in 2001 which resulted in one fatality. The residents felt that the fatality resulted from a collision with Bigfoot. The entire family maintained that the public was kept away from the scene of the nighttime collision, but these particular residents lived nearby and were able to approach the scene of the wreck by walking through the woods. From the woods, they observed the authorities burying something beside the road, scrubbing the pavement to remove copious amounts of blood and taking extraordinary measures to keep the public away from the scene.

The family had several sightings to relate to me on and around their isolated rural homestead. The wreck that they described was in an area of much prior Bigfoot activity. They called the area of the wreck, just off Highway 218, "Bigfoot Hill." It was easy walking distance from their house.

After the wreck and the mysterious burial they heard loud, mournful wails coming from the area for many nights. The residents were therefore very leery of visiting the location, not only out of concern for the fact that the creatures were still around, but for fear of being observed by locals who would wonder what they were after. As I recall, the mayor, who was also the undertaker, lived within sight of the location of the wreck. They sent me a detailed map to the location and I considered relaying it to a local investigator. Instead, I convinced the residents to try to investigate the matter more completely by themselves. Perhaps under cover of darkness they could probe the ground for an indication of what type of remains, if any, lay beneath the disturbed earth beside the road at the scene of the wreck

Eventually they were able to do just that, and they phoned me later with the news that the earth appeared to have been once again disturbed, the soil had an intensely putrid smell, but no identifiable remains could be found.'

I must say that after following up on plenty such reports in the past, I was not at all surprised by this news. Par for the course, really. While it was regrettable that the residents didn't get around to probing the ground sooner, such is generally the case. By the time such tantalizing reports reach us, it is generally too late to utilize the information even if it was accurate in the first place. But the credibility of the family was better than most situations: they lived near Mammoth Caves where many unmapped caves provide potential safe haven for any manner of reclusive creature, they were in regular telephone, U.S. mail, and e-mail contact with me, the woman was a reverend, and the different members of the family were in complete agreement about the details of the various events that they witnessed.

The family reported to me that they began to experience substantial hostility directed at them from unknown sources. Their property was vandalized. Someone tried to run them off the road. Someone tried to run over their son. The landlord wanted to evict them. Finally, they decided to move to another state.

Threats, persecution and even attempted murder by government officials? For accidentally running over a Bigfoot? Why? And what of. Barth's missing time? Truly the atypical reports seem a mystery clearly more science fiction than zoological. Barth says she hit it but felt no impact. Instead the car rose "up and over." This would seem, to even the most casual reader, an obviously implanted memory, as the creature's hair was sticking to the undercarriage of the vehicle, which sustained $700 worth of damage. Barth could not recall the exact point at which the engine had stalled, only trying to start it up again. Obviously, it took an hour and a half for the car to travel up and over the creature and come to a stop.

THE SPOTTSVILLE MONSTER
Spottsville, Kentucky, Henderson County, 1975

When I was nine years old my family moved into a small, isolated farmhouse very close to the banks of the Green River. My parents didn't realize that for the next 11 months we would be terrorized by a giant, hairy, red-eyed creature that would later come to be known as The Spottsville Monster. They were warned by the previous occupants, who reluctantly told my parents that one day the previous summer the man of the house had fired several shots through the back screen door at a large "hairy feller'" who was standing just outside looking in at him.

Red, my father, was a tough, intelligent, no-nonsense type fellow who was not easily scared by anything. He thought at the time that a .12 gauge shotgun could take care of pretty much any problem that might arise. Besides, the family had already had a run-in or two with what the kids called the Brown Man a few years previously, just across the river in Reed. It had ran away when fired at and eventually left us alone.

The new house on Mound Ridge Road seemed perfect at first. The property contained many types of fruit and berry trees and Dad planned on raising several acres of tobacco come spring. Rose, my mother, looked forward to raising a big vegetable garden. Us six kids could play in the big yard or artifact hunt in the many fields along the front and sides of the house.

That spring started out well despite the steady disappearance of dad's chickens, attributed to weasels

The Nunnelly farm on Mound Ridge Road, where the author's family endured a terrifying 11-month ordeal in 1975

and such at first. Then my older brother Dean and I, ages 10 and nine, began to find the carcasses of dead dogs in the fields when we were out looking for arrowheads. The bodies were strangely mutilated, being sliced from groin to gullet with all the internal organs removed as well as the eyes and tongues. No blood or footprints could be seen around these grisly discoveries, even though most were found in open, well cultivated fields. Also strange was the fact that no scavenger would eat the remains. Not even a fly would land on them to lay its eggs.

Before the episode was finally over in January 1976, my family would lose over 200 chickens, a goat, a horse and we would find the remains of eight dogs, a pig, and a goat - all mutilated. One day, my parents heard what sounded like something big drinking water from the small creek just inside the woods out behind the house. By the sound of the loud gulping noises it was making, dad judged whatever it was to be at least as big as a horse or cow.

Soon afterwards we began to hear strange noises coming from the fields and woods outside. Sometimes they would come from close by, sometimes far away. The two vicious and highly treasured guard dogs we owned could be heard bumping their heads on the floorboards as they scurried beneath the house in fear of whatever was making the sounds. This caused dad much concern. As a precaution, when my older brother Harold arrived that spring to add on a bedroom and an indoor bathroom to the house, dad invited him and his family to move their trailer and set it beside the house.

As dad was suffering from glaucoma and steadily losing his eyesight, he felt that we would be safer with another grown man there who could shoot a gun if the need arose. Harold could also help with raising the tobacco. They moved the trailer in soon after and placed it very close to the house under dad's direction.

One day a stranger came walking from the far tree line across one of the fields. He was holding a shotgun, broken down, and walking towards the house, his other hand up in the air in a friendly gesture. It took both the adults to finally calm down the dogs when the stranger approached and introduced himself as Roy C., a neighbor who lived less than a half mile up the road. He told my father that he had just been squirrel hunting in some nearby woods and had scared up something big and hairy that ran away on its hind legs. As it was heading in this direction and he hadn't the slightest idea what the animal could be or how dangerous it might be, he felt it was his Christian duty to come warn the family about the event. He didn't get a look at the thing's face, Roy said, but it was big, hairy and ran away like a man. Dad liked Roy immediately and invited him back for coffee when he had the chance. The two became great friends and this new acquaintance would play a pivotal role in the drama that was about to unfold.

The first sighting by someone in my own family happened around eight o'clock one evening when mom stepped out onto the front porch to call Harold and his wife and three children over for a late supper. Everyone had been working in the fields all day. She looked to her left and saw a giant, hairy shadow at least eight feet tall standing in the darkness near an old shed. It was looking at her. She screamed like a panther, then ran back inside and locked the door. Harold soon rushed over holding his rifle. Dad grabbed the shotgun. Shaking, mom called the police. After briefly looking around close to the house and finding nothing the state police left, most probably laughing at the crazy story. But they would be back several more times in the upcoming months as events escalated into an almost nightly visitation by the creature.

Eventually, even though it was later learned that sightings of a similar nature were taking place all along the Green River in towns such as Bluff City and Hebbardsville, the police refused to respond to any more "monster" calls and my family was left to defend ourselves.

Mom saw it again at dusk not long after as it ran from a field by the garden area and jumped an old fence-row. It chased dad and one of the dogs out of a tobacco field that dad was tending alone one day but it was my brother Dean who had the closest encounter. He was standing in the front yard one day trying to take some garden hoes away from a couple of the younger girls, when he heard a tremendous crashing through the trees out back, followed by a complete and unsettling quiet that came over the entire area. It was then Dean saw the monster standing in a small gully by an old truck. He described it as being muscular and tall, with a square jaw

The Spottsville Monster -- illustration by the author, based on witness accounts of the creature

and small, close set eyes. It was covered in reddish gray hair, thin and patchy in spots as if it was very old. All of us children saw it one morning while waiting for the school bus. It was standing in a cornfield out front. It towered above the full-grown corn and seemed to sway slightly from side to side as it stood there.

By this time the, local TV. news had heard of the events from the police band radio and decided to send a camera crew and sketch artist out to our house. The artist drew a hairy, man-like animal with no face and a segment about the affair was featured on the evening news. The next day a crew of reporters from the local newspaper descended on our farm to get the scoop. The morning edition of The Gleaner dubbed the beast The Spottsville Monster and the accompanying article treated the sighting fairly, despite some misquotes such as calling the monster green and misidentifying the road on which my family lived. Ironically, this brought the crowds of gun-toting "monster hunters" which then descended on Spottsville, searching everywhere for a location which did not exist. As I recall, not a single one of them ever made it to Mound Ridge Road.

A partial cast of the footprint of the Spottsville Monster, circa 1975. This photo originally appeared in the local newspaper

Meanwhile, Roy, the neighbor from down the road had agreed to try and track the monster down for the sake of the safety of the Nunnelly children. He encountered it one day at an old, abandoned house far back in the woods. It was stooping down, he said, looking out the window at him. He fired on it and in that instant it just vanished before his eyes. Shaken by the sighting, he went home where he dared not mention the incident to anyone, not even his wife. He didn't give up, however, and eventually claimed to have found trace evidence in the form of hair, a claw and a plaster cast of a partial footprint left in near-frozen ground. The print, though incomplete, was impressive and showed the clear impression of a large, four-toed foot.

When the news coverage began dad referred the reporters up to talk to the neighbor, which they did. His name appeared in print and he, like the my own family, suffered through an embarrassing period of public ridicule. The children were endlessly taunted at school, and the neighbor, who worked at a local fire department, fared much the same.

Strange things were seen and heard for the next several months but the events finally came to a conclusion, for my family at least, when Roy told dad about a bizarre encounter with the creature he had experienced a couple of weeks prior, followed by a short stay in the hospital. He had been looking for the thing one day, he said, when it started to rain. He was walking a tree line and there was a nearby, long-abandoned old barn into which he went seeking shelter from the rain. Little did he know the creature was also inside. He stood only for a moment at one end of the open ended barn, when suddenly the feeling that he wasn't alone washed over him, along with the sensation of the hair rising on the back of his neck and arms. He slowly turned around and found himself staring into a huge, hairy midsection. This neighbor stood 6' 3" tall but he had to look almost straight up to see the creature's face.

It was a horrible sight and deeply unsettling, he told me, with a short muzzle, long pointed fangs set into both its upper and lower jaws, black skin and strange red eyes that chilled and frightened him to his very soul. He reached for the rifle strapped on his shoulder but suddenly found himself unable to move as those terrible eyes froze him in their gaze. Roy thought that he was surely done for but the beast's alarming spoke to him without using its mouth at all, with some sort of mental telepathy.

It said, "Don't be afraid. I will not harm you." Then it turned around and ran out the end of the barn that was facing the open, plowed field, now muddy from the rain. It was a few moments before Roy could move again, he said. But at last he was able to shake his head and clear the vision of those red burning eyes from his mind. When he had composed himself somewhat, he walked to the doorway through which the creature had run, hoping to see the creature's tracks in the muddy field. There were none.

Dad, realizing this was no ordinary monster, asked Roy if he thought it might come up one night and try to steal one of his children. The man replied that it was not likely, as they had been there for nearly a year already and the thing seemed content with killing animals and merely scaring people. But, he told dad, if the creature ever did decide to do it, there would be nothing anyone in this world could do for them. They would be gone. Period. For weeks, dad kept a five-gallon bucket of kerosene and a mop near the kitchen door in case the creature tried to get in and attack the members of the household. In the event that he could not drive it away with bullets or fire it was his intention to kick the bucket of fuel over and set it ablaze, burning the house to the ground with the whole family inside rather than losing one or more of them to the creature and trying to live with the loss. Better, he reasoned, that they should all die together than try to live without a single member of the family. All of us agreed.

Soon after the talk with Roy, we found ourselves once again packing up our belongings and moving back to the safety of the city.

THE INTERVIEW

I interviewed Roy, the neighbor and my father's good friend, in February, 2005. It had been 30 years since I had seen him. He was older but still pleasant, intelligent and cordial. And extremely credible. He still lived in the same house that he lived in back then and is a God-fearing Christian with no reason to lie and no desire for any publicity whatsoever. After promising never to reveal his real name, and because I was Red's son, he agreed to grant me the interview and tell me everything that had happened to him during and after our ordeal in 1975. What he told me about his further encounters with the Spottsville Monster astounded me. He claimed that he had seen the beast several more times after my family left. Moreover, he said, that what he had seen with his own eyes went far beyond anything that he had ever dreamed possible

One day he was walking along an old fence line next to a field and he noticed a strange area that looked like heat waves rising from a hot, summer road. The area was only a few yards wide and to either side everything looked normal. According to Roy, as he was watching, one of the creatures stepped out of this strange wavy area like stepping out a doorway. One second nothing, and the next there it was looking right at him. It growled at him and, at the same time, screamed inside his head to "leave me alone!" Then it turned around and took a step back into the strange-looking "doorway" and disappeared.

After that, he began watching this area from a distance using binoculars as often as he could.. In all, he claimed to have witnessed several different monsters using this doorway a total of three different times, always appearing or disappearing, seemingly into thin air. These strange creatures would then be seen crossing his own property and tripping the sensitive motion detecting security lights in his yard. His last sighting was in August of 2004. When asked if I could see the trace evidence I received another revelation. Soon after the media coverage back in '75, he said, he was visited by members of the state police and a couple of other men whom he took to be Department of Natural Resources officials. He was shocked when they demanded that he turn over all evidence concerning The Spottsville Monster to them immediately, which he did. Moreover, he said they stated that if he ever talked to anyone else about the subject, especially the media, he would be arrested without hesitation and thrown into prison on a trumped-up charge and would never see his wife and two young daughters again unless it was looking at them through prison bars.

In addition, a statement had been prepared for the local paper in his name stating for a fact that what he had seen was nothing more than a large, black bear. Not easily intimidated he, at first, balked at the whole thing, reasoning that this was America and his rights were being grossly violated. But the officials were very persuasive and, in the end, he had little choice but to go along with the charade for the sake of his family.

Over the years he had tried to get the items back with no luck. One time he and his family came home and found a large freezer bag on the front porch. It held the remains of his plaster cast smashed into powder. The statement was released to the local paper which proudly proclaimed the mystery of the Spottsville Monster solved. The hoards of monster hunters melted away, leaving behind only the body of a dog, someone's family pet, accidentally shot by monster-hunting teens. Everything quieted down and the Spottsville Monster faded into memory. Roy never talked of the monster again, and he still fears the threats made 30 years ago, as he now owns a successful business and he does not wish to jeopardize it.

He blames the inability to speak of his encounters on a heart attack he suffered in 1985, which left him, for a brief time before he was resuscitated, clinically dead. He also claims that his near-death experience left him with a certain degree of formerly dormant mental abilities.

As I sat listening to his story and sketching the beast it struck me that here was a man who was highly successful and content. He seemed almost embarrassed by the whole situation and genuinely feared the possibility of his name being released to the public again and suffering through the treatment that he endured back in the '70s - or worse. Then why was he speaking to me about it at all?

His reply was simply because it was the truth and people had a right to know the truth regardless of how many choose to believe it or not. I honestly agree with him.

THE STURGIS VAMPIRE

Paranormal investigator Jan Thompson, whose name appears in other sections of this book, is certainly no stranger to the unexplained. Like other Kentuckians, enigmas seemed to just naturally cross her path. One did just that - literally - on Christmas morning, 1983 in Union County. She writes:

'It was while traveling these back roads between Sturgis and Morganfield, that a decidedly remarkable creature crossed my path. The incident left me in such utter terror that, from then on, I refused to drive alone at night along any deserted or isolated country roads again. This wasn't an apparition, a ghostly image, strange voices or unexplained poltergeist activity. There were no warning premonitions of something watching from the shadows, no omens, no mystic dreams, and no psychic sensations, but all that happened that evening, short as the encounter had been, would become intense memories of profound fear. One that still surfaces sometimes, like right now, sending chills all over my flesh, at the time of this writing.

It was snowing that evening along Highway 60 on my journey from Evansville, Indiana, where I worked at the time, back to Kentucky to see my family for the holidays. Although it was very late, close to midnight on Christmas Eve, 1983, the roads were well-traveled. Not bumper-to-bumper congestion, but enough of a line that it got on my nerves. The cars ahead of me evidently were not sure of the surface of the road as it snowed and they were keeping to an extremely safe speed, almost 30 mph below the limit. I could not see the beginning of the line as it stretched along into the darkness ahead, nor see the end that drew out behind me. It was just a steady flow of cars going about 25 miles per hour. On a normal evening with dry weather conditions all these cars would have been stretched far enough apart along the two-lane highway that no one would have known how many there actually were but, that night, we were clustered together going along at the unseen leader's pace.

I was confident that I could travel safely at a higher rate of speed, so I decided to take an old country back road that would cut around the parade of cars and hopefully leave me ahead of the traffic where it joined Hwy 60 again about 15 miles down. The old back road I chose ran past some of the abandoned Peabody coal mines, which made for an eerie picture against the peaceful snowfall. The snow itself had been powdery enough that it scattered in whirlwinds as I drove through it, revealing a relatively dry pavement underneath. The heavier snowfall must have stayed north of this road because Highway 60 had been much more slippery and slushy in spots. This allowed me to do at least 35 to 40 miles per hour.

The digital readout on the dash read 12:17, and I thought to myself, 'Merry Christmas.' At precisely that time, I caught glimpse of movement in my peripheral vision coming from a field on the left side of the road. My first impulse was that it was a deer running over the expanse of the field and leaping upwards and over clumps of brush. Being familiar with the road, I knew that up ahead was a very sharp curve to the right. Letting up on the accelerator and lightly touching the brakes I slowed my vehicle down to about 20 miles per hour to anticipate the 'deer' crossing my path, as it was traveling closer to my side of the road. It remained a murky object until it reached the beam from my headlights and I saw that this was not a deer. Nor was it a four-legged animal of any type. It ran on two legs - human-like legs.

As it deliberately moved towards the road from the field just inside the curve, I feared a collision would ensue. I hit the brakes, fought a few skids, then came to a stop a few yards in front of what had jumped onto the pavement and was standing at a halt in the beam of my headlights. It appeared to be a naked man, relatively tall. About six and a half feet in height, with milky white flesh that blended in with the snow. He was raised up on the balls of his large feet, with his legs slightly spread apart as if preparing to pounce, and his particularly hairy back was hunched over slightly with his arms elevated half way up from his sides for balance. Its muscles were tight solid outlines resembling the finely chiseled marble on a statue from a museum. One of the upper leg muscles trembled like a horse after a hard race. Its sexual anatomy was matted with tangles, uncircumcised and strangely hefty for a human. There was long, thick disheveled patches of dark brown hair protruding from his body in various odd places, mostly on the upper torso.

His head was covered with the same untamed mess that hung like a lion's mane over his shoulders and down his back. He just stood there staring at me through the windshield. His eyes were like red fiber optic lights, with no white around the pupils, and they seemed to have the same iridescent glow that an animal has when caught in the beam of headlights. There were large puffs of warm air coming fast from his mouth as he momentarily rested from running through the field. His nostrils were large and flared and seemed out of proportion for a human. Between the thick exhales of breath, I could see some color around his mouth, chin, and neck that went down to his chest. It too, was red, but this glistened in the light's gleam as something wet would. The large snowflakes fell around his hair, melting when it touched the red liquid that stained his skin. He appeared to have bled liberally recently from a wound somewhere in the face area.

My mind was racing with questions and possibilities as to what or whom it was that

Illustration of the Sturgis Vampire, created by the author based on descriptions given by the witness

stood there. Was I the victim of a practical joker? Was it a man who had been in an accident or been attacked and needed help? An escaped convict? Nothing made sense really as I took in more of his ragged features. His ribs were revealed with each heave of his breath as if he was malnourished. Patches of hair hung in clumps on the torso. A few scattered leaves clung to his unruly mane. His arms were as muscular as his thighs and were abnormally long and slender, and his hands ended in spindly fingers with long, ragged nails. They too, were covered with what appeared to be blood and dirt. In frightful silence I studied the figure and saw that the blood and dirt was spread sporadically over its abdomen and on its chest.

My eyes went back up to the face. His breath had slowed and more of his features were revealed. His mouth showed boxy, outsized teeth in what appeared to be a hideous grin, mixed with saliva and blood and stained pink. His lips opened wider in warning and revealed two large canines that were thick and longer then the other teeth. Then he licked its bottom teeth with his tongue, running it across his bottom lip. It still maintained an unblinking stare, with eyes that seemed to pulse inside its sunken sockets, as if pondering what action to take next.

It was in that one tense moment of direct connection when I truly realized the strong difference between beast and man. I was the unwary traveler who had interrupted his beastly movements and we were now at a standstill awaiting his decision of whether to pass over my intrusion and go onward or engage in an attack. It closed its mouth, snorted a hefty gust of air, then just as quickly as it had jumped onto the road a few moments before, jumped away to the other side with an uncanny grace, barely touching the ditch and running through the opposite field.

I sat there in my car for a few minutes more, looking back and forth at the tracks it had left in the snow, and from both sides of the road. The rest of my travels that evening where rushed, and a bit too fast for the road conditions. When it was time to leave the next day to return to Evansville, I opted to drive during the daylight hours and to stay on the main roads. Back at work that next week, several of my co-workers in the break room were discussing a series of cattle mutilations and farm animal killings going on in various surrounding counties. Some of the cattle were reportedly left alive, others ripped apart, and some just had certain organs removed. These incidents ranged from the farmlands of southern Indiana and down through western Kentucky.

There were several guesses as to what was attacking the animals. They ranged from coyotes to wolves and someone even suggested that aliens did it. I never spoke up as to what I had seen and silently kept the knowledge of that strange nighttime visitor to myself for fear of ridicule. Inside, I knew that the extraordinary creature I had observed that holiday eve could possibly be the culprit to all the carnage the farmers were experiencing.

Years later, after I moved back down to Kentucky, I came upon some other witnesses that had seen the same type of creature around the Sturgis area. It prompted me to do some research and I did indeed find that this scruffy biped had been given a nickname by the locals. They called it The Vampire of Sturgis. Over the years, I listened to stories of even more animals being killed, which included domesticated pets as well, supposedly snatched away from their own yards. Relatives or friends of the witnesses that lived in distant counties reported that the creature had been spotted as far away as Madisonville and then in the Marion and Salem areas of western Kentucky.

All the descriptions of the creature ran about the same; lean-looking, naked but for patches of long scraggly hair, humanoid but animalistic in features. Never had I heard it described as a Bigfoot type creature. It was only last year, 2006, that I was introduced to a plausible explanation from Bart Nunnelly, a noted cryptid investigator, that it could have possibly been a Bigfoot with the mange. Since then, I've also heard from other cryptozoologists with the same hypothesis and have read about other sightings with similar if not the same descriptions of what I witnessed all those years ago. I tend to agree with this theory as I compare my own portrayal of what I saw that evening with the features of the more commonly seen hairy biped.'

I offered to render a sketch of the creature she saw and pressed her for everything she could remember concerning the details of its appearance. She further commented:

"It had patchy hair, mainly in patches on the shoulders and back, and it had a full tangled head of hair spreading around its neck and patches on it's upper chest also. No tail and no hair in the genital area. It was thin and lean. You could tell it had a big boned structure but the flesh was thin on its body like it was unhealthy. The genital area looked like it had a rash or was being scratched on a regular basis as it was a pinkish color and it had large, hanging testicles with a thick uncircumcised appendage hanging loosely. When it did turn to run into the opposite field, the buttocks were muscular as well, even though it was rather thin. I would estimate its height to be somewhere between 6'2" and 6'5", and around 145 to 150 pounds in weight. I realize this is rather small to be classified as a Bigfoot, but maybe it had some sort of disease or malnutrition disorder. There were ribs showing, like it was starved. Also the area below around the hip area was slightly sunken in showing the pelvic bone structure.

The face was sunken and shallow. It had a wide nose, like a person of African descent, a large lip area around the mouth, and the canines were a bit shorter than the Beast of the Land

Between the Lakes'. I didn't notice any lower canines sticking up, and the face was gaunt, sunken in, the flesh sticking to the bone structure, the eyes were red but I'm sure that was from the headlights shining in its face. It did have blood around its mouth, on its teeth, and running down its chin and chest, and on its hands and lower arms. The eyes shown fiery red, with no white around the pupils, just solid red, glowing in the light like a captured animal's eyes in the dark. Wild, very long brown hair fell from its head in thick tangles along its white skin, down its back, over its shoulders. It appeared to be a man, and it was naked, its flesh as milky as the snow around its bare feet that were raised up on the toes, as if preparing to pounce.

Its back hunched over slightly. Its muscles were tight, solid outlines resembling finely chiseled Italian marble, no doubt they would have been hard to the touch, as well as cold. One of the upper leg muscles trembled like a horse's does after a hard race. It stood staring at me, through the windshield, I could see the exhales of breath, large clouds of warm air, coming from its mouth in fast rhythms as it rested from running through the fields. The hair on the neck and shoulders was in patches, like hunks taken out all over, there were sprigs of long hair hanging from the elbows and along the backbone from the neck down to the butt crack. Its hair was dark brown. and I don't know if you can add this but it had what appeared to be leaves stuck in it at places. It was a tangled mess, very unruly and the straggles that hung long by the face were twisted with blood at the ends."

WEREWOLVES IN KENTUCKY

THE DOGMEN

Of all the two-legged beasties which have been encountered in the Bluegrass State, none strike such utter fear and terror in the hearts of witnesses as the "Dogmen." Usually described as tall and hairy with a canine- type head, long pointed ears and cruel-looking fangs and talons, these frightening monstrosities resemble nothing so much as the widely-touted image of the classic Hollywood werewolf. In fact, many Kentucky old timers, when describing encounters with these canid curiosities, call them just that: werewolves.

Sightings of this nature are often mistakenly included in the Bigfoot category by many less-than- knowledgeable researchers, and referred to as "muzzled" or "dog-faced" Bigfoot, but it is clear that these creatures are something else entirely, bearing only a superficial resemblance to their equally mysterious counterparts in that they are tall, hirsute and usually described as possessing the ability to walk or run on two legs. Unlike their more gentle cousins, however, a commonly recurring theme in many Kentucky Dogman reports is an apparently fearless tendency towards aggressive behavior concerning both humans and animals. Indeed, if the common Bigfoot creatures actually have nightmares, then these Dogmen are what they are most likely dreaming of.

According to author and award-winning journalist Linda Godfrey, America's preeminent authority on the subject, these creatures have been seen in many mid-western and eastern states such as Michigan, Wisconsin, Illinois, New York, Pennsylvania, Virginia, Tennessee, Ohio and Georgia, but no reports from Kentucky have surfaced. Until now. Not surprisingly, the state of Kentucky, home to so many other reports of bizarre man-like creatures, seems to be a preferred haunt of these wolfish terrors as well. And their territory stretches from one end of the commonwealth to the other.

EASTERN KENTUCKY WEREWOLVES

Friend and fellow Fortean, the Rev. Joshua Sparks related to me that his aunt, Jeannie W. (Full name on file), had been badly frightened while driving to work one morning just before dawn back in 1975. She was a young woman that summer day in Boyd County as she took the shortcut from Ashland to Catlettsburg. Route 168 was a typical Kentucky country road, narrow and tree-lined and, for this reason, she wasn't traveling at a high rate of speed. As she rounded a curve, she noticed something moving off to the side of the road only a short distance away. When the vehicle's headlights swung around she saw what appeared to be some type of dark, hairy animal standing upright on its hind legs.

It had stopped abruptly when the lights hit it, and remained motionless as the car approached. On drawing closer, Jeannie saw that it was about six feet tall with "long, dark, shaggy hair all over it." It didn't appear scared and made no move to run away as the vehicle approached, but simply stared at her through the window as she drove by.

" I will never forget it," she said. "It looked just like a werewolf." It had an elongated nose, or snout, she claimed, like a dog's, and long, sharp-looking teeth. Strangely, as she drove by this creature and made eye contact with it, she was struck with the peculiar sensation that "time had just slowed down," like she was moving in slow motion. It was a very odd and frightening feeling even though the creature itself had never made a threatening move in her direction, nor any movement at all, as she passed by - just stood there glaring at her.

Of course she didn't stop.

Boyd County, especially the area in and around Ashland, has a history of hairy biped sightings usually associated with, and attributed to, the Bigfoot phenomenon. Strangely enough, reports of "Man-Apes" are often present in the same areas where "Man-Wolf" activity is witnessed. There can be no confusion between the two, however, when examining the many local werewolf legends to be found throughout the Bluegrass State. Ashland has its own legend concerning these nightmarish beasts which are said to be regular haunts of a local cemetery situated in the southern part of the city.

Of all the many strange things which have reportedly been encountered in this location, surely the werewolf is the most frightening. In all likelihood the legend is as old as human settlement in the area but, more recently, several bizarre events were said to have taken place in the Ashland Kentucky Cemetery back in the 1980s, when this creature seemed to be at its most active. Many who had seen this thing said that it could run both on two legs and on all four and was capable of leaping, from a standstill, completely over the 10-foot-high gate at the graveyard's entrance. The animal seemed to delight in chasing humans and, thankfully, stopping or turning away just before its prey was reached. Encounters with the beast invariably took place at night.

The local werewolf soon became the talk of the town and it didn't take long before the local police were sent to check out the scene of one of these disturbances. Once inside the gate they made their rounds, shining their flashlights among the headstones. Then the beast appeared in all its terrifying glory, at which point both of the armed officers turned and immediately fled for the gates and the safety of their patrol car with the werewolf nipping at their heels. To their great dismay, they found the gate inexplicably shut and locked, effectively trapping them inside with the creature. Several citizens, it is said, heard the terrified officers screaming for help over their police-band radios that evening.

One Dogman witness whom Sparks was able to interview claimed that he had seen the creature twice on different occasions while crossing the cemetery at night. The first time he saw it, Sparks said, he was walking through the graveyard when the lights from a passing car shined on an "evil-looking thing with a wolf head and fangs" as it ducked down behind a gravestone. Sparks bravely walked over to investigate but there was nothing there. His second encounter cured him of any notions of bravery concerning the beast however. This time, he was accompanied by several friends and family members when, according to Sparks, the creature appeared and began to chase them on all fours. They all ran through the surrounding woods all the way to the Southside swimming pool before the werewolf turned away and disappeared back into the trees. They all said that it ran very swiftly and probably could've caught them easily if it had wanted. The same could be said for many, if not all, other Dogman encounters, I'm sure.

Another sighting took place in nearby Greenup County only a few years ago. A young man and his wife were driving home one night in two separate vehicles. Because her car had been acting up lately they were using a pair of two-way "walkie talkies" in order to stay in constant contact with each other should something go wrong. When she began to slow down, the husband asked her what the matter was. She told him that something was running down the middle of the road in front of her, coming in her direction. Then she suddenly slammed on the brakes and screeched to a stop. The thing wasn't moving now she told him, just standing in the road, and it was some kind of monster. He could tell by the tone of her panicky voice that she was definitely not joking. He was only a few seconds behind and, as he approached his terrified wife's automobile, the "thing" she was looking at bounded up and over her car, landing in the road behind it, and started running towards the second vehicle.

It was very swift and in a flash it was upon him, he told Sparks, but he was able to get a good look at the thing before it leapt over his own car and disappeared into the darkness. It was a big "werewolf-looking" thing, completely covered with shaggy hair. It had cruel looking eyes, pointed ears and long fangs and claws. He screamed into the radio for his wife to "Go! Go! Go!" and they both got out of the area as fast as possible. The werewolf had looked at him just before it jumped, he said, and it was a terrible feeling. Both witnesses claim that they will never forget that night as long as they live.

Several years ago Shirley Elkins sent a letter to Bigfoot researcher Bill Green of the New England Bigfoot Information Center, who forwarded it to Ray Crowe of the International Bigfoot Society. The letter concerned an event which took place back in April of 1944 in Paintsville, Johnson County. The incident is notable here not only due to the description given of the creature in question, but also in that it involved aggression in the form of a physical assault on a patient at a hospital where Elkins was working as a nurse on the night shift. She wrote:

'I was on night shift at the hospital in my hometown in April, 1944. That night a young man was in the waiting room to see the doctor. He was all a mess of scratches and his mother was telling him to just say he fell down and to not mention anything about being in a fight with a tall, man-like hairy thing. They kept him overnight at the hospital, and later that night, someone phoned us about an accident caused by a tall hairy creature that was in the road. A year passed and I went to work at a restaurant and there was this man I'd seen at the hospital. He was the owner's son and he became my husband on June 7, 1945.'

His name was Ellis and he later told her what had happened that rainy night back in April. It had been dark and rainy all day, he said. He had gone fishing and had caught a pile of catfish for the restaurant. He was out back cleaning them on a table lit by a 25-watt bulb, when up from the riverbank came what looked like a man only he was (covered) with dark hair, long and shaggy all over. He thought it was a teenager dressed in some outlandish costume at first. But then it growled at him, pushed him and made a grab for the fish.

Ellis grabbed a bottle and promptly hit the creature, knocking it into a rain barrel that was kept outside for cleaning purposes. The creature jumped up, growled again then grabbed Ellis and shook him like a rag doll before hurling him to the ground and running off with the fish.

"Mom didn't believe it," Ellis told Shirley. "She thought the staff at the hospital would send for a shrink if I told this to them. It had small, aqua-colored eyes- like a cat. Heavy scattered eyebrows. Looked like a young teen only was very bushy with hair of a shiny slate color. He wasn't over 6 feet tall, slim, long body, short legs. He had large, long feet, long claw-like nails like overgrown human ones. Its tail bushed when it saw the fish! It looked like it smiled, but it still growled. It had sharp, long, pointed teeth."

The creature reportedly left five-toed footprints complete with the impressions of claw marks in the mud.

Although no mention is made of a muzzle, or elongated snout, the other features such as long, sharp fangs and claws, and most especially the bushy tail which bristled at the sight of food, seem to argue against the more mundane notion that this beastman was merely another Bigfoot. Perhaps it was a juvenile Dogman and, if so, it's not the only example of an apparently immature form of these creatures to be seen in Kentucky.

The following report was submitted to kentuckybigfoot.com on July 30, 2006:

Name: Chris
County: Harrison
Year: Fall of 1991
Time of sighting: 9:00 p.m.
Nearest City: Cynthiana
Duration of sighting: Less than 20 seconds
How many witnesses: 2 including myself
Describe your encounter:

'I was driving on a gravel road with one of my friends in an area of the county that is somewhat quiet and off the beaten path. The area is forested with mixed pasture. We were only driving about 15 miles an hour when a creature about three feet tall ran in front of the car from left to right and jumped down into the brush adjacent to a woodlot. The thing that got me about this thing was that it was on two feet, but the legs looked to be lupine (wolf-like). It, however, was not a wolf or a dog. My friend looked at me and asked if I saw that. We had both seen something that scared us enough to get out of the area.'

Describe the animal:
'The creature was about three feet tall and walked on two legs. The best description I can give is to imagine a slightly shaggy monkey with lupine legs. This thing was very fast.'

Additional comments:
'I used to be a forester and I'm used to seeing deer, turkey, barking squirrels and all the other critters out there. This was something different.'

Surely a onetime forestry official, well versed in and familiar with the local fauna, would not mistake a more common animal for something extraordinary. The point becomes moot when one considers that there are no animals whatever indigenous to eastern Kentucky which might easily fit the description given by this man. But these creatures are, by no means, only to be found in the eastern parts of the commonwealth. Across the entire breadth of the state they seem equally, if not even more so, at home in western Kentucky as well.

WESTERN KENTUCKY WEREWOLVES

I've spent many an hour talking to fellow Kentucky Bigfoot researcher, Mark M. (full name on file) from Trigg County, about his experiences with Man-beasts in his area. After months of discourse I finally persuaded him to submit some of his encounters to kentuckybigfoot.com.

Website Submission on Nov. 26, 2006:

Date: Early Spring, late March, early April
Location: Trigg County
Weather Conditions: Sunny, calm afternoon. Very light breeze
Time: Between 3:00 and 4:00 p.m.

Events:
'I had been researching the Bigfoot phenomenon for some time. I still classified myself as a novice in understanding the nature of these creatures. I hadn't come across a whole lot of findings up until this point. It seems that, for some reason, my encounters of Bigfoot activity seemed to increase after the day's events. From this point, my research yielded several encounters with these creatures. Even thought the account below doesn't contain a sighting, it is important to note that this event not only happened to me but someone else as well. When I learned of the event from the person it happened to I was very surprised. The fact of the matter is that this person had no knowledge of what happened to me on this day. What concerned me very much was the fact that there were small children living in that environment that hadn't been there previously. The events that took place with this person were almost identical to the events described below. The exception is that, when the creature reached the spot where it stopped howling on the day I encountered it, it turned and moved deeper into the forest, howling as it moved along its course.
In the Spring of 2001, a nice, warm, sunny afternoon in western Kentucky near Lake Barkley, I had gone to visit a friend. I didn't expect any "out of the ordinary" events to take place. I arrived at my friend's house and was talking to him outside. It was typical for me to visit on Saturdays and we would discuss the week's events. Not long after I arrived, he told me that he needed to use the phone and that he was going down to the shop where he worked to do so. He asked if I wanted to go with him and I said, "Well, if you're just going down there to use the phone and come right back I will stay here." He said he would be right back. He then

got into his truck and pulled out onto the highway going towards the shop.

I sat there on the back porch smoking a cigarette and watching his truck go down the road until it disappeared. It wasn't long after his truck went out of my sight that I heard a distant sound. It was kind of hard to judge exactly how far away from me it was but it sounded like maybe a quarter of a mile or so. When I first heard this sound I thought it was a coyote. Sitting there, I began to realize that, if it was a coyote, there was definitely something wrong with it. Most times you will only hear coyotes at late evening, night and early morning. I heard it howl again. This time, it sounded like it might be closer and moving through the woods that ran behind my friend's house. I wasn't real sure of its direction of travel, so I sat there patiently, hoping to catch a glimpse of the animal crossing through the neighbor's pasture.

The howl sounded again and this time I could tell that it was moving closer. I realized that it was moving along the edge of the woods towards my friend's house. After the fifth howl I realized that it wasn't a coyote. If it was it was like no coyote that I have ever heard before. With each progressing growl it moved closer to where I was sitting and the howls got louder and louder as this thing moved through the woods towards me. After each vocalization I got a very uneasy, sick feeling in the pit of my stomach. It's very hard to describe or explain but, I assure you, it will never be forgotten.

I was sitting there wide-eyed, looking for whatever this creature might be. I had heard about eight howls when I guessed the thing to be no more than a hundred yards away from me. At this point I had heard, fairly well, its direction of travel and it really didn't take long at all for it to have covered the distance it had traveled since I first heard the vocalizations. Sitting there patiently on the porch I heard one last howl that sounded like it came from the top of a ridge just behind my friend's house. My eyes were scanning the woods looking for any sign of this thing. I could see no movement at all and the sounds had completely stopped at this point. There were no more howls. What happened? I thought to myself. Where did it go? I then began to think about what might be taking place. I have hunted those very woods for the last five years and have never really seen anything out of the ordinary. I do know that, from atop the ridge where the last howl came from, the house and back yard are easily visible. My guess was that, whatever it was, had stopped up on top of the ridge to figure me out. What I was doing. Or maybe it knew I was there all along somehow.

I sat there waiting for anything to happen, hearing and seeing absolutely nothing. I was in a very nervous state, feeling extremely uneasy, which is unlike me, at not being able to see what this creature was. It seemed like forever, but then I heard the sound of my friend's truck turning into the driveway. I was glad that the stalemate of sorts was now over. I didn't mention anything, at the time to my friend about what had happened while he was gone. I didn't stay much longer that day as I felt very unnerved by what had happened. I have heard of the Beast of LBL but never really paid much attention to the story until that day.'

Only a couple of months later, in June of 2006, Mark got his first tentative glimpse of the "monster" that was frequenting his research areas. It was a cool, starry night between 9:30 and 11:00 p.m. and slightly hazy when the following incident took place. Mark writes:

'The area that I had been researching has a large piece of property in the center of it that is leased to a hunting club. That left me with the possibility of only researching on some of the private property that bordered this large tract of acreage. My findings in this area were somewhat limited due to not having access to the majority of the property there. Nonetheless, I continued my research where I was able to. I stopped by to see an old friend who was a member of the hunting club. We got to talking and, out of the blue, he asked me if I would be interested in going camping. I said "Sure. Where do you want to camp?" He replied that he was thinking that we could go to the hunting camp on the club's property.

I was somewhat ecstatic as I had wanted to gain access to that property for a while to see if I could find something of interest there relating to Bigfoot. The rest of the afternoon was spent gathering camping gear, research equipment and such. Later, just before dusk, we headed out on four-wheelers to the campsite. We arrived and unloaded our gear. Once that was done we decided to build a fire in the fire-pit. Tending the fire and roasting some hotdogs I could hear a lone coyote calling southwest of the camp. I listened as it moved behind the camp in an easterly direction, calling to its brethren. My companion seemed to pay this little attention as we sat around the fire. It was a normal-sounding coyote, unlike the vocalizations I had heard a couple of months previously, and added to the outdoorsy atmosphere that I loved so much. A few minutes passed and he asked me if I wanted to go for a ride. I was agreeable so we started up the four-wheelers and took off into the night.

As we headed out across the vast wooded lease I had no idea where we were going. It was dark and I was unfamiliar with the property in the daytime, let alone at night. We rode for a long time, it seemed, out across this immense piece of land. One thing I did notice was that, during the entire ride, I never did see any animals of any kind, even though this area is usually covered with deer, rabbits, raccoons and other creatures that move about in the evenings here. It seemed like the area was totally devoid of these nocturnal animals. I suspect that it may be due to the presence of the one creature which we did encounter that night. A creature unlike any of the usual forest animals.

We topped a large hill and started down the incline. My friend was a good distance ahead of me by 60 yards or so. He was hauling ass when he reached the bottom of the hill. The trail leveled out for a short distance and then began to elevate gradually into about a 20-degree slope. When I reached the bottom of the hill my friend was already at the top of the incline ahead of me. All of a sudden, and without warning he quickly turned off the trail to his left, drove about 30 yards or so then stopped. I remember thinking, where the hell is he going? but I focused my attention back onto the trail as I started up the incline ahead of me.

I then noticed something at the top of the hill which was unlike anything that I had ever before seen. It was a pair of large eyes. They had a very sinister look to them. I realized that I couldn't see a body, or even a silhouette to go with the eyes. The headlights from the ATV were not hitting it directly so I attempted to turn enough to hit it squarely with the headlights. As I did so, I could see this creature's head turn to its left as a human would turn his head. The lights still reflected in the thing's eyes from the side profile as I turned in its direction. It then rapidly left the trail and went into what I thought was a wooded area.

The eyes were just below the tree branches which hung over the trail about seven or eight feet from the ground. They were a solid amber color with no distinction of eye-banding, iris or pupils like you find in normal animals eyes. They were large. Only slightly smaller than the diameter of a snuff can. They never blinked, at least that I noticed. They were set at such an angle to imply that they belonged to a creature that possessed a snout, or muzzle. The head's movement was fluid, with only a slight bob as it turned its head. As it left the trail, its eyes never bounced but moved in a straight horizontal line.

I reached the top of the incline and turned in the same spot as my friend had turned. Pulling in behind him I stopped. His four-wheeler had evidently stalled and he was busy trying to get it started again. I asked him two questions: Where the hell did he think he was going? and, did he see those eyes at the top of the incline? He told me that when he reached the top of the hill, he had thought there was a trail to the side there, but was mistaken and had partially lodged his ATV on a bent-over tree limb. He claimed that he didn't see any eyes but I knew that he was not being honest with me as we bushwhacked a different route back to camp, totally avoiding the previous one. Instead of going back the way we came, we cut across a power line right-of-way that led us back.

We arrived back at camp and sat around the fire thinking about what had happened. Thirty minutes or so had passed and, from out of nowhere, I started getting this overwhelming feeling of dread. It was like my inner being was telling me that I didn't need to be there at that place and that I should leave. After a short discussion about it we decided to leave, so we packed up everything in a hurry and got the hell out of there. The return trip home was uneventful.[']

A Kentucky werewolf, illustrated by the author and based on actual witness accounts

In 2005 I was contacted by Jamie Woods, of the Henderson County Paranormal Society, who had heard of my interest in the many cryptozoological mysteries of the area. He asked if I was familiar with the local werewolf legends of Henderson County. I had been aware of them for some time, I admitted. But on a personal level. I had never seen the subject referenced in any printed material.

Years ago, my mother had told me a strange story regarding an incident which happened to her when she was a 10-year-old girl living on Wilson Station Road in Henderson. The year was 1951. Some relatives had come to visit her parents and all the kids - mom and her four cousins - had congregated in the living room away from the grown-ups. As they socialized with one another a large animal leaned up against the window and looked into the room from outside. My mother, who was closest to the window, got a good look at it before her screams mingled with the other kids.

It looked like a large dog in the face, she said, hairy, pointed ears, muzzle - but it was hideously disfigured with what looked like numerous terribly deep scars. It fled when the children screamed - as did the kids - in the other direction. The adults were incredulous of the account despite the obvious fear on the children's faces. By the time anyone made it outside the animal was long gone. It was a horrific sight, my mother told me, one which gave them nightmares for some time to come. When prompted, she was able to provide more details concerning the creature's appearance. She said it was much bigger than a dog and its head was at least as big as a man's, if not bigger, and covered with dark brown to black hair. It was huge. Its muzzle was neither long nor short, but of medium length. The ears weren't standing straight up, she said, but lying halfway flat on its head. It had large, dark eyes. Dog eyes. The most bizarre aspect of her sighting, however, was that the thing looked like it was wearing a dirty white shirt or blouse.

I knew that Kentucky was once named "Transylvania," so it was no surprise that some of the older European werewolf legends may have made their long voyage from the home country to arrive here with the early settlers. According to Woods, some members of the historic Transylvania Company settled here back when the county was founded. One of these renowned men was a Pennsylvanian named L. Talbott and, after this man's death and interment into the Bethel-Talbott Cemetery, encounters with the frightening, wolf-like humanoids began. Some even believed that the werewolf was actually Talbott himself, returned from the dead in a wolfish body to spread fear and calamity across the countryside.

Many years ago, when I was a teenager, I heard a similar legend concerning a heavily forested area next to the John James Audubon State Park known as "Wolf Hills." This place, legend claimed, was named after the early werewolf sightings and even now, it was said, if you drove out to the woods there and parked at midnight on a full moon night and howled like a wolf, the werewolf would answer you.

Soon after I heard this tale I found myself driving a vanload of friends out to the location to test this local legend. We found a very isolated spot along a narrow, forest-lined side- road and parked with the full moon shining down from the frosty sky. It was just after midnight. We got out and I then did my best imitation of a wolf howl straight out of an old Lon Chaney film. We were not seriously expecting anything to happen, of course but, to our surprise, after only a few seconds had passed, something did answer back in the same wolf howl. We were a long way from any houses and this didn't sound like a coyote, but rather a perfect imitation of the call I had just made.

After a few seconds I was urged to have another go at it and, again I was answered. Only this time it was much closer. The retort left the girls in bad shape, and we were forced to evacuate the location at a pretty good clip. Sounds fanciful indeed but, lest you dismiss such things immediately as so much nonsense, there is a Bethel-Talbott cemetery in this county. And one of the gravestones does bear the name L.Talbott.

Peculiarly, this is the same name given (with only one 't' on the end) to the lead character in Universal Pictures' 1941 classic "The Wolf Man" starring Lon Chaney, Jr. The film, written by Kurt Siodmak and probably the most influential werewolf movie of all time, introduced into popular culture many of the misconceptions regarding werewolves which later became dogma concerning the subject in both literature and film, like their aversion to silver and the need for a full moon in order to transform - all concepts created by Siodmak for his fictional screenplay.

Could all this merely be a matter of coincidence? Possibly. But it is interesting to note that during the 1920s and '30s Henderson, Kentucky, was considered the richest city in the nation and boasted more millionaire citizens than any state in the U.S. It drew in the rich and famous like bees to honey back then, including many well-known Hollywood folk. If, perchance, Siodmak visited the area as well and was exposed to some of the local folklore, the inspiration for his now famous movie certainly would've been available. Perhaps Siodmak even drove out to Wolf Hills and parked beneath the full moon, just as I did some 50 years later, to test for himself the mettle of the legend. Like me, he probably even felt a little silly standing there in the dark and howling up at the moon. That is, until the Wolfman answered back.

Hollywood dogma aside, what could these creatures be? Fantastic misinterpretations of common wolves? Although no wolves have been seen in Henderson County for over 150 years, I have no doubt that something which very much resembles them are still around. My brothers and I once watched a very large wolf-like animal (see Kentucky Kryptids) chase a black panther out of a creek in broad daylight back in the 1980s. But no common wolf, of any species, can account for the many Dogman sightings where the beast is actually seen to use bipedal locomotion.

The ancient people of Kentucky were also aware that there were "beastmen" in their midst, as evidenced by this rock art that was found in a cave in Edmonson.

THE BEAST OF LBL

Paranormal investigator Jan Thompson, like myself, has had many brushes with various unknowns. These experiences served to inspire her to begin a search for others who have witnessed the unexplained. One of her most frightening encounters concerns a Dogman which attacked one of her cousins one day during summer vacation at their home near Kentucky Lake in Livingston County, an area known as The Land Between the Lakes, or LBL. Here is what happened in her own words:

"It was one of those typical sultry July late afternoons, back in 1978 in Grand Rivers when this encounter with the inexplicable creature transpired. I had come down to stay at my aunt's house for a few weeks of summer vacation and spend some time with my two cousins. Her home was surrounded by generously wooded and hilly acres and sat at the end of dead-end road. There were several trails throughout the woods that had led to more than a few places; a long out of service railroad track that went on for miles, an old, abandoned sawmill, a large section of rough rock bluffs and a lonely stretch of shoreline on Barkley Lake. Most of the trails were made by my cousin Joe's dirt bike and were well defined.

As it was on almost every day I was visiting, Joe, 13 at the time, was out riding on his bike through those woods. His younger sister, Ronda, who was around 10 at that time, and myself were sitting outside on the porch swing waiting for their mother to come home from grocery shopping. I was 17 years old.

The stillness of the afternoon was interrupted by the distinct sound of Joe's dirt bike in the distance screaming through its gears, echoing inside the trees. I knew he must have been on his way home because his dad had forbidden him, or anyone else in the family, to be out in the woods after dark. I could hear the sound of the bike's motor as it approached us at full throttle. I was expecting him to slow down, but he didn't. Still at top speed he reached the trail opening at the top of the driveway and burst towards us, actually going airborne for a few feet. The front tire crashed down on the pavement and he continued his descent, struggling to keep the bike upright. He hit the brakes hard to avoid going past the driveway and down an embankment, slid the bike sideways and jumped off in a daring maneuver. He had a look on his face, like something terrible had happened. His eyes were wide with fright and his body shook from the adrenaline. Sweat was rolling down his face and he drew deep, rapid breaths through his mouth which was drawn taut in a strange grimace. Tears were coming down his cheeks, mixing with the dusty trail dirt, and his eyes remained unblinking as he turned to stare at the top of the hill and the end of the driveway in fearful anticipation.

The basset hounds that their parents raised began barking wildly which turned to growls and then to whines. They were kept in a pen across from the driveway and all of them seemed to panic at once, digging and gnawing at the fencing, desperate to escape. All this happened in a matter of less than a minute, taking Ronda and myself by complete and utter surprise.

"IT GRABBED ME! LOOK AT MY LEG!" Joe screamed, making us jump with alarm at the sound of dread in his voice. His Levis were scratched all the way through to the flesh, leaving bloody marks on the skin. The claw marks were larger then what a grown man could have made.

"IT WALKED ON TWO LEGS!" he yelled, scaring us again, as he was trying to tell his story in between huge gulps of air. "It was following me...through the woods...along the path...from the old sawmill...hairy...it was so hairy...and it had a snout...and it walked on two legs...it ran on two legs..." his voice was sputtering, and I could see his pulse throbbing under the skin of his temples.

In that moment the howling began. It came from the woods at the top of the driveway. We all stood deathly still, even the hounds had suddenly grown silent and still. It sounded at first like a mournful wolf's howl, but more profoundly chilling and, as it came closer, more threatening. Joe began pushing us towards the front door, demanding we go inside when it came out of the woods above.

With the sun just going down, it turned the creature into a silhouette of hairy blackness. It stood maybe a foot taller then a good-sized man and was twice the breadth in the shoulders and chest, which was heaving quickly like someone who had just finished a long distance race. When it raised its head, as well as its arms, up into the air to continue its guttural vocalizations, I could make out the shape of a snout; not as long as a canine but not a nose either. The security light overhead popped on and suddenly illuminated the creature, making it raise one of its arms to shade its eyes, which appeared a bit oversized for its face and solid black in color, from the glare.

We tore the screen door trying to get into the house all at once and started barricading the main entrance. Then we heard another howl just outside, coming closer, and we all retreated into a back bedroom and barricaded that door as well. The basset hound they had inside as a pet had smelled around the front door, then tucked its tail and ran along with us. The other dogs outside were going absolutely crazy again as we heard items being thrown around on the porch, continuing all around the side of the home as well. There was also the unmistakable sound of a window being shattered just before we heard my aunt's car horn blare as she drove down

The Beast of LBL -- illustrated by the author based on witness descriptions

the road. We didn't budge to help with the groceries.

Later that evening my aunt relayed our frenzied tale to my uncle. He was skeptical but, when he went out and witnessed the broken window and the huge mess outside the house, he decided to go out the next morning into the woods with a rifle on his shoulder. He returned a few hours later with such a look on his face that left no doubt he was now a believer. He warned us all very sternly to stay out of the woods. He had found several large pits that had been dug and filled with animal bones and parts of rotting carcasses along the path that led to the old sawmill. He also saw where something had dug holes, which looked like deep caves, big enough for a man to hide in, in the sides of the bluffs along the hills that overlooked the mill. There was a rank smell in the area which was unlike the stench of rotting flesh. It literally turned his stomach but he could not identify it.

He related further that years before, when the old Boy Scout camp used to be on the other side of Grand Rivers, an unexplained two-legged creature with wolf-like features was seen along the water's edge close to the camp sites, and that he and his son had witnessed it themselves one evening on the Kentucky Lake side.

When summer was over and school resumed, Joe would venture gradually back into those same woods on his dirt bike, with a pistol on his belt for protection. There were many times he felt it watching him and would actually turn and see it again, heavily jogging towards him with a warning howl. For safety's sake Joe decided to make some new trails on the other side of the woods. At night though, after all was quiet and everyone else was asleep, sometimes the dogs outside would start acting erratic, trying to get out of their pen again. And more then a few times, when Joe had fallen asleep in the living room floor watching TV, that familiar feeling of something intently watching him would cause him to awaken. He would look over at the patio doors that were open to let the cool air in, and see the creature leaning down and staring at him through the screen door.

In the early '90s, Joe and my dad, who had come down to visit, would both travel on foot into those same woods and go all the way back to the old sawmill. They found old as well as freshly dug dirt pits with animal bones in them. The holes in the bluff were still there and they both experienced the feeling of being watched and felt uneasiness that something just wasn't right. The area where the sawmill stood seemed to have no life stirring around it; no birds, no squirrels, crickets, bugs, etc. Even the small pond that lay separated from the lakeshore stood still and lifeless. And all around it smelled like a combination of skunk and wet dog. When a large shadow moved from inside one of the holes in the bluff, the men retreated, walking backwards for awhile before turning to make haste back home.

Today those trails have either grown over or they are bulldozed away at some places. Construction crews came in where the sawmill was and demolished acres of the land to make room for condominiums and new homes. My aunt's home still stands at the end of the road but even further neighborhood advancements are taking place all around them. I'm sure the creature we saw all those years ago has left for more quiet surroundings and hunting grounds, but it must not have moved far, as there are still local sightings of it a few times a year."

When I contacted Thompson, she was able to offer even more details concerning the physical description of the terrifying beast that the three youths witnessed.

"The beast I saw at my cousins' house resembled more of a Bigfoot, except for the pointed ears and longer snout and claws that it had. It was kind of a cross between the werewolf and Bigfoot. The nose had wider nostrils at the tip, more human-like coming down from the bridge of the nose and was hairy and it was either the thing did not have a neck or that it blended in with the tall head. (It had) wide shoulders, a thick chest...no muscle definition that I could see, mostly hairy, but there was a slight curvature to the calf muscles. I had a large, top-heavy chest. The ears were laid down towards the back - not standing up, like a dog's does when they are agitated or angry. The nose didn't appear to be a glossy black nose like a canine, but part of the facial skin. The teeth between the long canines were large and square, top and bottom. There was short hair around the muzzle and facial features and then it got longer and straggly, especially in the chin area. The lips were more of a black, smooth outline with no curvature on top like the muzzle of a dog where it meets the end of the nose."

Under the witness' direction, and much effort via trial and error, I was able to render a detailed sketch of the Beast of LBL. Thompson also claims to have witnessed this creature, or others similar to it, on more than one occasion in the general area and has extensive knowledge of local folklore and events concerning these wolf-like anomalies. One such event that she claims to be aware of personally is extremely disturbing and involves the gruesome killings of a vacationing family in the LBL area back in the early 1980s. She writes:

"I believe it was around the beginning of May, just before the tourist season would start on Memorial Day, when the following event occurred. I must make note here that this story was never published in the paper, or on the news, nor did it have any media attention at all. All the witnesses to the facts were contacted shortly after the incident and strictly instructed not to repeat anything they saw, share any information, or disclose where the actual location was. A few particular individuals said in later interviews that some high-ranking government officials threatened to take away their jobs and pensions if they ever disclosed any aspect of this particular case. So, for nearly two decades, most of the people that were involved kept silent.

Two local police officers, (I'll call them Adam and Bill to protect their identities.) came in while I was on duty at the service station. They usually came by during the night, got coffee and a snack, chatted a bit and then left. But on this particular night, I soon discovered, they had just come from a crime scene in LBL and had been there for over eight hours. It was around three in the morning and they both appeared particularly shaken, pale and acting curiously bewildered. Adam sat on the curb next to some gas pumps expelling his stomach contents, while his partner, Bill, came in to get coffee for himself and water for Adam. Being a slow night, I went outside with Bill to see if I could offer some assistance. Fifteen minutes of hushed silence passed, except for the occasional dry heaving sounds from Adam. They both appeared in a disorientated stupor and it was Adam who spoke first.

"I can't believe it...it's not possible...I just can't believe it..."

The conversation that followed was in broken sentences at first but, ever so slowly, fragmented descriptions of their recent ordeal were revealed. Finally it was Bill himself who divulged the whole frightening account.

They had gotten a call to help with an investigation at one of the many rural campgrounds down in LBL. Several types of law enforcement were already there; state troopers, sheriffs, deputies, etc., when they arrived around sundown. Also present were several coroners, each from different counties. A young married couple that was camping in the area had discovered the scene and reported it to the authorities from a payphone in Grand Rivers. They had only given directions to the crime scene and their names, the officer said. They had flat out refused to return to the LBL area.

A motor home was discovered with one of its doors hanging by one hinge, along with bloody hand prints along the metal outside walls. Ripped and bloody clothing and the remains of three bodies were also found on the property. The gouging wounds found in what remained of the bodies were made by thick long claws, and the deep teeth and bite marks were made from some long incisors, according to one of the first examining coroners. The rake marks in the flesh were made up of four distinctive long strokes with an additional smaller digit stroke, like that from a thumb, and its span was much wider than that of a man's hand print.

The theories that a bear, wolf, mountain lion or coyote could have done the damage were dismissed as the injuries were clearly made by a much larger animal. (Bears are not native to the area.)

Along with all the evidence collected there was also found a clump of long gray and brown hairs in the hand of one of the victims. From the clothing that was examined inside the camper the authorities presumed that the victims had been a family consisting of a father, mother, a young boy and a small girl, yet there was one body missing - that of the little girl. It was Adam that inadvertently discovered her up high dangling from a tree, positioned on a limb. Parts of her body had been leisurely eaten. Some of the same long, gray and brown hair was found sticking in the bark of the tree near her body.

About a month after this incident, Adam and Bill stopped by during one of my midnight shifts. They seemed to have aged quite a bit, with streaks of gray in their hair and beards which had not been there before. Their faces showed signs of stress. They told me in confidence that they got word that the tests results from the hair samples and saliva taken from the bite marks, came back with an "unknown species of origin. The closest animal the source could be compared to was a canis lupus - a wolf."

So, just what are these things? No one can say for sure. Theories are as plentiful and varied as the people who posit them. Some claim they are flesh and blood animals. Others think they are some type of genetically engineered hybrid between the more common Bigfoot creatures and dogs, the creations of either demented factions from our own government or extraterrestrial beings from the Pleiades Cluster. Some even feel the creatures are demons straight from hell. While it is beyond the scope of this work to attempt to offer vindication to any of these theories, I think it is a safe bet that all Dogman reports are not the result of disingenuous eyewitnesses or hoaxers. Linda Godfrey writes in "Hunting the American Werewolf" (Trails Books, 2006):

'There is still no handy, definitive answer to give a waiting public about this creature. But I think that with these further sightings, descriptions and even evidence such as footprints, we have come much closer to gaining a true understanding of this furry Unbelievable.'

THE LIZARD MAN

In Louisville, back in the year 1878, the Louisville Metropolitan Theater exhibited a most unusual creature. It stood six and a half feet tall and was humanoid in appearance. It was also reportedly covered from head to toe with fish-like scales and had eyes twice as big around as a human's. The theater claimed the monstrosity had been captured down in Tennessee. The whole affair was reported in the Oct. 24 edition of the *Louisville Kentucky Journal* but no records of the eventual fate of the Kentucky Wildman, as it was called, have ever come to light. So was this thing a single freak of nature or an entirely separate species of hominid with a viable breeding population? While this creature may well have been a showman's hoax designed to separate the gullible from their hard-earned coins, other Kentucky Lizard Man reports are more believable.

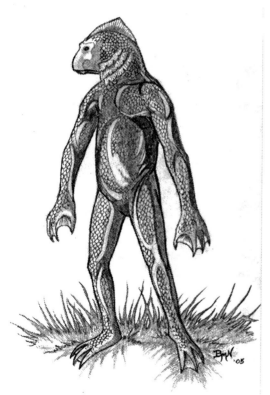

The Kentucky Lizard Man, illustrated by the author and based on witness accounts

Nearly a hundred years later in October 1975 in Milford, Trimble County, 13 years after the "monster scare," another monster appeared to frightened residents. Clarence Cable reported seeing a giant lizard near his junkyard which he described as nearly 15 feet long with a foot-long, forked tongue, bulging eyes and black and white stripes and spots covering its body. Other witnesses reported the thing as looking like a giant lizard that walked upright and was tailless. The town of Milford sits on the banks of the Ohio River.

Report Submitted: Sept. 13, 2006 by Joseph (full name on file)
Date: 1966; early fall
County: Breckinridge
City: Stephensport
Time: approximately 1 a.m.

Encounter:
'When I was around nine years old living in Breckenridge County I had the most hair-raising experience of my life! One night while fast asleep in my bed I woke to a loud commotion outside my bedroom window, as if something hit the side of my house. I sprang to the window and looked out but saw nothing. So I ran to the living room and pulled back the curtains on the window of the front door and came face to face with the strangest creature! I can best describe it as a "lizard-man," although the only "human" thing about it was the fact that it stood on two legs and was about 5'6" to 6' tall. As you could image we really startled each other! It quickly turned and ran for the creek next to my house and I jumped back from the window. I then ran to an adjacent window to catch a glimpse of it as it ran away on two legs towards the creek which was about 75 yards from my house. I lost sight of it as it disappeared into the darkness.'

Description:
'It was very amphibious-looking with scales covering its entire body. I could definitely see that this creature had webbed feet and webbed hands. Its color was a dark, brownish green. What I remember the most about its face where these huge rows of gills which flared out on both side of the face. Its face was very "hard" looking with little dark eyes, similar to a snake or lizard. I can't recall a nose or lips as the face-to-face encounter only lasted a second or two. There was this ridge-like feature which started on the forehead and ran back over the top of its head, kind of peaked at the top.'

Other Information:
'Our house is located on an acre where Sinking Creek meets the Ohio River. Sinking Creek originates 15 miles upstream in Big Springs. An interesting fact, this creek is the only natural trout/spring fed creek in Kentucky. Just past the town of Sample, it disappears 12 miles underground (thus the name Sinking Creek) and then resurfaces in an area farther upstream in an explosion of bubbling water. As far as I am aware, nobody has ever dared to dive far enough down to determine its true origin. This creek is believed to connect to the vast underwater system which connects the many caverns of western Kentucky, the most noted being the caverns of Mammoth Cave.

The witness was interviewed by Bigfoot investigator Charlie Raymond, who wrote:
"Joseph" appears to be very credible. He is now 49 years old, married, with two children in college. The details of his encounter remain true to his online report. He kept stressing how "amphibious looking" the creature was and that it definitely ran on two feet. He added that its body was proportionate to a man's but neither muscles nor genitalia were noticed. What struck him the most was how quick it was! Still to this day he can't even imagine someone having a costume that lifelike, not today, not 40 years ago, especially not in the remote parts of Breckinridge ,Kentucky.

THE GOATMAN

From time to time, reports of a Goatman, a creature with the upper body of a man and the lower body of goat, surface from varying parts of the country. It should come as no real surprise by now that this odd entity has even been seen in western Kentucky. Although this creature seems to be the rarest of all the Beastmen, I did interview a neighbor of mine, Mr. Stapleton, back in 1993, who claimed to have witnessed such a being with his own eyes. Stapleton and his entire family, including his wife and parents all claim to have seen the Goatman on their farm in Smith Mills, Henderson County, in the late 1970s. They described it as having the familiar traits. It had long, shaggy hair falling down to its shoulders with two short horns growing from its forehead. It had a hairy chest and arms with the hair thinning out around the abdomen and entirely covering the creature from its narrow waist to its split-hoofed feet. Its eyes, according to the Stapletons, were a glowing yellow color.

Two of the men were brave enough to approach it but it vanished right before their eyes when they drew to within a few yards. Interestingly, the Stapletons claimed that the house they were living in at the time of the Goatman sighting was haunted.

The Goatman has been seen in several parts of the U.S., most notably in Maryland, where it is considered aggressive and dangerous, but is most well know within the Bluegrass State in Jefferson County, where ,back in the 1940s and '50s, it was rumored to live beneath a railroad trestle over Pope Lick Creek in the Fisherville area of Louisville. It was dubbed the Pope Lick Monster by the locals and was said to hypnotize area youths onto the trestle late at night to their deaths either beneath the wheels of oncoming trains or from the 80-foot fall into Pope Lick Creek. The numerous deaths which have, indeed, occurred there are a matter of public record.

Area farmers complained of finding livestock ripped to shreds there decades ago and there is even one account of the creature chasing a Boy Scout troop from the area, screaming at them and throwing stones. Oddly, the Pope Lick Monster was commonly considered to have the upper torso of a man and a goat-like head and some even consider that it may have been a Bigfoot creature with mange.

Paranormal Investigator Jan Thompson shared some research notes about the Goatman. She wrote:

'The Goatman of Livingston County legend, in Tiline, Kentucky, goes all the way back to the mid-1840s when there was a working iron ore mine in the area. There were local iron furnaces in the area that would leave mammoth-sized holes in the earth to extract the natural ore. One in particular was dubbed 'The Red Hole' and was famous for its size, its rust-colored dirt and the dangers surrounding the opening. Supposedly, it was surrounded by quicksand, and after it was no longer in use it quickly filled up with water. Its depth was reportedly unknown. Anything or anyone slipping on the muddy steep sides of the hole would meet an untimely end. After its abandonment, stories abounded that the work crews had dug so deep they had unearthed a slumbering demon. It's been said that many of the miners that had worked that particular hole mysteriously died just before they closed it. Moreover the rumors attributed these deaths to arousing the quiescent devil. A few years afterwards, bright red eyes were seen at night by passing horse and buggies, and hoof prints were found in the dirt that were over five feet apart.

Many attributed this to pranksters but there were rumors of a terrible giant ogre haunting the area that was half man and half goat. The stories continued over into the next century and were added to as the sightings increased. One belief is that it ceremoniously appears once a year on the eve of its awakening to wreck havoc on the close-at-hand residents, farms and the nearby highway. According to local tradition, the Goatman goes on a rampage, killing anything in its path, eating it raw then throws the bones back down into the infamous red hole. No one exactly knows what date this "awakening" took place on, but teenagers often go out there at night during various times of the year in hopes they have the correct anniversary of its rebirth. Today the area is all dried up, except for a small lingering puddle.

Ironically, this same area is still known for some unexplained sightings of something nearly eight feet tall, partially hairy with other parts of its body being dirty pink skin and scabby. Its description is more akin to a Bigfoot with an obvious

The Kentucky Goatman, illustrated by the author and based on actual witness accounts

skin deformity. It has been spotted in the Red Hole area but mostly resides in the vicinity of the wooded area surrounding it. The undocumented reports are sporadic and from what I've been told there were several incidents back in the 1970s with only once about every five years from then on. Some of these sightings involved the creature raiding some burn barrels on the back of rural properties. (These are metal 50-gallon drums used to burn household garbage and trash.) However, more have seen it crossing some of the rural narrow roads or just standing by the ditches and watching the people drive by.

This animal allegedly does not have horns growing from its head, nor does its hind legs bend backward like a goats, but I'm sure it's been tied in with the Goatman sightings just to keep the legend alive.'

VI. MYSTERIOUS KENTUCKY KRYPTIDS

KENTUCKY'S BLACK PANTHERS AND OTHER PHANTOM FELINES

It is a commonly held zoological fact that no species of melanistic pumas exist in North America - yet sightings of black panthers are relatively common and have been reported in numerous cryptozoological outlets as well as mainstream scientific journals and newspapers for decades now. Just like many other creatures that "officially" don't exist here, the Black Panther is a very real animal. Although currently scientifically unrecognized, these large predators are evidently fairly numerous in the Bluegrass State as they have been, and are often still, encountered by citizens in various locales throughout the entire state. The reclusive panthers have been seen within Kentucky's borders since the state was first settled by rugged pioneers over 200 years ago. Just to attempt a complete listing of the names of eyewitnesses would be an impossible task. The frequency of the early settlers' encounters with the panther is evidenced as well by the many locations which bear the panther's name. An entire county in western Kentucky was named thus because of the many sightings of the beasts by early residents. It would seem that the academics who would scoff at the notion that these big cats exist here should merely travel to the bottomlands of the Bluegrass State and see for themselves.

Since this book attempts to cover many other species of mysterious Kentucky wildlife as well, we will touch only briefly on the mystery of the black panther which, to many researchers, isn't much of a mystery at all and will simply be a matter of time before some bewildered hunter shoots a black panther in the wild and puts the controversy to rest.

I have personally seen these rare animals on two separate occasions, many years apart, and have no doubts whatsoever as to the reality of their existence here. One of these encounters took place in broad daylight, which is highly unusual given these animals' nocturnal natures. Both sightings involved multiple witnesses. The first time I saw one, I was just five years old sitting in the front seat of the family car with my mother. It was around 9 p.m. and completely dark outside. We were returning home to Collins Road in Reed after a PTA meeting at Spottsville Elementary. My older brother and sister, Dean and Diona, respectively, were sitting in the back seat.

As we rounded a curve in the long gravel road that led to our isolated country home, there bounded into the high beams the sleek, totally black figure of a big, slender cat. It was around four to four and a half feet long from nose to tail. My mother immediately screamed. She had seen the black panthers before and heard their frightening screeches in the night, which never failed to send her into a panic every time. In the blink of an eye and two graceful strides the panther crossed the road and disappeared into the night, leaving our shaken mother to drive the remaining distance to our house in terror. We were hurried inside as quickly as possible. I remember clearly the cat's red eye-shine in the headlights. This happened in 1971.

I remember hearing the panther's bone-chilling screams many times as a child. They were high and piercing and sounded for all the world like a woman screaming out in terror or pain. One time, just at dusk, my mother went to call Dean in from the back yard when a panther scream broke the stillness of the quiet country evening. She was so terrified by the sound that she ran back inside and locked the door - with my brother still outside!

My only other experience with these beasts came during a midday stroll near a creek bed in Stanley, Daviess County, with two of my brothers in 1988. We were artifact hunting, walking three abreast along the edge of a field overlooking the creek. It was high summer and the creek was nearly dry, retaining only small, rapidly shrinking puddles of stagnant water every 50 yards or so. On the other side of the creek to our left was a short expanse of trees and thickets which lay very close to the banks of the mighty Ohio River. We were about a quarter mile away from the car, walking in the field with our heads bent and our eyes scanning the ground when suddenly it sounded as if we had startled up a large deer or something from the brush to our immediate left. We all looked up, expecting to see a buck or large doe as it fled into the thicket but what we saw running away from us was something entirely different. To this day, none of us are entirely sure what it was. It resembled a big dog running on all fours, although larger and heavier than just about any dog I've ever seen. It had a long, thick, bushy tail and thick brownish-gray matted fur - not hair - and moved with a surprising speed for such a large animal. So fast was it that, when I looked up, all I saw were its hindquarters as it took two big strides and disappeared into the trees. It made no sound as it retreated, other than its own footfalls in the dry brush, neither growl nor whimper, and I could see heavy muscle masses working the hind legs as it ran. It looked basically, to me at least, like an oversized canine with a wolfish looking tail. I decided it was a large gray wolf. My older brother Dean, who was positioned closest to the creek and, therefore, was afforded the best view of the animal, disagreed. He still states that the creature's front legs were smaller than the back ones, and that its head reminded him, not of a dog at all, but more of a wolverine. Short muzzle. Small pointed ears laid back on its head. He said it must've weighed around 200 lbs.

We immediately began to debate the animal's possible identity and whether or not we should leave the area. After all, we were a long way from the car and not so much as a pocket knife or walking stick between all of us for protection. I was of a mind that since whatever it had been, timber wolf or mutant wolverine, had ran away from us, I saw no reason to let it ruin a perfectly good arrowhead hunt. We decided to go on for a little way farther. So we continued our walk, still excited and not getting much hunting in for all the jabbering - and having no idea at all that something even more bizarre was only seconds away from happening.

About a minute later, a huge dust devil swirled up from the creek about a hundred feet in front of us. The dust cloud drew all our attentions and, although we heard no sounds, we thought it must have been caused by the thing we'd just scared up, so we halted in our tracks. Then, to our complete astonishment, up from the creek leaped a six- or seven-foot-long black panther. We all saw it very clearly and there was no mistake as we stood there, all six eyes wide and three mouths gaping, and watched it lope across the field taking what seemed like leisurely strides of 10 to 12 feet. There was absolutely no doubt in anyone's mind as to the identity of the animal. It was long and skinny, had short, dark hair and a very slender three-foot-long tail.

It looked old and possibly malnourished, covered in dried dirt and dust which gave it a dark gray appearance. Three quarters of the way across the field it leaped over a wide ditch without much visible effort. During its flight from the creek-bed it had turned its head in our direction a single time. We were sure that it had seen us but it continued on without hesitating. However, once it had cleared the ditch, it took only a couple more strides forward and then began to half-circle back in our direction as if it had changed its mind about us. This was pretty much unheard of since we were three in number and it was broad daylight but this didn't change the fact that here we were without weapons of any kind facing the   dilemma of possible attack by a large predatory cat. We were all aware that these cats were not supposed to exist in Kentucky, or the entire country, for that matter, and one might imagine that we all felt somewhat foolish to find ourselves in a predicament of this nature, being both defenseless and about to be run down by a fictional, though hungry-looking, mystery feline but, I assure you, the scientific plausibility of this animal's existence never entered our minds at all.

We were scared as hell as we watched the cat loping forward, not quite so leisurely now. Being unable to come up with anything better, we followed our older brother's example and began to jump up and down screaming at the top of our lungs and generally making as much noise as we possibly could. To our immense relief the tactic worked. All the commotion caused the panther to stop dead in its tracks. It stared at us for a few seconds, then turned around and trotted away, soon disappearing into the large expanse of forest on the other side of Laketown Road toward which it had been originally fleeing.

This time no debate was called for. We beat as hasty a retreat as was possible back to the car and got the hell out of there.

No matter how oft-debated the subject may be by modern academia, the acceptance of the black panther's existence in Kentucky grows with each new witness. Many people who live along the numerous forested watershed and bottomland areas throughout the state are already convinced. Aside from my own personal experiences I have spoken to dozens of other reliable eye-witnesses and heard scores of accounts from all parts of western Kentucky and surrounding areas. Place names and believable reports, however, do not comprise the entire body of evidence concerning the Kentucky panther. At an ancient petroglypic site in Johnson County, a panther is reportedly pictured alongside other animal and human figures. These ancient works of indigenous art support the notion that cats of this nature have roamed the area for an extremely long time.

So are they real, or simply phantoms - variant manifestations of some cosmic trickster having its way with human consciousness? I personally believe, based on what my own experiences, that these animals are real, biological creatures, although I do not dismiss the notion of phantom felines. The town of Russellville, in Logan County played host to a very mysterious feline that was, seemingly, of a different nature. The event ranks as the strangest Kentucky big cat account that I have ran across in recent years. A "Phantom Tiger" was reported there in 1823. It was witnessed more than once, by many local residents and was described as being of gigantic size, striped, with a long tail and eyes the size of dinner plates.

One shaken witness further stated that it had the biggest eyes that he had ever seen on any animal. Shots were fired at the beast, some by excellent marksmen, but no one ever seemed to be able to hit it or, if they did, the bullets had no effect. This gave rise to the notion, as well it should have, perhaps, that the creature was spectral in nature and could not be killed. It was last seen heading south toward Tennessee. To my knowledge, this giant, spectral feline was never again seen in Kentucky.

In Harlan County, a black, saber-toothed panther, complete with 15-inch-long tusks, was seen in the '70s. It reportedly killed a pet cat, and attempted to get in a house by ramming the storm-door, behind which the terrified witness was standing at the time, with its head. Fortunately, the atypical panther was unsuccessful and eventually left. It returned one week later, however, where it was seen by both the heads of household. Strangely, both sightings were accompanied by bizarre, loud clicking sounds, like crickets. No explanation for these unusual feline encounters readily presents itself.

HYENAS IN KENTUCKY

On Aug. 10, 2006, James Berry, 25, a construction worker, was returning home to Uniontown, on Highway 316 shortly after 5 p.m. when he saw what he at first took to be a fawn or a large fox cavorting in a field next to Highland Creek. As he drew closer he realized that the animal he beheld was something he had never seen before. It was brown with black patches, had a tail and was obviously canine. Its ears were dog-like as well, only quite a bit taller. Most peculiar, however, was the way the back sloped down like a giraffe's to the animal's back legs, which were much shorter than the front ones. What Berry was looking at, it immediately occurred to him, was a hyena. There could be no mistaking the animal now frolicking in the field to his right for anything else. Of that he was certain.

When I spoke to Berry, he was convinced of the animal's identity and that he had made no mistake with his observations. It was only about 20 yards away, he told me. In broad daylight, acting as if it was perfectly at home in western Kentucky even though the witness knew good and well that it most definitely was not. He had never heard of anything like it around these parts and it was the last thing he expected to see. Even so, there is some precedent to such sightings of hyenas, or hyena-like cryptids, in the Bluegrass State. The following is from eyewitness Emily Edwards:

"On 4 December, 2004, my husband and I were driving along the expressway near Lexington about 1 p.m. There was a car with emergency flashers on ?the right shoulder. I slowed down as I approached the car and passed it. About 10 feet in front of the car, on the grassy area next to the ?expressway, we saw a strange creature. It looked like a hyena, bluish-gray fur with blackish spots or splotches. It was crouched down as if going to pounce. As our car passed it looked over at us. Its face had a snout and long teeth. It bared its teeth at us and we were so shocked we just drove on. I can't imagine what it was. It was about three feet tall at the shoulder with a sloping back and narrower haunches. Its head was big and it had a fur 'fringe' along its back."

I contacted Edwards regarding her encounter and asked if there was anything else she could add, in retrospect, to the report. She replied:

"You are more than welcome to use (the report). I don't know what else I can add, except that now, nearly two years later, my husband and I are still freaked out by what we saw. It was really a strange feeling to see something so out of place in broad daylight."

Could there be a relict population of hyenas in the Bluegrass State? Some feel that the explanation is simply coyotes or other canids which suffer from a medical condition that withers the hindquarters. This does not address the tall, upright hyena-like ears that were observed, however. It would be no fantastic stretch to suppose that, at some point in Kentucky's past, hyenas might have escaped from captivity and thrived just as the indigenous populations of feral commonwealth canids do. Much the same might be said for the occasional appearances of...

GIANT SNAKES IN KENTUCKY

Some people claim that giant snakes also exist in the Bluegrass State. Snakes of such enormous proportions that the mere sight of one can turn a brave man's heart to stone with fear. They are usually sighted in or very near large bodies of water. Not surprising since snakes of great size such as the boa or anaconda must rely heavily on water to support their large bulk and transport them over long distances. While these types of snakes do indeed grow to enormous lengths, they are not native to North America. There are no known species of great snakes, such as the anaconda, in North America. They have been found here from time to time but, in nearly all instances, it has been assumed that they were merely examples of one-time pets either having escaped from captivity or deliberately set free for one reason or another. This is the accepted zoological viewpoint. But could science be wrong? Does North America have an indigenous species of giant snake? Some say the answer to this question is yes. Although rare, reports of snakes reaching in excess of 20 to 30 feet do exist in this country, and even within the boundaries of Kentucky.

For example, during the Trimble County "monster scare" of the 1960s, residents of nearby Hazel County were out hunting for a 28-foot long snake that was seen there by several witnesses. A snake of this size, they knew, posed a very real and immediate danger not only to livestock and family pets, but to people as well. Especially children. Skeptics, of course, scoffed at the very notion of such a snake. A mistake had obviously been made, they asserted. After all, the hunting party failed to kill, or even see, a snake of that description. Perhaps the locals had seen something normal, a log maybe, and simply mistook it for something else altogether. Although the witnesses actually believed they saw a snake, what they actually saw was, more likely a log. At any Kentucky lake, stream or river, anyone can see snakes that look like sticks and sticks that resemble snakes, but a 30-foot log that can fool more than one person into believing it to be a gigantic snake must surely be one of nature's most amazing anomalies, perhaps even more startling than the notion of the creature itself. Logs, while sometimes clever, stand little chance of evading armed search parties.

Years later, attention was turned to central Kentucky when residents living near Reynolds Lake reported witnessing another unusually large snake - or log, if you prefer. These poor, deluded souls were actually keeping their pets indoors, at least until the hungry log had passed, for fear of them being eaten. Similar reports of possible giant snakes have also come from the Kentucky Lake and Herrington Lake areas.

Many years ago, back in the 1980s, I remember my late uncle James O. Nunnelly telling us that one time, while he and my Aunt Helen were picnicking near a small farm pond in Stanley, Daviess County, the couple had been badly frightened by a movement in the still water. On closer scrutiny they were stunned to see the body of a huge snake slowly sliding over a log. It was a muddy brown color, Uncle Jimmy said. He could make out some type of pattern on its back resembling a rattler's.

"It was the biggest damned snake I ever saw," he told me. "As big around as a six-inch stove-pipe. I had a little ole' .22 pistol with me and Helen jumps up and says, 'shoot it, shoot it!' And I told her, 'Hell no. That would only make it mad. Get to the car.' We watched that ole' snake for awhile before we peeled out. Never did see either end of it."

Another giant snake was allegedly seen in Henderson County, also in the same time period, beneath the Fifth Street overpass across from the old saw mill. Joe W. (full name on file) and a companion claimed to have seen the serpent as it disappeared into its hole. It was also

compared in size to a six-inch pipe. Although rare, snakes of prodigious proportions have been seen in other parts of Kentucky as well but, again, animals such as these have been escaping from their owners, from whatever state, for decades now. Without a carcass to examine, no change in official opinion is likely. Paranormal investigator Jan Thompson shares some interesting accounts concerning this subject. She writes:

'The local stories say that there was a snake that surpassed the famous size of the Amazon anaconda that use to haunt and hunt in the swamps closest to the river. The actual legend I was told began back in the early 1800s when the local Native American tribes warned the new settlers moving into the wetlands territory to keep all their livestock gathered together for safety and not to let the small children wander off too close to the creeks. They told of a giant serpent, the "losa sinti," that slept during the day under the waters and did evil at night by devouring the deer and coyotes. The next day you would find whatever it ate the night before in a disgusting pile where it had spit out the bones.'

Even though these tales of gigantic-sized reptiles abound all throughout Kentucky and have for some decades, no one has obtained a photo of one to date, nor has anyone found a shedding of its skin. Many chalk these accounts up to being just a part of Kentucky's legacy of tall tales that are widely ridiculed, even though most witnesses appear extremely truthful with their reports. Maybe this is the case for this one, as I have yet to interview anyone from this area who has actually seen this anomaly, but I have talked to those who have had relatives who claimed to have seen it. Their descriptions repeated from family traditions varied as to length. Some said it was between 18 to 22 feet; others went all the way up to 30 feet in length.

Another story I heard was that it would come out of the river at night and would follow the swollen creek beds in search of cattle, small game or deer. In each case I listened to, over the course of several years, most of the story contributors did have one similar description in common; it's coloring was black, with light gray triangles repeating down its back, and had a dirty yellow belly, one person added, with black speckles.

One woman of Chickasaw ancestry, whose family originated in the area, told me her grandfather had seen it while plowing their fields one early morning. About a week before, he noticed a single smooth track that traveled arbitrarily through his freshly tilled dirt. This puzzled him, as he knew a motorcycle hadn't made it, because motorcycle tires were too wide, and there hadn't been any tread marks, either. A few mornings later, he discovered what looked like a stack of tractor tires lying out close to the edge of the field. He proceeded to drive his tractor up to inspect the pile, all the while wondering why someone would come all the way out there just to dump some old tires. When he got within 30 feet of them, the three black rubber spheres slowly uncoiled and slithered off into the shadows of the trees.

The woman went on with her story: "There was a solitary fishpond where my mom and I caught a creepy looking fish. It was near the end of autumn one year when we decided to take another shot at fishing there. This time she brought along her snub-nose .38 police revolver because we remembered that we had ran into a few of the local reptiles the last time. We both lugged our tackle boxes and fishing gear back across the fallen tree that served as a makeshift plank that led across a small creek to the side of the pond. Although it was fairly peaceful, a whooping crane startled us once by swooping down and grabbing some dinner from the stagnant water. Nothing was really biting that day so we amused ourselves by carefully working our way around the edges on separate sides. Most of the leaves had already fallen, creating a colorful carpet all around. As we walked we were vigilant to look where we were stepping and took special notice of the ground area around us. Even though winter was right around the corner, this part of Kentucky had very mild autumns and it was still warm enough for the snakes to prowl around. While we were ambling a few feet at a time, both of us noticed that there were a couple of large holes around the pond, I had even placed my tackle box over one of them. They were too large for a frog or a snake, and not quite large enough for beaver. I even placed my foot over one to measure its size and found that it was between seven and eight inches across. We threw suggestions back and forth while casting out our lines, guessing animals like muskrats or otters may have made the holes until I had to go back to my tackle box a few yards away.

Before I reached it I saw that it was gradually vibrating and moving off kilter. After laughing out loud with surprise I hollered over at my mom and jokingly said, 'I think I've trapped a critter in its hole!' She told me to go behind it and lift the handle up with a stout stick just in case whatever was under it might come out pretty ticked off. I obeyed my mom's suggestion and, after lifting the box up about 12 inches, I let it slam back down jumping backwards at the same time with a loud scream. I shrieked out a few choice cuss words and yelled at my mom that we needed to get the hell out of there, 'NOW!' She scrambled gathering up her gear and came around to meet me to see what was going on. We both eyed the tackle box and watched it lightly bounce up and down a few times then it ceased. 'What the hell was under there?' she demanded, and went forward to check it out herself, drawing her gun at the same time. I pleaded with her not to but she persisted and promptly picked up the box. An empty black hole stared back at her. Then she turned her head to look at me questioningly. I explained that I saw the head of a snake, a black one, and it was as almost as big around as the hole. There was no hesitation from then on and we left the pond quite hurriedly and never went back. We assumed that the other holes were either the one snake's alternate routes or there was more then one living in the area. It didn't matter, we were familiar with the breeds of snakes in Kentucky, and knew that they just didn't get that huge.

When we got home and told my stepdad about the incident, we were met with laughter and got poked fun of. But sometime later a few of the neighbors sat and listened with intent and had some stories to tell of their own. Some of the local teenage boys said they used to go down there fishing also. Used to, until they saw the massive snake come in from the woods, ignoring the fishermen, and slide down its muddy inlet. They didn't stay to see how long it was because they ran away as quickly as they could but one did say that it was still slithering downwards by the time they had crossed the plank to the other side of the creek. A farmer's wife down the road said that years ago they found a couple of bizarre tunneled holes out on their property, large enough that a pig could have fit into. Once in a while a young calf, or a runaway pig would be missing but it would show back up a few weeks later as a pile of rotting bones, close to those burrows. Her husband had taken a backhoe down there one time and pushed a rotted carcass down in the hole and then covered it up. About a month later while on a 4-wheeler in the same area he saw the hole opened back up and the left over bones pushed back out."

MORE STRANGE BEASTS

Rowan County, June 1, 2005

Witnesses in the Pine Hill area observed a strange animal as it climbed down from a nearby tree one evening. It was described as being 'bigger than a cat, but smaller than a cougar,' or about the size of a dog. It also had a row of spikes running lengthwise down its back. No possible identity of this climbing critter has been offered. The area has a history of both UFO and cryptid sightings including a giant owl that gave off a yellow glow seen there in November, 2006

GRAVEDIGGER

Occasionally, for the cryptic hunter, coincidence and blind luck combine at just the right moment and bring forth unexpected fruit. Such was the case when, in March 2006, I was contacted by Rose Sinkhorn who had heard mention of my ongoing attempts to collect reports of Kentucky's more mysterious fauna. Sinkhorn had never seen anything of that sort herself, she said, but her first cousin, Terry, had seen some strange things in his life. I was given the contact information by this wonderful lady and, after a couple of attempts, finally succeeded in reaching him. Soon thereafter, we were chatting on the phone like old friends. I found the man to be extremely cordial and easy to speak with. In fact, one year after the initial report below was posted on the kentuckybigfoot.com website we still call each other from time to time to discuss all manner of Forteana and our own personal experiences with these mysteries. A man of devout faith in God, and a damn fine guitar picker, that everything he told me was in the utmost of sincerity I have absolutely no doubt, and I am honored that he calls me "old friend."

Boyle County, 1970
Report from actual witness, Terry. (real name on file)

"Me and a friend went fishing one morning. It was in the spring about 1970. We had to walk a few miles east on the L&N Railroad tracks from Shelby City, Kentucky. It is now Junction City, Kentucky. We would sneak to this pond to bass fish. I had to be home before noon one day, so I started back by myself and left my friend fishing the pond. On the way back down the tracks, this creature landed on the tracks in front of me. When I say landed I mean jumped, because all I saw was a blur and then there it was. It stood about four feet tall and stood or squatted on two legs. It was covered with real fine fur on its fat body. It had a little round head that moved like an owls head almost in circles. It had little round eyes and a mouth full of razor sharp teeth. Its teeth were almost transparent, kinda like a bat's. It sorta favored a bat in the face. It had small ears and a small nose. The thing didn't have any lips, just teeth. Its arms looked like they came out of its chest and they were spindly. It had long fingers and a thumb on each hand with long claws. Its arms didn't have any hair or fur on them. They were slick and oily looking. The thing couldn't see good in the daylight, because it squinted a lot and it never did see me when it landed in front of me. It acted like it was watching for the trains. It would rub its tiny head on its arm every now and then. It looked right at me and couldn't see me and I was only about 30 or 40 feet from it. I could see its fur moving. The creature never made a sound.

I was dumbfounded. I'd never saw anything like it before and haven't since. I wasn't scared at first, but I wasn't really sure what to expect. I had a tackle box in one hand and a fishing rod in the other, but I did have my hunting knife with me. As I tried to switch my fishing rod over to my other hand so I could get to my hunting knife, I rattled my tackle box and that's when this thing heard me. It leaned forward and squinted its eyes and when it saw me it reared back and kinda puffed up. I thought it was going to attack me, so I jerked my knife out. When I did this thing took off so fast it was like a blur. In one leap or jump it cleared a fence about 40 feet away and was gone. I shook my head because I couldn't believe how fast this thing could move. I took off running up to where it leaped the fence but I never saw it again. I never did see this thing's legs, because it squatted all the time, but they sure were powerful. This thing could have easily gotten me if it wanted to. I believe it only comes out at night and just by chance I got to see it. Maybe it was headed to its home or den after a night of hunting or whatever it does. I have thought about it and I believe it burrows in the ground like a groundhog. Because not far from where I saw this thing is an old family cemetery plot with slab graves and a rock wall around it. There are huge holes all in this cemetery under the graves. If a groundhog had dug these they couldn't see anything sneaking up on them because of the wall around them, but it could still be ground hogs I guess.

My grandmother told me of a thing the old people call a "Gravedigger" and it moves real fast and digs in graveyards but I don't know. I know I saw this strange creature and it has to stay somewhere. Another man I know saw it one night run across the road in front of him and it only paused for a second to look at him and then it was gone. The way he described it, it was just like what I saw. He said he's never seen anything move so fast in his life, especially on two legs. This was also on the L&N Railroad tracks about 12 miles from where I saw it. It was in Parksville, Kentucky, where he saw it. The strange thing, it was near a cemetery as a matter of fact. That's where it came from when it ran in front of him. When I saw this creature it was a beautiful spring morning, the sun was shining and I watched it for what seemed to be 10 minutes or more, I could have watched it longer if I hadn't made any noise. If I'd only had a camera."

I spoke to Terry on March 31, 2007, during the course of a couple hours long phone interview. He is sure of what he saw and, with further correspondence, I was able to produce a sketch of the animal under his close direction. Although the legs and feet rendered are purely speculative as the witness' view of the lower portions of the creature was blocked by a length of railroad tracks, the upper portions of the body are exact. I urged him to provide all the details he possibly could and he further related to me:

"The creature's arms looked like they came right out of it's chest, it didn't have shoulders. I couldn't see its legs because it was squatted and its feet and legs were hidden by the rail. When it landed in front of me it just crouched down. Its legs couldn't have been very long, but they sure were powerful, to move like it did. It didn't have a tail. I couldn't make out the pupils of its eyes, its eyes were very small and round and they were very dark, maybe not completely black but almost. Its face looked mean and curious. The thing blinked a lot, it would squint its eyes as if it couldn't see very good in the daylight. Its snout or

Sketch of the Gravedigger that was done by the witness

nose didn't protrude, it had a pug nose and was dark brown, no fur on it. It did favor a bat in the face. Its teeth were razor sharp and very close together. It had perfect teeth and a bunch of them. They were almost clear. I guess they looked like that because they were so sharp and thin. Like a bat's teeth. It looked like they were all the same length, but the upper teeth almost covered the lower ones up. It had a fat body, its head looked too small for its body and there was no neck.

When it finally saw me, it leaned forward quite a bit and squinted at me like it was trying to make out what I was, then it was gone like a speeding bullet. This thing's head turned like an owl's head almost in a complete circle. It had long slender arms and very long fingers with long black sharp claws, actually thy looked like fingernails. It had knuckles on its fingers. There were three fingers and a thumb. Its skin on its arms looked oily and real dark brown, about the color of used motor oil. Its fingers moved constantly. Its fur was real fine I could see it moving when the wind blew. Every now and then it would raise its arm and rub the side of its head like it was scratching, but it always moved its head towards its arm, it never would move its arm very far, it always kept them straight out in front of it. Its ears were little and short. I could barely see them above the fur. Its fur was darker on the ends and the closer it got to the body the lighter it got. Some places were grayish in color. It looked like it didn't have any lips at all. Just mostly upper teeth in a straight line and extremely sharp. Its nose was just a small button like nose with two nose holes. It didn't have a chin. This will be hard to describe, but its thumbs were on the bottom on both hands, it almost looked like it had two right hands, its fingers were on the top and it looked like its arms came out of its chest, and they were closer together. I guess its hands looked like they were backwards, but it had long slender fingers on top of each hand and a thumb on the bottom and both thumbs were on the same side if you know what I mean."

His parents and grandparents knew of this thing as well, Terry told me, and, according to them, it was called a "Gravedigger." It was common belief, among the older folks of the area, that these things traditionally made their homes in old graveyards and survived by eating the decomposed flesh of cadavers. They were also said to be nocturnal in nature, and it was an extremely rare occasion to see one.

The actual length of time during the sighting and the amount of details concerning the creatures appearance is unprecedented and, as I was preparing the sketch of this animal under his direction, it struck me that I had never before heard or read of anything resembling it in over 20 years of cryptid research. This was something totally new on the cryptozoological lists and thus seemed likely a highly localized phenomenon. Perhaps these strange creatures exist nowhere else on earth but central, Kentucky. One wonders.

"I was only about 40 feet away from this thing," Terry told me. "I couldn't see any legs at all. They must have been folded up in under it. All I saw was its body sitting on the ground and the rail wasn't tall enough to hide much. It's been over 30 years since I saw it. I was only about 15 years old and I was dumbfounded when I saw it. I couldn't believe what I was seeing and, after all these years, I still lie in bed at night trying to envision this thing again. I guess it put me in a daze when I saw it."

The animal seen was apparently myopic or, at the very least, near sighted which tends to support the belief that it may spend most of its time in low lighting conditions such as would be expected underground. Far more difficult to explain, however, is the extremely unusual, even bizarre, way the it was described to move around. No animal of this size, to my knowledge, is capable of producing 40-foot jumps from a complete standstill. Moreover, Terry later explained that when it jumped, or hopped, these great distances it accomplished the feat in such a quick manner that it appeared to him as "just a blur" of motion. It moved so fast, and quietly, that he never even saw where it came from. This unnerved him most about the encounter. He just couldn't see how a natural animal could move like that. It seemed impossible.

So, could there be any more reports of these creatures from the Bluegrass State? When we first posted the Gravedigger sighting I was in hopes that it would encourage other possible witnesses to come forward and, occasionally, a report is submitted that does bear at least a partial resemblance.

The following cryptid report was sent to kentuckybigfoot.com on April 16, 2006. It has been edited for spelling and grammatical errors.

1. Your first name: Billy
2. Which county: Pike
3. Estimated date : June 1990
4. Estimated time: between noon and 3 p.m.
5. What city, or nearest city: Dorton on Caney Hill

6. Length of time the encounter lasted:: 10 minutes
7. How many witnesses: just myself'

8. Please describe your encounter:
'When I was a young teenager, I was walking up in the hills behind my parents' house. Their house is nestled deep into the mountainside down in a valley in the eastern Kentucky hills. So any way that you walk, you walk pretty much straight up into the mountains. After making the uphill climb, the ground levels out a bit and goes on for miles of very thick, dense forest. I spotted what I thought was a very large white dog from behind about 20 yards from where I was standing. It was just a quick glimpse and I didn't know at the time that what I had just seen was much ,much bigger than a dog. It was broad daylight and summer so the brush and trees were very overgrown, and I would occasionally see glimpses of it again making its way through the forest. I began to call out to it, "here puppy," and follow it up into the hillside.

It must have been moving pretty fast because I then lost sight of it for about five minutes and continued to walk in the same direction. It was then that I came to a very large bush. The bush was directly in my path, so I had to go around it. When I did, I was in for the surprise of my life. When I peered around the corner my heart stopped. There in front of me, less than five feet away, was a creature I had never before seen or imagined. This was NOT a dog. It was white and covered with hair. It was standing up on two legs hunched over with small arms very high on its body. It didn't really have shoulders. The arms were much like that of a kangaroo. It was at eye level with me but in quite a hunch, which puts it at about 7 feet tall if it were standing fully erect. We stood face to face and made full eye contact for what feels like hours, neither one of us moving a muscle. The encounter probably only lasted five to 10 seconds before I turned and ran as fast as I could down the mountain. I was terrified. Its eyes were fire red and the way they stared into mine felt as though it was taking something from me. The terror took my breath away.

I kept this story to myself for quite some time until I met another guy who began to tell me of his experience with a similar creature. Over the past 16 years I have gradually heard several other stories here in the hills. Right now I am actually aware of eight or nine other people who have had personal experiences with this creature or one like it in the surrounding area where I live. It still doesn't make me less freaked out by what I saw. As far as I know, I have had the closest encounter with it.

Here are a few brief details of other stories I have heard from people in this area: Several men had seen this creature on railroad tracks up near Penny Road in Virgie. A friend of mine used to tease me about my experience until he saw it perched in a tree at Dark Holler up near Penny Road off of US-23. He then apologized! Another friend saw it from behind running down the creek. A friend's mother and sister saw a white creature on two legs jump off a ledge in the cut-through and bound across the four-lane right in front of them. (This was on US-23 at Esco.) It turned and looked at them before it headed down into the ditch and out of sight. As I am writing this, I'm aware at how crazy this all sounds! And how surreal. It's not something we talk about much around here, but these stories come out from time to time. And then you hear other people who have had, or know people who have had, encounters with a mysterious white beast.

Another thing to note is that all of these sightings took place within five to 10 miles of each other. They were all near railroad tracks and/or coalmines. I was remembering this experience tonight when a friend of mine decided to look up online any stories about a white

A Kentucky Gravedigger, illustrated by the author, based on the accounts of eyewitnesses

creature in the hills. Needless to say we happened upon this site. When I saw the story about the Gravedigger I nearly lost it. I never had a thought about the graveyard at all. But, (it's giving me chills to type this right now and to realize this tonight) my sighting was between 50 and 100 yards from a very old family graveyard up in the hills. I know what I saw was real. Before I had heard the other stories, I wanted to keep it to myself, and still not many people know my story.'

9. Describe the creature with detail:
'The best way to generally describe this creature is that it was human-like and animal-like at the same time. Its body was about 7 feet tall, with a long, oval-shaped canine-like torso mostly covered in thick white hair, much like the hair of a long-haired dog. It had a human-looking expression. When I first saw it from behind I noticed a tail. Its head was shaped much like a human head. It had long white hair, longer than on the rest of the body. Its face was sort of pug-like, similar to the snout of a bat. It had less hair on face than on the rest of body (more skin like.) The skin on face a bit darker in color and rough-looking. Its eyes were pure bright red, like fire. Its nose was very much like a bat nose. Its ears were very human-like and small on the sides of the head with a bit of white hair as well. I couldn't see any lips really just a closed mouth under a snout-like protrusion. Its arms were short and very thin- kangaroo like. Its hands were bony and thin, yet covered with thin tufts of white fur/hair. (Kind of like a very hairy man's hands only white) The palms were curled under so I didn't get to see the fingers, but from first glance they were more human-like than animal-like. Thin legs with less hair than on the rest of the body but it was a softer more fine hair than on the back. The creature was hunched up on hind legs. The fur on the legs was much like the underside of a dog's belly The feet were long and human-like with fine thin fur much like on the legs. It didn't make a

sound or any movement at all once we were face to face. When I think of its deep breathing I get chills. It was not panting, and it was not afraid. It was curious and seemed as shocked as I was.'

10. Additional Info: Area, Sounds, Etc.: 'Thick dense forest area in the hills of eastern Kentucky. There are railroad tracks and a graveyard nearby. I would not have thought to mention these, but so many other encounters seem to have the same details.'

Aside from obvious differences in height and length of hair, this creature sounds much like a Gravedigger. Until you consider the description of the eyes. "Pure bright red eyes like fire." Since this encounter happened in broad daylight, one would expect no eye shine of any sort to be mentioned in this instance. Yet Billy was very adamant when I spoke with him that he had described the appearance of the eyes accurately. They were very frightening and, after looking into them, all he could think about was getting away from them.

"Glowing red eyes," although largely atypical, are more commonly reported during sightings of this nature, especially in Kentucky, than many researchers seem willing to admit. Roughly one-quarter of Kentucky reports include mention of apparently self-illuminating eyes. What this means, of course, is a matter of conjecture, but this trait is historically, and most typically, reported in association with manifestations of entities regarded as being supernatural, or even demonic, in nature.

In any event, I forwarded the report to the original Gravedigger witness and this was his response:

"I enjoyed our talk today on the phone. I also read the encounter you sent, it sure sounds a whole lot like what I saw. Maybe it's of the same species but different, like monkeys. You know they can look different and come in different sizes. I have relatives that live in the eastern part of Kentucky and there's a lot of thick forests for a critter to hide in there. Maybe more people than we know have seen the Gravedigger.

My buddy called me today and said that lady showed him how to get to that graveyard, So we went and checked it out. We found a graveyard but it's not the same one I found. Actually I already knew about this one and it's not that far from the other one. We did take pictures of the old tombstones and sunken graves. All of them were in the 1800s. I don't know the name of this graveyard though. I found it years ago and it has Civil War soldiers buried there.

We decided to drive to the airport and ask if we could look for the Givens Graveyard, that's next to where I saw the critter. They let us look, but the man said the graveyard was gone, because they extended the runway. He was right it is gone. He said they moved it, but he didn't know where to. I couldn't find a trace of it. I believe our best bet is to look along the creeks nearby. I doubt if the airport would let us camp on their property anyway. They extended the runway for what looks like a mile. Nothing is the same there now. There is a six-foot-high fence all around the area where I saw the critter. But you never know, it might not be far from where I saw it, because there is still a lot of places around nearby for it to hide. I still think our best bet is the creek that is nearby. Who knows that might be where it lived anyway and I just saw it coming in from a night's hunt.

Getting to the original place where I saw it is practically useless now, there's nothing there but an airport runway. Though where the tracks used to be there is still tree lines, like there was, but mostly grassland. The farmers have really cleaned the place up. I'm gonna keep checking the creek nearby. Thanks for sending the story, I really enjoyed it. Mister

(Above) A possible Gravedigger print from Boyle County. The knives and coins are included to show the scale and size of the print. (Photo by witness)

(Left) A close-up view of the print.

Gravedigger has to be around here somewhere. All we have to do is find him."

At my request, Terry revisited the scene of the encounter to explore the nearby creeks for evidence of possible cryptid activity. Below is the update that was posted soon after:

'Earlier this month (April 2006) Boyle County witness T.W. returned to the area where he had seen the Gravedigger over three decades earlier. He was accompanied by a longtime friend who brought along his video camera to record anything of interest such as possible tracks. While they were walking down the middle of a creek, just across the Lincoln County line, they came across a large fish laying near the bank. It was gutted and the head had been devoured. None of the meat had been eaten. They left the creek and walked up into an adjacent field where they discovered two strange-looking tracks situated over five feet apart. The prints were measured, recorded on both video and still camera and show a four-toed, clawed impression four and a half inches long by four inches wide. It resembles that of a large dog, or wolf, with some peculiar differences - like the spacing between the toes, which is awkward, and a squared-off heel.'

Canids are known to walk toes first and their prints often reveal indistinct heal marks (see red wolf photo.) In contrast, the Lincoln County print looks as if the heel touched the ground first and rolled forward. A careful search of the field yielded no more prints, which suggests to some that whatever left the two tracks probably walked bipedally and was apparently capable of jumping some distance. The witness stated that he weighs approx.180 lbs. and he hardly left any impression at all in the dirt.

The investigation remains ongoing.

Later, after reviewing the video his friend took that day, they noticed an anomalous dark figure standing a good distance out in one of the adjacent fields, although neither of them had seen it at the time of their visit to the location. Both witnesses feel sure that it is something unusual, perhaps even the animal which made the prints but, unfortunately, it is standing too far away from the camera to make out any details. I viewed the footage a couple of weeks later and found it inconclusive at best. However, since the area of the area has a history of cryptid and other phenomenal activity, more visits, with camera in hand, are planned for the Spring of 2007.

The following report was submitted in mid-December 2006:

1. Your first name: 'A.' (real name on file)
2. Which county: Martin County
3. Estimated date: 2001
4. Estimated time: 1 minute
5. What city, or nearest city: Inez
6. Length of time the encounter lasted: five minutes
7. How many witnesses: 4

8. Please describe your encounter:
'Dad and I were coon hunting. We stood outside our truck that was stuck in the mud. We called for the dogs to come back, however, the dogs would only come so close to us and the truck. They turned around and ran. We heard something going around in a circle like it was hopping. So dad and I got in the vehicle. Two friends of the family were on the ridgetop signaling with headlights of their vehicle to find where we were at. Dad turned on his headlights to signal back and when the lights came on the creature appeared standing in front of the vehicle. We stared at it and IT stared back.'

9. Describe the creature with detail:
'It was a creature of about 6-1/2 feet tall (hunched over.) The creature had yellow eyes, with a long snout, and sharp teeth about three inches long. It walked on two legs, but hopped like a kangaroo. Its fur was long and dark brown.'

10. Additional Info: Area, Sounds, Etc.: Nat's Creek, Ky. Hops instead of footsteps'

During a follow-up interview conducted by my kentuckybigfoot.com partner and fellow bigfoot researcher Charlie Raymond, a series of questions was asked.

Thursday, December 14, 2006 8:24 p.m.
Subject : encounter

1. Did it look more like an ape, human or kangaroo?
It had the body of a kangaroo, kind of hunched over.

2. If you saw its teeth, was it because it was angry?
I don't think so. We caught in the headlights so it may have just been startled.

3. Did it have a conical shaped head, long arms and was it muscular?
It had the snout like a dog, not as long as some. More like a boxer (with) a kind of smashed nose.

4. Did it have hands and feet?
Yes it had hands. I didn't really see if it had feet at the time.

5. Did it have pointed ears on top of its head, like a dog?
Yes, it basically was a kangaroo-bodied dog.'

A kangaroo-bodied, bipedal dog? It is interesting to note that in the previous two reports both witnesses remarked on the apparently kangaroo-like features of the animals they saw. It is possible that these are not related to the Gravedigger creatures at all, despite the resemblances, but belong to the "Phantom Kangaroo" group. These sometimes terrifying beasts have been reported sporadically across the midwest for many years. One 1934 account from Hamburg, Tennessee tells of a "giant kangaroo" which was "lightning fast" and fond of killing and devouring large dogs.

Noted cryptozoologist, author and publisher, Chad Arment, in a personal communication, had this to say concerning the Gravedigger subject:
'Interesting story. First impressions: doesn't sound morphologically like a burrowing animal. The holes sound like groundhog holes (and being familiar with groundhogs, they don't really care where they dig.) The Gravedigger folklore is an extension of European folklore, probably passed down from immigrant relations (there's a cryptozoological/folklore mystery animal over in the U.K. called a cemetery dog or something like that, its in one of Karl Shuker's books). The animal itself, if thinking where to look for it, I'd say look for ecological/morphological similarities: think similar to aye-aye, possibly tree dweller. Long fingers for grubs in dirt or tree-bark, etc. Lots of small primates have sharp teeth. Would explain the leaping. You know, Ron Schaffner looked into a medium-sized or small leaping primate report from southern Ohio, I can't remember what Loren Coleman put it under in his field guide to mystery primates, maybe devil monkey. That might be a possible southeastern state correlation. Hard to say.'

Though the whole affair may sound a bit "folkloric" to most people, it is wise to remember that there is often some basic kernel of truth in much folklore.

Perhaps creatures such as these were responsible for the European "ghoul" legends of old, passed down, as Mr. Arment suggests, from one generation of new world settlers to the next. There is no doubt, however, that with such sharp teeth and lightning quickness, these things could, and probably do, eat pretty much whatever they choose to. Good thing for us living Kentuckians, then, that they are content with their alleged consumption of the flesh of the dead.

DEVIL MONKEYS

In 1831, in Jessamine County, a man named Patrick Flournoy reported that, while descending a cliff on the east side of the Kentucky River, he came upon a most unusual creature in seeming repose on a ledge below him. On reaching the ledge, Flournoy saw that it was large and hairy with a long, bushy tail. It sprang up into a nearby tree when approached, using its tail to climb as well as its hands and feet. Bizarrely, it had only one large, white eye set into the middle of its forehead.

In Clinton, Kentucky, in 1973, a man named Charlie Stern witnessed a similar creature with a bushy tail attack and kill his livestock. This one had two eyes, however, and was apparently immune to gunfire. It ran away on two legs leaving nine-toed tracks behind.

In 1991 I was squirrel hunting with my brothers and friends in a densely forested area beside the Ohio River known as Horseshoe Bend, in Henderson County, when a similar animal, though on a much smaller, less frightening scale, presented itself to my view. We had all spread out to cover more ground and I took the outside left position. All the hunters were at least 20 yards apart and after a few minutes of walking I could no longer hear or see anyone else from my group. I remember hunkering down for a brief rest when I heard a noise to my right. I turned and saw an animal running in my direction which I at first took to be a large squirrel that the others had managed to scare my way. As it drew nearer, however, I could see that it was something that I'd never seen before in all my years in the

An illustration of the Devil Monkey that was witnessed by the author in 1991

woods. It was about three times larger than a squirrel, dark-haired with lighter colored hair - almost white - on its undersides. It had a long tail, nearly twice the length of its body, which it held straight up as it ran. The hair on its body was much shorter than the hair on the tail. I was immediately struck by the unusual way that it ran, which wasn't at all like a squirrel. It bounded along in great leaps with all four feet touching and leaving the ground simultaneously. It saw me as I stood up, thumbing back the hammer of the 12-gauge, and bolted out in front of me and to my left, instantly doubling its speed.

Reacting as a hunter, I gave chase and managed to squeeze off a shot at the animal but apparently missed as it never wavered a single stride. I was astounded at its swiftness and by the way it so easily outdistanced me. A few seconds later I broke into a small clearing just in time to see the critter leap well over 10 feet up into the branches of a large tree and, without the slightest pause, jumped a couple more times upward and was lost to view. I could here it jumping from tree to tree, racing away like a bolt through the upper branches.

Admittedly, this animal struck me as resembling more of a rodent than anything else. But when it reached the trees it seemed even faster and more at ease than on the ground. Its ability to utilize the trees as a method of travel in such a way as I witnessed was amazing and would've put any monkey on the planet to shame. I have never seen any animal capable of such rapid locomotion and, to this day, still have no idea as to its possible identity. Do you?

Website submission on March 19, 2007:

1. Your first name: Jeff
2. Which county: Jefferson
3. Estimated date: Jan. 29, 2007
4. Estimated time: 9:50 p.m.
5. What city, or nearest city: Jeffersontown
6. Length of time the encounter lasted: about two minutes
7. How many witnesses: 1

8. Please describe your encounter:
'While getting in my car to go to work I looked in the street and saw what appeared to be a large dog walking down the street about sixty feet away from me walking towards a dead end. As I said, at first I thought it was a large dog so I started to walk towards it just to see what it was. There are not many street lights out so it was hard to see. I got within about 20 feet of it and it ran between two houses. It never turned towards me or acknowledged my presence in any other way'

9. Describe the creature with detail: 'It was about three and a half to four feet tall and pretty thin so I would say it weighed about 70 or 80 pounds. Its front legs were shorter than its back legs and it walked with its rear end in the air. It had a flat face with no visible ears or a tail. It was too dark to tell if it was covered with hair or not. If it was it had to be short. It walked like a person would if they tried to walk on all fours. '

10. Additional Info: Area, Sounds, Etc.: 'Two days later I decided to go looking around the neighborhood to see if I could find anything or see it again. I didn't see it but I did find a strange footprint in the mud about a half a mile from my house. I made a plaster cast of the foot and it doesn't look like anything I've ever seen. I run my own paranormal investigation

group and I put the picture on my website along with a report .

It is probably possible that it was a sickly animal of some sort but then I don't know where the print came from or even if it's from the same animal. I don't think anyone would go through the trouble to plant this print by my house but, if they did, then they sure baffled me.'

Nelson County - mid-1800s

MYSTERIOUS ANIMAL AS SEEN BY HARRY SMITH ON THE SALT RIVER:

'Smith and Tom Hardman were fishing on a creek known as Dutchman Creek, 23 miles east of Louisville, which empties into the Salt River. This fishing tour was in the night. After fishing for some time, a terrible noise was heard like distant thunder. Rocks and pebbles could be heard tumbling down the bank. The earth trembled, and looking down the creek from the bridge, they discerned a huge animal resembling a dog. It was spotted and about eight feet in length, and four feet high. It was coming up to them on the bridge. The animal had no head or tail, and nothing seemed to stop it in its course. On went this mysterious animal up the creek, rocks were heard tumbling a mile away. This mysterious phenomenon was, and is to this day, a wonderful mystery to Smith. As he never could account for its appearance. He being a man of great nerve it did not frighten him as it would many others.'

Could this early account be referring to a possible Bigfoot walking on all fours? Since it was dark at the time of the sighting, it is possible that the head was simply in such a position as to render it unnoticeable. Furthermore, as it was described as being eight feel long and four feet high, the chances of any type of canine identification for this animal seems very unlikely. Smith, a runaway slave, might be forgiven for comparing this creature to one with which he was more familiar.

From: *'Fifty Years of Slavery in the United States,'* by Harry Smith

CRYPTIDS ON THE WING: KENTUCKY THUNDERBIRDS

Report Submitted to www.kentuckybigfoot.com on Oct. 10, 2005

Date: 2005
County: Bullit
City: unknown
Length of Sighting: 30 seconds
Number of Witnesses: 3

Encounter:
'After returning home from a trip to Bernheim Forest on a very windy day, I looked out the window to see a large bird in a field with some cows. The bird was standing just a few yards from an Angus bull that was full-grown. The ground was very level so the (following) measurement in height is very accurate. A gust of wind came and the bird leapt up in the air and started flying away. I saw it flying for about five seconds so I had time to judge the size

because one wing was longer than the bull.'

Description:
'It was 4½ to 5 feet tall (and) had a falcon's head and feathers, not skin, covering it. There was black on the top of it and brown on the belly. The tail was white and there were white speckles on the wingtips. The wingspan was 14 to 16 feet in width. The talons were very dark and I didn't look at them very well but the wings were just like a predatory bird's not a scavenger's - as in made for speed. They were in a triangle unlike the box (shape) that vulture's wings form.'

Additional Information:
There were other very common birds in the area as well because the wind made it a good day for large birds to fly.'

I spoke to E.D. (real name on file) on several occasions soon after the report was filed. He seemed to be an intelligent young man and was very sincere about what he'd seen. All three people in the car, he told me, saw the thing and were sure that it was no ordinary bird of any type.

It was absolutely huge. When it spread its wings to fly, the bird was easily twice the size of the bull, which he estimated to be about seven feet long. He was familiar with the different birds common to the area and was absolutely sure that this was not one of them.

Of all the personal sightings of unknown animals that I have been fortunate enough to experience throughout my life, the one my wife and I saw in the skies of Smith Mills, in Henderson County, easily ranks as, hands down, the strangest thing that I've ever seen. If there was ever one time that I truly regret not having a camera of some sort with me, this is it. It happened on Saturday, April 11, 1998 and yet it seems like only a couple of years, at most, could have passed since the incident took place. At the same time, what we saw was so bizarre that it's almost as if it were a dream. It would be much easier to explain if it were, but we both know, for good or ill, that it was real.

We were, on that day, enjoying a leisurely country drive through the bottom lands on the outskirts of Henderson County just outside Geneva, on Klondike Road in the little hamlet of Smith Mills. We were familiar with the area, as we were with nearly every back road to be found along the Ohio and Green River bottoms in Henderson, having roamed these places nearly my entire life in search of prime fishing and/or Indian artifact hunting spots. As occasion would have it, a series of strong tornadoes and thunderstorms had ripped through the area only a couple of days previously, leaving a terrible swath of destruction and tragedy in their wakes. The fields were still muddy from the heavy rain, the road saturated and we drove along slowly, careful to avoid the ruts in the gravel road and the occasional downed tree-limb. We stopped briefly at a pull-off at the edge of Highland Creek to enjoy the forested, swampy scenery and skip a few rocks on the water before returning to the car and heading back. Our four-year-old son was at the babysitter's and I was always hesitant about being away from him for too long at such a tender age. We had driven only a few minutes when my wife, who was looking up and out the passenger window, said, "Look at this crazy idiot. Who does he think he is, the Red Baron?" I paid her little attention at first, occupied as I was with driving and all. We had been together for nearly 10 years at that point and, I'm somewhat ashamed to admit that I had, very cleverly I thought, almost perfected the art of ignoring her completely without her even knowing it. A few seconds later, still looking out the window, she reiterated her request and added " What the hell...is that a hang-glider?"

I knew there were no hang-gliders anywhere near Henderson, it being primarily low ground, but there were plenty of ultra-lites and this was what I had already, almost instantly, concluded that she was seeing. This puzzled me. We had seen the contraptions hundreds of times as they made their noisy way about the

An early depiction of the legendary "bird who devours men", the Piasa Bird of Alton, Illinois. Such aerial anomalies have also been reported in the Bluegrass State

western Kentucky skies. I wondered why she was having trouble recognizing one now. City girls..."Look honey," she said again. "Is this an airplane or what?" Seeing nothing to do but oblige her, I grudgingly leaned toward her and glanced quickly up and out her window. It was only a quick glance, mind you, but what I saw startled the hell out of me. So much so that I looked again, trying not to run off the narrow country road and into the ditch. What I saw sailing above the trees across a field some 60 yards away was no hang-glider, ultra-lite or airplane, but some sort of giant, bird-like "thing" as it casually glided down toward the treetops as if preparing for a landing. It was completely red in color and unlike anything I had ever seen before. I stole another quick glance in utter astonishment. "That's no plane," I said. "It's some kind of bird!"

I slowed down and looked again as the thing banked to the right, still descending at about ten feet above the treetops. By the time I got the car stopped it was rapidly disappearing over the trees and was soon completely out of sight. From the few brief glances I managed I could see that this creature had no feathers either on its wings, body or legs. Its skin was leathery looking and wrinkly like an elephant's and reflected the sunlight somewhat. It's legs and feet were like those of any large raptorial bird such as an eagle or hawk, but smooth. The only growth being a line of reddish-brown hair about five or six inches long that encircled its feet just above the ankles. I could tell it was hair because it rippled in the wind. The wings of this thing struck me as quite being quite odd. They seemed far too long and skinny to actually attain and/or sustain flight. They were shaped atypically as well. A fairly close comparison would be to a plucked chicken wing stretched out to its full length. I could also see why my wife had at first taken it to be an airplane of some type - its wingspan had to have been at least 20 feet!

Whereas I was only able to get a few quick looks at the creature my wife had the opportunity to study it almost at leisure. Due to its immense size she just could not associate it with any living animal until I told her that was what it was. Then she became very scared. As it did appear to be coming in for a landing in the trees I wanted to get out and give chase but she wouldn't hear of it. Looking back, that was probably the best advice I'd had all day. Since I wasn't able to see the head and tail of this thing I immediately began asking my wife questions regarding what she'd seen. The head looked prehistoric, she said. It had a short, thick neck - not skinny - and a long, stout looking beak. On top of its head was a bony looking protrusion about a foot long, knobby and round. Its tail was "like a lizard's," only tightly curled into a loop beneath it. The tail ended with a short phalange on top. She could also see that the wings were thin, with blue veins showing near the tips. I was stunned that she had just described a pterosaur to me.

I cannot honestly say that I know what this flying mystery animal was other than it resembled some type of modern day pterodactyl. We never reported the sighting to authorities, needless to say. Who would've believed us? And I'm aware of no others who claim to have seen it in the area. In fact, as of this writing, I know of not a single other instance of pterosaur sightings within the boundaries of the Bluegrass State. Regardless of this, I must conclude due to personal experience that these aerial anomalies are present in Kentucky or, at very least, make the occasional rare side-trip here.

DOG ATTACKED BY "BIG BIRD"

Burlington, Kentucky (AP) - A five-pound puppy remains in critical condition today while wildlife experts try to decide whether it was attacked by an American bald eagle. ?Mrs. Greg Schmitt, Rabbit Hash, Kentucky said the beagle was snatched from her farm and dropped in a pond 600 yards away. Mrs. Schmitt said she did not see the incident but that a seven-year-old neighbor boy did. He said it was a "big bird" which took the puppy skyward. The veterinarian, Dr. R. W. Bachmeyer, of Walton, Kentucky, said wounds on the puppy might have been caused by talons. Source: *Cincinnati Enquirer*; Sept. 2, 1977

From paranormal investigator Jan Thompson:
"I was told from a third party, that this event happened about three years ago along the Trace, the main road that travels through he middle of LBL It was a sunny afternoon in late summer, and two elderly women where traveling south towards Cadiz to do some antique shopping. They had just passed the Golden Pond area. Up ahead about a quarter of a mile, they suddenly noticed what appeared to be a man standing in the middle of the road facing them. As they drew nearer to him, they realized that he was not going to move and the driver started slowing her vehicle down. The closer they got to the figure the more perplexed they became as his image developed into something more sinister, which they later described as a "demon from Hell," It stood well over 7 feet tall, was of a well-defined muscular build, and didn't appear to have any clothes on. Its skin was a dark grayish-green with a bumpy texture like ostrich hide but one of the women reported that some of its flesh had a scaly appearance like a carp. They said it had huge ruby eyes, the size of eggs, that bulged outward from its brow, a large flared nose and ears that were pointed upwards along with a wide pencil thin mouth. The car almost came to a complete stop within 20 feet of this entity when both women were greeted with an even more astonishing image. The creature rapidly threw out its arms from its side revealing a set of leathery wings, jumped up into the air, swooped directly over their car and flew away behind them.

The rest of their journey was hurried until they reached the outskirts of Cadiz. There they stopped at a small diner to sit in bewilderment and mull over what they had just been through. Some nearby patrons saw how upset and shaken the two women were and asked if they could be of some assistance. The women readily told their story, crying all the while with obvious fright. The two sat there for nearly two hours until they felt calm enough to proceed with their trip but they did not do any shopping that day. Witnesses said they asked for directions back to where they had driven to avoid going back up the Trace.

There are other reports around the same area of a being, or beings, of a similar description. One notable story came from a truck driver back in the mid 1970s and the details are about the same. Another story was from around the 1920s but this time it was seen further north up the Trace closer to Grand Rivers."

VII. THE MOST MYSTERIOUS KENTUCKIAN

Since Kentucky became the 15th state on June 1, 1792, hundreds of Bluegrass natives have gone on to become world-renowned personalities in areas such as politics, film, music, literature, art and sports. But, without a doubt, the most mysterious, enigmatic and influential person ever to walk from the Kentucky foothills and emerge into public scrutiny was a man named Edgar Cayce.

Edgar Cayce

He was born on March 18, 1877 on a farm near Hopkinsville in Christian County, and achieved fame not in politics, sports or the fine arts, but by the immense and seemingly boundless psychic abilities which he only seemed to possess while asleep. Abilities of which he retained no memory when conscious. Abilities which still serve the good of mankind even now, more than 60 years after his death.

What was so special about this individual which set him apart from all the other self-proclaimed spiritualists of his day? For one thing, while in a self induced trance, or sleep state, Cayce discovered that his unconscious mind possessed the uncanny ability to travel to any location on earth and describe it in perfect detail. Remote viewing is nothing new, you may say, but that's not all. When given only the name and address of any individual anywhere in the world, Cayce's sleeping mind could somehow locate that person, examine him (or her) both internally and externally and diagnose in minute, extremely accurate detail and precise medical terminology every physical ailment that existed in that particular body as well as the medicines and methods needed for a complete recovery. No illness or its cure, whether minor or complex, was out of this Kentuckian's view or beyond his dissertations.

As word of his abilities spread like wildfire, thousands of people suffering from all manner of medical afflictions from the common cold to major diseases such as polio, cancer, tuberculosis and multiple sclerosis, called upon the humble man to perform his unconscious medical miracles. He was equally at ease diagnosing cases of mental illnesses, and often cited psychological unbalance as merely a symptom of physical disturbances such as blows to the spine and head. He was also able to list each ingredient in the medicines that he prescribed while asleep, how they should be prepared and administered and even the nearest locations where they could be purchased.

The voice that issued from the entranced Cayce, who was quickly dubbed the "Sleeping Prophet," was reportedly very different from his own and spoke of being able to draw information from an omniscient "Universal Mind" which was roughly the unconscious sum of every living thought from every sentient being since the beginning of time. While the depths of Cayce's medical knowledge was then (and largely still is) unequaled, the very nature of the boundless reserve of knowledge he claimed to draw from made him capable of so much more than just healing the sick. Since there was no information in the universe that his mind was not privy to, Cayce could see with equal ease all that lay hidden deep beneath the oceans of the world, or watched unseen from the heavens above. Even the barriers of time itself seem to unlock at the will of this one man allowing him to view, unhindered, all that is normally veiled and hidden forever from the eyes of ordinary men. He could see and accurately describe every event that had ever transpired in mankind's past, present and, allegedly, even his future. He predicted many events that would later come to pass and many more that have yet to. He could shift his gaze at will from the very beginnings of the universe to the end of the world as we know it and clearly describe all that he saw there.

Although he seemed predestined for worldwide notoriety with nickname's like "The Kentucky Nostradamus," "The Father of Holistic Medicine," or simply "The Greatest Clairvoyant in History," Cayce began life as the unremarkable son of ordinary, deeply religious and dirt poor parents. As a child he was a dreamer and an academic dullard who frequently failed at his lessons. He was quite prone to be, more often than not, off playing with his imaginary friends instead of studying. He shared a very strong emotional bond with his mother, however, and she alone knew early on just how special young Edgar really was. She alone was well aware of the fact that Edgar's playmates were not imaginary for she could see them as well. She would often watch from the house while he played with the strange children that only the two of them could see. They came from out of the forest as if attracted to the boy. Sometimes only a couple of them would appear, she later said, other times there would be over twenty of them at once running, laughing and cavorting about with her son. Sometimes they would be all boys. Other times they would be all girls. Edgar would later say that, if he looked real hard, he could see through them. They told Edgar that they lived in the woods by themselves and didn't like to come out and play with anyone but him. At the end of the day they would disappear back into the woods from which they came. Young Edgar's mother was also aware that her son received periodic visits from and conversed with his dead grandfather, Thomas Jefferson Cayce.

As Cayce grew, so did his extraordinary mental abilities which soon became obvious to other family members. He often performed amazing feats for them using only his mind, such as making a broomstick dance away from the wall untouched and lifting the dinner table simply by placing a finger on its top. By the closing of the 19th century, Cayce had become a well-known dowser, or "Water Witch" as they were called then, and he is credited for the locations of many of the early wells dug in Hopkinsville. Unusual traits seemed to run in the Cayce family and these might account for the early psychic abilities inherent in young Edgar but he did not become world-renowned for his power to find water or speak with the dead, but for his singularly - if not unparalleled - healing ability. Although this ability would baffle the population forever it was no mystery to Edgar. It was simply a gift from God.

Cayce, described by those who knew him best, was always completely selfless towards others, going out of his way to help someone in need if he could, regardless of personal hardships or gain. This trait stayed with him throughout his entire life and, even when his abilities were in the greatest demand later on, he refused to charge those in need for his services. He loved to disappear alone for hours on end to his favorite secluded spot, a grove of old weeping willows which stood beside a small stream, to read the Bible and contemplate the scriptures. Though he kept it a secret from the public at first, Cayce later claimed that, one day around 1890 as he sat beneath the willows and read, his meditations were interrupted by the sudden appearance of what he took to be a celestial being made of intense light. In a melodious voice this being spoke to Cayce, telling him that all his prayers had been heard and he had but to name whatever his heart desired most and it would be granted to him. Edgar, though startled, incredulous and uncomprehending as to the full nature of the event, had needed only a few seconds of thought before giving his answer. What he wanted most, he said, was to be able to help sick people and, in particular, sick children. At this the entity disappeared and the boy ran home to tell his mother of the strange visitation. She assured him that it had, indeed, been an angel of the Lord come to reward him for his caring nature. Though neither could guess as to what way or form the gift might manifest itself, it was surely a special blessing from heaven just for him. They hadn't long to wait, however. That night, as his father attempted to teach him his spelling lesson, Edgar showed his usual academic shortcomings, unable to get even a single word correct. His father, known locally as "The Squire," was a stern man. Although he loved his son greatly, the boy's lackadaisical efforts at schoolwork were completely unacceptable and he soon lost patience. However, even after the boy had been knocked from his chair, he was still unable to correctly spell the words in the lesson. Then, according to Cayce, he heard the voice of the angel telling him that everything would be all right if he just went to sleep. He begged his father for a small break so that he could take a fifteen-minute nap. Perhaps then, he reasoned, he would be able to think more clearly and have better luck with his lessons. The Squire, though frustrated, could tell that his son was really trying hard despite his failures, granted the request and left the room saying that all the foolishness had better cease on his return or else. Edgar immediately lay his head down on his spelling book and went to sleep.

His father returned thirty minutes later, giving his son the extra time in hopes that it really would help him. Edgar could quote passages from the Bible with accuracy and ease, but when it came to schoolwork he seemed helpless as a babe. It was painfully obvious that his heart just wasn't in it but giving up was not one of The Squire's lessons. He woke the boy and, to his utter amazement and delight, found that Edgar now knew every word in the lesson and spelled them all impeccably. But that was not all. Edgar had somehow memorized the entire book while asleep and could quote, without error, every word on any given page, spell them correctly and also describe any pictures that might happen to be on that page. Every printed word within the book's covers, right down to the copyright dates, were at the boy's disposal. From then on, as might be expected, Edgar's studies improved at an alarming rate. He just slept on the schoolbooks! In no time at all he became quite the scholar even though he was later forced to quit school in the sixth grade to go to work. The Squire was so proud of him and impressed with his sudden abilities that he showed him off to everyone and even tested him publicly for one of his political friends.

Later, while suffering from a sudden bout of laryngitis, Edgar once again fell asleep and began speaking in a strange voice, describing the cause of his affliction and the cure. It worked and the rest, as they say, is history.

Though he languished in uncertainty for years as to its true purpose, Cayce's gift astonished all who beheld or came into contact with it. As word of his gift spread requests for readings began pouring in from sick people from all over the country in desperate need of a miracle. When strictly followed, the sleeping Cayce's prescriptions proved incredibly beneficial to those in need, he was a reluctant healer, fearing that something he might say while asleep could be misinterpreted and end up actually killing someone and branding himself a murderer. He retained no memory at all of the sessions when awake and seemed disinterested and unimpressed with the difficult medical terminology which he uttered when asleep, not knowing the meaning of the words. He was skeptical of the significance of the gift at first, and only hoped that he was actually helping people. He always refused payment for his work even though he was very poor, feeling it to be his Christian duty to help his fellow man if he could, regardless of anyone's ability to pay. The few times that he accepted money for his readings his body reacted violently and he suffered crippling headaches for days at a time until he was certain that he was not meant to use his gifts in that manner.

With encouragement from his mother, Edgar continued this work but soon became worried that, since he had no recollection of what was being asked of him during his self-induced trances, he could not know if they were asking him questions concerning health or monetary gain. It was rumored that some of his patients unexpectedly became rich by sneaking in questions such as, "Which horse will win the race?" Also, while asleep, Cayce was entirely at the mercy of whomever was present at the reading. The final straw came when he was persuaded to give a demonstration before a committee of doctors. While unconscious, the physicians became curious as to the depths of his trance and poked pins through his cheeks and the soles of his feet entirely without objection or response from Cayce. Not satisfied, they then procured long hat pins and repeated their ministrations on the helpless man. One even went so far as to surgically remove a nail from one of Cayce's fingertips. The knowledge that the sleeping Kentuckian demonstrated astonished every doctor present but when Cayce awoke in agony, he berated them for their barbaric treatment and vowed never to give another reading unless accompanied by someone he trusted and every word written down so that it could be checked and rechecked by qualified professionals.

Though plagued by personal turmoil, Cayce's fame grew with each life he saved. He became a sensation and his alleged powers were the talk of the day. Although he achieved a measure of fame, something that he'd never wanted to begin with, fortune seemed to forever elude him. He was so poor that, after proposing to his wife, they had to wait six years before he could afford to marry and support a wife. He always had faith however, saying that God would provide for the needs of his family - and God always did.

It was his lifelong dream to establish a free hospital where his reading could be correctly administered to those in need. Sadly, this dream would be denied him in life, but after his death the A.R.E. Research Center in West Virginia was founded and built to house, word for word, over 14,000 transcribed readings which are still being used by physicians and laymen alike to diagnose and treat all range of illnesses.

Edgar Cayce was an American wonder, perhaps the greatest psychic and healer in the history of the world, who was equally at ease discussing events from the earth's distant past - such as the sinking of the legendary lost continent of Atlantis - or events that were yet to come in the future - such as the date of his own death in 1945 - which he predicted correctly down to the day.

SELECTED BIBLIOGRAPHY

Every search into the mysteries of the unknown should begin at home or in your local library. Many of the incidents contained in this volume can be investigated further by reading the following distinguished works:

1. Mysterious America - Loren Coleman
Faber & Faber, 1983
2. The Complete Guide To Mysterious Beings - John Keel
Doubleday, 1994
3. The Complete Books of Charles Fort
Dover, 1974
4. The Locals - Thom Powell
Hancock House, 2003
5. Mysteries of Time and Space - Brad Steiger
Dell, 1973
6. Monsters You Never Heard Of - Daniel Cohen
Pocket, 1998
7. Beyond Belief - Brad Steiger
Scholastic, 1990
8. Unexplained - Jerome Clark
Visible Ink, 1993
9. Mysteries of the Unexplained
Reader's Digest, 1992
10. Haunted America - Mike Norman & Beth Scott
11. Notes on the Spread of Ice-Age Mammalia in Kentucky - Willard Rouse Jillson, 1970
12. Strange Encounters - Curt Sutherly
Llewellyn, 1996
13. World of Strange Phenomena - Charles Berlitz
Fawcett, 1988
14. In Search of Prehistoric Survivors - Karl P. N. Shuker
15. History of Henderson - Edmund Starling, 1965
16. Searching For Hidden Animals - Roy P. Mackal
Doubleday, 1980
17. Rock Art of Kentucky - Coy, Fuller, Meadows, Swauger
Univ. Of Ky. Press, 1997
18. Monsters Among Us - John Lee & Barbara Moore

Pyramid, 1975
19. Weird Stories From Real Life - Marjorie Burns, ed.
Scholastic, 1977
20. Beyond Earth - Ralph & Judy Blum
Bantam, 1974
21. Sightings - Susan Michaels
Fireside, 1996
22. The UFO Book - Jerome Clark
Visible Ink, 1998
23. Mysteries of the Unknown
Time/Life, 1992
24. The Truth About Flying Saucers - Aime Michel
Pyramid, 1956
25. Passport To Magonia - Jacques Vallee
26. The Mothman Prophecies - John Keel
Illuminet Press, 1991
27. Strange Stories Amazing Facts
Reader's Digest, 1976
28. Fate Magazine
29. Fortean Times Magazine
30. Ancient American Magazine
31. The Bigfoot Files - Peter Guttilla
Timeless Voyager Press, 2003
32. Forbidden Archeology
Torchlight Publishing, 1993
33. Strange Creatures From Time and Space - John Keel
Fawcett, 1970
34. The National Directory of Haunted Places - Dennis W. Hauk
Penguin, 1996
35. Tragedy At Devils Hollow - Michael Paul Henson
Cockrel, 1984
36. Mothman and other curious encounters - Loren Coleman
Paraview Press, 2002

ABOUT THE AUTHOR

Cryptid researcher and investigator B.M. Nunnelly, a self taught writer and artist, was born and raised in Henderson, Kentucky where he spent decades searching the bottom lands of the Bluegrass State for evidence of its diverse natural mysteries. His wanderings have brought him face to face with such creatures as Bigfoot, water monsters, black panthers, out of place wolves and other mysterious cryptids including a Thunderbird in 1998 - something no other living researcher can presently claim.

He co-founded kentuckybigfoot.com, a website devoted to the collection of Bigfoot and other unknown animal sightings in Ky., with partner Charlie Raymond in 2005 and his cryptid art has appeared in numerous publications including children's books. He spends his time writing books, documentaries and feature films in Henderson, Kentucky where he now resides with his wife and teenage son.

Visit Bart online at his website

www.kentuckybigfoot.com

The premiere site for collecting strange accounts, cryptid reports and Bigfoot sightings all over the state of Kentucky.

WHITECHAPEL PRESS

Whitechapel Productions Press is a division of Dark Haven Entertainment and a small press publisher, specializing in books about ghosts and hauntings. Since 1993, the company has been one of America's leading publishers of supernatural books and has produced such best-selling titles as **Haunted Illinois**, **The Ghost Hunters Guidebook**, **Ghosts on Film**, **Confessions of a Ghost Hunter**, **Resurrection Mary**, **Bloody Chicago**, **The Haunting of America**, **Spirits of the Civil War** and many others.

With nearly a dozen different authors producing high quality books on all aspects of ghosts, hauntings and the paranormal, Whitechapel Press has made its mark with America's ghost enthusiasts.

Whitechapel Press is also the publisher of the acclaimed **Ghosts of the Prairie** magazine, which started in 1997 as one of the only ghost-related magazines on the market. It continues today as a travel guide to the weird, haunted and unusual in Illinois. Each issue also includes a print version of the Whitechapel Press ghost book catalog.

You can visit Whitechapel Productions Press online and browse through our selection of ghostly titles, plus get information on ghosts and hauntings, haunted history, spirit photographs, information on ghost hunting and much more. by visiting the internet website at:

www.prairieghosts.com

Or call us toll-free at 1-888-446-7859 to order any of our titles.
Discounts are available to retail outlets and online booksellers!